THE SOUL OF IT ALL

My Music, My Life

MICHAEL BOLTON

CENTER STREET

NEW YORK   BOSTON   NASHVILLE

Unless otherwise noted, all photos courtesy of the author's personal collection.

Center Street
Hachette Book Group
237 Park Avenue
New York, NY 10017

www.CenterStreet.com

Printed in the United States of America

RRD-C

First edition: January 2013
10 9 8 7 6 5 4 3 2 1

Center Street is a division of Hachette Book Group, Inc.
The Center Street name and logo are trademarks of Hachette Book Group, Inc.

The Hachette Speakers Bureau provides a wide range of authors for speaking events.
To find out more, go to www.HachetteSpeakersBureau.com or call (866) 376-6591.

The publisher is not responsible for websites (or their content) that are not owned
by the publisher.

Library of Congress Control Number: 2012944592

ISBN 978-1-4555-2365-8

This book is dedicated to my mother and father; my beautiful daughters, Isa, Holly, and Taryn; and my gorgeous granddaughters, Amelia and Olivia "Gwenny," who have directed my course and continue to bring me back to the soul of it all.

Contents

Introduction   *ix*

Part I: The Climb   1
Chapter One: This Is the Tale of
    Captain Jack Sparrow   3
Chapter Two: Finding My Voice   9
Chapter Three: Band of Brothers   27
Chapter Four: Coming of Age   39
Chapter Five: The Epic Struggle   65
Chapter Six: Mad Dogs & Mites   83
Chapter Seven: Higher Stakes   101

Part II: The Rewards   119
Chapter Eight: The Talent I Didn't Know I Had   121
Chapter Nine: Songwriter Shangri-La   141
Chapter Ten: Feeding the Hunger   173
Chapter Eleven: The Soul of It All   203

CONTENTS

Chapter Twelve: Trials, Tribulations & Triumphs   229

Chapter Thirteen: Friends & Lovers   247

Chapter Fourteen: Reaching Higher   263

Chapter Fifteen: Singing On   277

Acknowledgments   317

Index   327

About the Author   335

Introduction

Know then thyself, presume not God to scan;
The proper study of mankind is man.

—Alexander Pope

Hello, I'm Captain Jack Sparrow. At least that's how I am known to those who've racked up more than ninety million views of my viral music video with the Lonely Island guys from *Saturday Night Live*.

For reasons I'll explain later, Andrew "Andy" Samberg, Akiva "Kiv" Schaffer, and Jorma "Jorm" Taccone now call me Lord Boltron, while the people from my home state of Connecticut know me by my family name, Bolton.

If you are a radio listener, you know my voice from Top 40, rock, adult contemporary, and R & B stations over the last four decades.

If you were around the Yale or Berkeley campuses or Greenwich Village in the 1960s, you may have known me as the hippie kid who played guitar and sang on street corners for meal money.

Anyone who regularly traveled U.S. Route 66 during that same decade may have seen me along the roadside, either hitchhiking cross-country with my buddies and bandmates or trying to push-start a vehicle that looked like a cross between a Wonder Bread truck and the Beatles' Yellow Submarine.

My fans know that I've won a couple of Grammy awards for Best Pop Male Vocal Performance and sold millions of albums and singles—more than fifty-three million so far. Still, the truth is, very few people know me as well as they know my music, and even fewer know just how much of a crazy, arduous, and rewarding adventure my life has been.

Not many are aware, for example, that my mom had to sign my first record contract for me because I was not quite sixteen years old when it was offered. To have a record deal at such a young age sure seemed like a great running start, but it was only the beginning of a long trek.

You see, I didn't have a hit record until eighteen challenging years later.

By the end of the 1970s, I was a struggling rock singer, husband, and father of three, facing eviction because my rent checks kept bouncing. If you have keen hearing, you may figure out that I finally found a way to pay the rent by performing scores of jingles for radio and television in the early 1980s for anything from Budweiser beer to Dr Pepper, Subaru cars, and the U.S. Army.

Remember *"Be all you can be"*? That was me.

Around that same time, I also established myself as a songwriter. I've written more than 220 songs, many with co-writers, including Bob Dylan, Lady Gaga, Diane Warren, Desmond Child, Walter Afanasieff, Billy Mann, Kenneth "Babyface" Edmonds, Robert John "Mutt" Lange, Lamont Dozier, and Ne-Yo, among others.

My name appears as a songwriter on records by diverse artists such as Conway Twitty, Kanye West, Jay-Z, KISS, Barbra Streisand, Cher, John Legend, Marc Anthony, Patti Austin, Wynonna Judd, Joe Cocker, Kenny G, Peabo Bryson, Kenny Rogers, Patti

INTRODUCTION

LaBelle, Laura Branigan, Gregg Allman, the Pointer Sisters, and many more artists from the country, pop, R & B, and rock genres.

And while I may be known for singing romantic songs about looking for and finding love, anyone who reads the tabloids and gossip sites knows that I've made some pretty good runs at romance. Very few people understand how lucky I've been in love despite my current single status, but if you keep reading, you will learn that love is still something I believe in very much. You will also gain insight into what it takes to relentlessly pursue and achieve a dream, to endure and learn from failure and disappointment, and to build upon that success over a long and rewarding career.

I'm a million miles from perfect. I've made many mistakes and done things—and not done things—I'm truly sorry for; but I have also experienced countless and cherished moments of joy, love, and laughter, and I have no regrets for putting my heart and soul into a career in music—one of the greatest gifts we all can share.

This book is about *the soul of it all,* which includes the deep emotions and vital forces experienced in a lifetime spent developing gifts and pursuing passions. It's about recognizing the purpose, the point of it, whether in times of great joy or deep sorrow, in times of sacrifice or celebration. Alexander Pope said, "We are immortal souls in human frames." I also believe the soul of it all far transcends the human frame. For me, the soul of it all and the true meaning of life are one and the same, and are found in everything from the joy of creating music to treasured moments with loved ones to giving back to others.

I may not know you any more than you know me, but I am confident that reading this story of my journey will not only entertain you but also, I hope, inspire you to persevere in your own quest to achieve your dreams.

There is one more thought I want to plant in your mind before you read my story: I didn't dream as big as my life has become.

PART I

The Climb

Chapter One

This Is the Tale of
Captain Jack Sparrow

S omewhere in my forty years as an artist and performer, I
picked up a reputation for being a serious guy.

Many of my fans don't realize that I was never bar mitzvahed
because I was the kid betting on the dreidel in Hebrew class and
smoking cigarettes during breaks. If you were beaned by a water
balloon or splattered by a flying tomato in Greenwich Village in
the 1960s, it was likely launched from the rooftops by yours truly.

You may be surprised to learn that I'm secretly a prankster and
a fun-loving kind of guy.

That's why I did not hesitate when *Saturday Night Live*'s Lonely
Island crew called me to join them in a music video.

Well, maybe I hesitated a little. I mean, these are the guys who
convinced Justin Timberlake to put his dick in a box—and sing
about it. He was freakin' hilarious, and of course Justin made it
look fun and easy, just as he would any other video.

Justin's video won a Creative Arts Emmy for outstanding original music and lyrics, and he seemed to enjoy himself doing it. I

was a fan of the Lonely Island guys and thought it would be fun working with them, though I worried what they might have me do. As hilarious as Justin's video was, I found it a little scary to contemplate what they would come up with for me. Justin sang in the Baptist choir as a kid. I sang on crusty street corners for spare change.

The *SNL* guys assured me they wanted to build a hip-hop song around me singing "a big sexy hook." They thought I'd be perfect for the job.

Jorm later told an interviewer who asked about my role in the video, "You can't fake funk like that."

From the start, Andy, Kiv, and Jorm promised to come up with a shocker skit that people would want to watch again and again, and they did just that.

The next thing I knew, I was in a crow's nest on a pirate ship decked out like Jack Sparrow, doing Forrest Gump on a park bench, cross-dressed as Erin Brockovich, and flashing my guns as Scarface.

And that was the tamest idea they came up with.

Initially, the mad geniuses of the Lonely Island presented me with a "Lord Boltron" song and video concept that involved violating laws of nature and each of the Ten Commandments, repeatedly.

It was hilariously funny, but really, really raunchy.

Now, that's what I expected from these boys without borders, the creators of family classics such as *I Just Had Sex*, *3-Way*, and *Jizzed in My Pants*. I loved those videos and the Lord Boltron bit, too. But I was concerned that the proposed Lord Boltron video might slightly upset my fans, because the first script was more than disturbing.

So we met for a creative session in L.A. to try to come up with something not quite so dark but still funny. When we met, I told Andy that my daughters were excited we were working together.

"My mother feels the same way about me working with you," said Andy.

We hatched out some more ideas for our music video at that meeting. Honestly, they were so busy with *SNL* and all of their movie and record projects, I didn't know if I'd ever hear from them again. But over the course of an approximately eight-month period, they somehow found time to come up with a script I could do. When they showed me the final Jack Sparrow concept, I loved it!

We met in New York City for two seventeen-hour days of filming the video. Our locations were the Buddakan restaurant in Manhattan and Brighton Beach, Brooklyn. Andy, Kiv, and Jorma were a pleasure to work with—funny, entertaining, respectful, and thoughtful—despite the tight deadlines. This is a team of guys who collaborated so well on every detail. Andy, Kiv, and Jorm also went out of their way to include me in making decisions. They kept coming up with new twists and gags on the spot. Then they'd run them by me and make sure I was on board, and they had trusted me to ad-lib and stack harmony parts all over the choruses of the catchy little ditty they wrote.

They kept me laughing through the whole process. I think all three of them were shocked when I agreed to a traumatizing scene in which I dressed as Erin Brockovich and breast-fed a doll. Unfortunately, that scene didn't make the cut. It may have been too over the top even for the Lonely Island team, but I would have voted to keep it.

To my amazement, they had the music video ready for prime time within forty-eight hours. I went to the music video's premiere on *SNL* in New York. I was too nervous to sit in the audience, so my manager Christina Kline and I watched from the back of the house. When they introduced our video, I couldn't breathe until the first waves of laughter came from the audience.

They loved it!

A fellow Connecticut resident, the phenomenal singer, songwriter, and guitarist John Mayer, was on the set when the video premiered. He was certain that it would go viral and become a huge hit.

"People are going to go nuts," John told me. "They won't expect this from you, and new fans who don't even know your music will...well, you'll see in the morning."

My daughter Isa, an expert on social media, began monitoring the video's views on YouTube as soon as it aired. When I walked downstairs the next morning, she looked up at me and said, "You are not going to believe what is going on." Jack Sparrow was already approaching a million views. She read me comments that included "OMG, I can't get this song out of my head!"

Just as John Mayer predicted, my music video with the Lonely Island guys went viral and, at last count, had more than ninety million views on YouTube.

Sometimes you have to take risks in life, and this one paid off in a huge way. Ours was the third-most-viewed video on YouTube in 2011, and it received an Emmy nomination, so we were invited to perform it live at the awards show for millions of viewers around the world.

Now I can't walk through an airport anymore without receiving high fives and fist bumps from eighteen-year-old guys screaming, "Captain Jack Sparrow! Dude, you rock!"

Andy, Kiv, and Jorm, you can call me anytime to do another music video.

So there you have the tale of my latest adventure in a music career that I began seeking at the age of nine while singing in my bedroom closet. What follows is the backstory. You will find many twists and turns—some of them as wild as those in the Jack Sparrow video.

You will also learn about the "soul of it all," the passion, hard work, striving, sacrifices, joy, and faith it takes to keep the dream alive. It has taken all of that and then some to build and sustain an incredibly rewarding career for more than four decades.

Chapter Two

Finding My Voice

My older brother, Orrin, calls himself "the original Bolton," which refers to the fact that he was the original rock star of our family. In the early sixties, he worked as a roadie for the Shags, one of the many New Haven bands formed in garages and basements in that musical decade. The Shags were among the few local groups to sign a record deal. A couple of their songs, "Don't Press Your Luck" and "Breathe in My Ear," received national radio play. Orrin brought some of the Shags to our apartment when I was ten or eleven. He bragged to them that I could sing.

"Michael may be a scrawny Jewish kid, but he sings like a chain-smoking, whiskey-chugging seventy-year-old black bluesman," Orrin said proudly.

One of the Shags, Carl Augusto, who played guitar and later taught me basic bar chords, patted my mop of curls and said: "Maybe someday you'll have your own band, little bro."

I was four years younger than Orrin and still in elementary school when my brother moved on to playing drums and singing in his own bands. Orrin was an enthusiastic early adopter. The Beatles, the Rolling Stones, and other great bands of the sixties inspired a major cultural shift, leading millions of American male teens to grow their hair longer and form their own groups—and my big brother went all in.

One day he was a high school jock. The next he was a hippie flower child rock 'n' roll sex god. Women of all ages wanted to sleep with him. Guys wanted to be him. He was a very popular guy, though not with the teachers. My first day of junior high was marred first by kids picking on me for my long hair and second by a teacher whose opening salvo to me was "Don't think you can get away with everything your brother got away with."

Orrin was a mysterious figure, even to me and my buddies. He would disappear for weeks and months, then pop up with an exotic beauty on each arm and, at one point, with his eyelids darkened by plant oils he discovered in India.

Upon his return from each of these long absences, Orrin would share tales of adventure in faraway places and show us treasures from his import-export business. My brother was our magical mystery tour guide into the music world, too. Orrin had an anthropologist's interest in the history of the blues especially. He knew of bands like England's John Mayall and the Bluesbreakers even before Eric Clapton joined the group. He shared his extensive collection of albums with us, explaining that the Beatles, Stones, and Clapton were actually mining black American rhythm and blues and playing it back to U.S. audiences. Their heroes, he explained, were long-neglected black musicians like Howlin' Wolf, Robert Johnson, Little Richard, Chuck Berry, B. B. King, John Lee Hooker, and Muddy Waters.

All this was enlightening and inspiring to me, and it didn't hurt that Orrin's record collection also included albums featuring Chicago's Paul Butterfield and Mike Bloomfield—a couple of Jewish guys like me. Orrin and I were known as the first "heads" in our circle of friends. We had long hair and were into the blues before everyone else. It seemed only natural that I would follow Orrin into music, just as I'd followed him into baseball, running, vegetarianism, and martial arts classes. Like him, I was a good athlete, but after our parents divorced, I dropped out of sports.

Instead, I put all of my energy into growing the longest hair of any male in the public school system, playing in bands, and pretending I'd had sex. ("The first time I had sex, it was very scary. I was alone." Thank you, Rodney Dangerfield.) My mother had custody, but controlling her wild-child sons was another matter. She had her hands full with three willful teens.

I took to the streets, wandering from teen hangouts like My Brother's Place and On the Green in New Haven, on the fringes of the Yale campus, to Greenwich Village. Its Bohemian blend of beatniks, painters, poets, and folksingers was then transitioning into the East Coast epicenter for sex, drugs, and rock 'n' roll.

Well, not so much sex for me, at least not right away. I was barely in my teens when I began wandering the streets of the Village with my brother and older friends. Orrin got all the girls in the early days. Even when I began hooking up with my share of women, I often suspected those who came my way were really after my brother, the legendary charmer. I may have seen myself as the scrawny younger brother with John Lennon wire rims, but I was never in danger of becoming a twenty-year-old virgin.

For the record, I lost my virginity at thirteen to my first cougar. She was all of fifteen and smokin' hot, but more on that later.

Divided Family

Before we dive into the history of my love life, I should provide some of my family background. Let's begin with the full disclosure of my true identity: In February 1953—two years behind my sister,

Sandra, who was two years behind Orrin—I was born of Russian Jewish heritage into the Bolotin family, pronounced *Below*-tin. Many years later, I switched out a couple letters and pared it down to Bolton so radio deejays, fans, and telephone operators would have an easier time pronouncing and remembering it.

Orrin took the name Bolton, too, even though he considers it a curse when he is mistaken for his kid brother—unless there is a better seat or a beautiful woman involved. The Bolotins-slash-Boltons always have been an idiosyncratic bunch. Ours was not the Ozzie and Harriet 1950s idyllic familial unit sporting cardigans and kitchen aprons.

We were way ahead of our time: In the '50s and '60s, we had all the dysfunctions of the '70s and '80s. As I was growing up in New Haven, Connecticut, my childhood and teenage years unfolded on the same schedule as every baby boomer's, but in that time of social upheaval, the Bolotins were upheaving with the best of them.

My parents seemed to get along fine until I was about eight or nine years old. I wasn't aware of any conflicts until then. My favorite childhood memories are moving into our big house at 1592 Boulevard with its huge backyard, where all the neighborhood kids came to play baseball, basketball, and football. In the winter freeze, we'd turn on the hose spigot and create a skating rink. Orrin, Sandra, and I regard those as our happiest times, but then things changed.

Lacking the counseling resources and marital guides of today, the marriage of George and Helen (née Gubin) began to disintegrate before our young eyes. Both of my parents were beloved by nearly everyone who knew them, but they couldn't seem to get along with each other.

Dad was a big bellows of a guy; tough as a steel-belted radial tire but one of the most tender, kind, and accepting men I've ever known. My father was big in local politics, a behind-the-scenes guy mostly. He was the longtime Democratic chairman of the Twenty-Fourth

Ward and property manager of the never-ending redevelopment project in New Haven's downtown. Dad enjoyed doing things for people in our community, where he was well known and respected.

Mom has always been an unfettered free spirit, a live-and-let-live, creative, artsy, and generous soul, who my buddies thought was the coolest mother in the 'hood.

I don't take the blame for my parents' divorce, but I do carry some of the inevitable scars. They verbally flailed at each other in the marital ring of fire for a couple years, but we never expected them to divorce, especially at a time when most couples still stayed together for life.

Most of us, if we are lucky, spend our childhoods in a protective bubble insulated from the struggles of our parents. We are free to focus on issues important to us, such as the condition of our baseball gloves and who will pick us up from band practice.

Only later did we see that Mom and Dad were growing apart and struggling with the day-to-day challenges and demands of middle-class parents. To some extent we are all sold a story that our lives will have happy endings. The prince and princess ride off into the sunset and the credits roll, but the movies rarely mention that the next day the fairy tale turns from something like Disney into something more Grimm.

I did have a happier marriage model in the family, thanks to the fifty-year union of my mother's parents, Rose and Isadore "Izzy" Gubin. They, too, railed at each other, mostly in Yiddish, yet their jabs were always followed by laughter and long hugs. They would throw the barbs without scorn, giggle, hug each other, and then explain to us in English that Grandpa had just called her "an old cow" and Grandma had just called him "an old horse."

We all thought this was hilarious, of course.

Grandpa Izzy was a plumber, a proud Mason and Shriner. He smoked big cigars that smelled like burning gym socks. He never really retired as the neighborhood handyman, and, I'm fairly certain, he helped financially support my mother and the rest of us after the divorce.

We assumed they would just continue their warfare while we went about the business of growing up. We were stunned to learn that Dad had packed up and moved out. He was long gone when Mom sat us down and said our father was no longer in residence. I was confused and deeply disturbed.

Later, I began spending many days in solitude, holed up with my guitar, playing for hours upon hours. I found particular comfort in my bedroom closet. Door closed. Lights out. I worked on my guitar chords and I wrote songs. I'm a loner by nature, which has served me well on long train rides, flights, and many nights in hotel rooms on the road. I still seek out my own quiet, private spaces when I want to create something. When I was writing songs as the kid in the closet, I didn't have any inkling of what I was doing. I barely knew what chord changes were. I was at the very beginning of my music life. Maybe I felt safe and secure in there, and free to express myself singing and playing without worrying what others would think or say. I can't recall many of the lyrics I wrote in those early "closet" days, but I'm sure they expressed my hurt and fears over the divorce and the changes it forced upon my life.

RELATIONSHIP ISSUES

Both of my parents assured me in separate conversations that Dad would still be there for me in the stands for Little League, giving the umpires a hard time if he thought I'd been robbed on a call. As I look back, I recall that one of the lingering memories of that time was how much I missed sitting around the television to watch *The Ed Sullivan Show* as a family.

Our parents retreated to separate corners and separate lives, bruised, battered, and never to marry again, not to each other or to anyone else. They simply grew apart and lost feelings for each other, like so many couples, but they were ahead of the wave, which didn't help us in dealing with the family breakup. Divorce was not yet the so-what shame-free norm. I didn't have a big circle of buddies dividing up their weeks between Mom's apartment and Dad's place. I didn't know another kid in my school whose parents were divorced.

I felt the burden of something I was far too young to comprehend. Years later, in therapy, I'd realize that the tension between my parents created a deep impression and planted fears and angst that I would grapple with as I struggled in my own relationships. My mind unconsciously stored snapshots and scenes from their hostilities at the kitchen table, complete with the harsh tones and tensions. Just recently I was somewhere in the world far from my own bed, numb with exhaustion after a concert and trying to sleep, when some memory cell more than fifty years old opened up and invited me in. I saw my mother storming into a room where Orrin and I were, yelling and carrying on. Maybe we were up past our bedtimes or just being typical brothers. I had this very clear and close vision of her face, and I could sense her exhaustion and distress. My mother, who'd wanted to sing and write songs and live as an artist and performer, clearly was not experiencing the life she'd wanted or expected.

She filed for divorce, and I certainly understood her reasons, but from that point on my young brain was imprinted with the fear that a woman could walk away from a relationship at any time. That perception didn't serve me well as a teen or as an adult. In my teen romances I tended to be highly possessive. Securing a lasting and loving relationship has always been important to me, as it is with most of us. It's interesting that my career as a performer flourished when I began singing more about seeking love ("Soul Provider"), finding love ("When a Man Loves a Woman"), understanding love ("How Can We Be Lovers If We Can't Be Friends"), losing love

("How Am I Supposed to Live Without You"), and never giving up on love ("That's What Love Is All About").

I'm also very big on making home a safe place to be for everyone. Although most of my charitable work has been aimed at protecting women and children from physical abuse, there was none of that in my family. My father didn't drink, and he was very much about remaining in control. He often lectured Orrin and me about this, saying that men who physically abused women were shameful and unmanly. Still, my mother and father did not shy away from taking verbal shots at each other before and after the marriage.

Orrin, Sandra, and I tried to ignore or laugh off the insults and animosity they aimed at each other. But we had sympathy for both. Today, there are all sorts of guides to conflict resolution and "healthy divorces," but my parents didn't have them. By the time I went through my own marital split twenty-five years later, the Divorce Universe was vast. Couples decoupling were common and well schooled on not disparaging each other in front of the kids, because children translate "Your mother is bad" or "Your father is bad" to "I'm bad."

My parents did not agree on much, but they had one thing in common. They both loved us dearly—of that we had no doubts. Mom was given primary care of us, but Dad was still a strong presence, though probably not strong enough as far as our mother was concerned. She took on a load. Mom became the head of the household as well as a single parent who worked a full-time job as a secretary and somehow managed to put up with and love her rebellious children.

I may have cost her many hours of sleep, but my mom was my hero because she made sure we felt protected and loved, even as we snarled and ran from her. She worked hard to give us a home, which we even visited now and then. After the divorce, the four of us moved into a town house on Whalley Avenue. Orrin and I tended to roam at will.

Mom never had much of a chance to establish control. Mostly, she surrendered. She was, and remains, a beautiful, loving, always fashionable, and free-spirited woman. When she and my father were still together, the only way Mom could rein us in was the six-word stopper: "Wait until your father comes home!" When Dad was no longer home, she had no leverage over the bold Bolotin brothers. Orrin and I immediately crossed every boundary and pushed every button.

Sandra, the well-mannered and high-achieving child in our family, obeyed Mom, finished high school, and went off to Berkeley University for her master's in psychology. My sister has the sweet personality of our grandmother Rose. Sandra also has a generous heart and never says an unkind word about anyone. She has done an incredible job raising her son, Adam, a talented musician who is determined to make a difference in his community.

Mom stressed out a lot, for good reason. One night while she was ranting at her wilding sons to clean up our acts, she stopped midsentence and fainted, dropping to the floor at our feet. If she didn't have our full attention before—and she didn't—she won it then. It was a frightening moment, but she was fine about ten minutes later. Within a few hours Orrin and I were back to our defiant ways.

THE FATHER-SON GAME

My dad was a rugged, chain-smoking man's man. Hard-nosed, barrel-chested, and jut-jawed, he was a handsome and imposing guy with many friends of all races and income levels, and, despite the gruff exterior, he was a loving and affectionate father. In my younger days, he'd grab my face with his huge paws and kiss me over and over until I managed to squirm away. Sometimes I didn't try all that hard to break free. I loved my dad.

He was a devoted liberal, but no softie. His job as the property manager for the New Haven Redevelopment Agency meant he had the keys to the city, or at least to every downtown building. He'd played some small-college football, where he earned the nickname

"Bullet Bolotin" for his tenacity and toughness, which served him well in his work and in politics. Part of his job was to collect overdue rent from the tenants of city-owned buildings in New Haven. He wasn't popular with those who fell behind in their payments, which is why a patrol car was often parked outside our house. I think.

After the divorce, Dad stayed in touch with Orrin and me mostly through politics and sports, his twin passions. He knew all the Democrat and Republican players, big and small, across Connecticut. Many of the future leaders of the Democratic Party found their way to our front door. Orrin and I were their foot soldiers. We'd walk door-to-door or ride our bikes around town distributing campaign flyers for candidates, setting up chairs and tables for events.

Years later, after I came to know politicians like Dick Gephardt and Bill Clinton, they'd sometimes comment on how comfortable I seemed in their world, and they were right. Before the family upheaval, our home was a gathering place for local pols. The two-story house on Boulevard in New Haven's working-class Beaver Hills neighborhood—just a mile and a half from the Yale University campus—had big porches on both levels, and there were often nights when they sagged under the heft of Connecticut Democrats plotting domination of the Nutmeg State. Many a morning I'd have to dig out my homework and schoolbooks from under their residue of cigar ash, coffee cups, and liquor bottles.

I have many great memories of playing catch with my father in the front yard of the Boulevard house. Those were happy times. I practiced pitching to my dad. He always reminded me to follow through to increase velocity and accuracy.

"Finish the throw," he'd say.

Sometimes, my adrenaline would kick in and I'd throw it over his head, which meant I had to run down the block to retrieve the ball. Having to chase my own bad throws was a major incentive to improve my accuracy and deliver the ball to his glove.

Many years later, I thought of those games of father-son catch after one of our Bolton's Bombers celebrity softball games, when former New York Yankee Clete Boyer, a childhood hero of mine, asked, "Where'd you get that arm?"

"From my father," I said without pause.

The house was not huge, but the backyard seemed to stretch forever. It served as our own sports triplex, with a baseball and football field and a basketball half-court at the far end. All the neighborhood kids seemed to regard it as their playground, too, and the games ran from morning to dusk in my memories of those idyllic times.

Politics aside, sports provided our biggest connection to our father. Dad was present at a lot of our baseball and basketball games. Orrin and I were both good athletes, and Dad cheered us on. No fan of the longhair trend, he still rose to my defense when my sixth grade teacher said I couldn't play softball with the class during recess if I didn't cut my shoulder-length locks. I was captain of our sixth grade team, but the teacher said I was a danger to myself and others because my hair was always in my eyes.

Dad had a talk with the principal, demanding that I be allowed to play while I wore my hair as long as I wanted. Dad won. The principal was no fool. He was aware that my father knew people who knew people. Dad, who was not shy about betting a hundred dollars on a bowling match, was intensely competitive, a trait his sons inherited. I used to race Yale students on their green for lunch money, and my friends always bet on me to leave the Yalies in the dust. I was my father's son, and he advocated the "Winning is everything" philosophy, especially if the victory was sealed with a grand-slam home run, a slam dunk, or a knockout punch.

Dad liked big wins, but when we lost he always encouraged us, saying, "Keep your chin up, you'll get 'em next week." He sent us off to each game or match with sports metaphors ringing in our ears, exhorting us to conquer and vanquish. He was of the Knute

Rockne, Vince Lombardi, and Woody Hayes old school. He also believed practice made perfect, and he drove my brother and me to practice our sports religiously.

Well, maybe *religious* is not the right word, since I was booted out of our temple's Hebrew school for not taking my faith seriously enough. Neither Dad nor Mom practiced their Jewish faith, even though they sent us off to give it a try. Maybe I should say we practiced our sports as if they were more important than religion.

Even though we were born Yankees fans, my father used to speak highly of iconic athletes that our beloved Yankees competed with, like Rocky Colavito of the Cleveland Indians or Al Kaline of the Detroit Tigers. Then there was the unforgettable team that shut us down in the 1963 World Series: the Los Angeles Dodgers, with Don Drysdale and Sandy Koufax both pitching as well as any team or true fan of the game could ever witness. And what could you ever say about the great Ted Williams, even when he was batting against the Yanks? Was he not worthy of our highest praise? What I came to believe at a young age was that there are people who achieve a level of true championship—like our rival Red Sox, one of the greatest teams I've ever seen. There wasn't one moment, even with a solid Yankee lead, that I didn't have huge respect for that Boston lineup, and I never counted them out. Sometimes your team is going to get beat because the other side rises to a level of excellence when it really counts. All my life (long before free agency) getting past the Yankees in the postseason meant you deserved to be there. My respect for players and champions in all sports who perform at such a heightened level allows me to enjoy sports more. So I've never understood and never will understand the mentality of the haters who appear from time to time in a baseball stadium, in the stands, or courtside. That's not what sports are about. Honoring the game means recognizing the athleticism and the spirit that it takes to be a champion, no matter what team you're on. To me, great performance earns and deserves due respect. That's part of the soul of it all.

One of the things Dad drilled into Orrin and me early on was that the most effective way to break out of a tackle while playing football was to keep your legs moving, because the big leg muscles are the most powerful in the body. "Just keep your head down and keep your legs moving and they will have a hard time stopping you boys," he'd say.

My football was limited to neighborhood games, since I never played in the local leagues, but I took that philosophy and ran with it. My approach to challenges typically has been to put my head down and bull ahead, refusing to surrender. I didn't become the star athlete that my father had hoped for, but as much as I may have rebelled in other ways, I did adopt his strategy and apply it to the greatest force in nature—passion. In my case, it was a passion for singing and performing.

No one will ever accuse me of holding back, either in my live performances or in the recording studio. For me singing is about expressing passion. Female fans, especially, seem to respond to this aspect of my performances and, oddly enough, so have several big-name male athletes, including some I know, such as Barry Bonds, Joe Carter, and Andre Agassi. They've said that they can relate to the intensity of my voice when I sing certain notes because it reminds them of the same explosiveness they strive for in swinging the baseball bat or tennis racket. Maybe it's just the Bullet Bolotin in me, always pushing for the "out of the park and onto the railroad tracks" grand slam, trying to get a cheer from my dad in the stands.

OUR MOTHER'S PASSION

Orrin's theory is that he and I played sports mostly to please our father, and we embraced music with even more enthusiasm because it was our mother's greatest passion. Mom played the keyboards, and she wrote many songs in hopes of making a career in music. We often joked that her best songs had titles like "You Kids Are Killin' Me!" and "I Hope You Have Kids as Bad as You Someday!"

Mom did have a love for music. Whenever a singer would appear on *The Ed Sullivan Show*, she would say, "Did you hear that note? That was a high C" or "Did you hear the vocal variation there?" I believe her running commentary and the music she sang and played throughout our childhoods helped me develop a musical ear, a strong sense of pitch, and a passion for singing. Many people of my generation remember the Beatles' first appearance on *The Ed Sullivan Show*. What struck me and stayed with me from that landmark event was not just how the Beatles performed, but how I heard it. When I listened to that show and my first Beatles records, I found myself sharply focused on their harmonies and how their voices interacted. My musical training was limited to saxophone lessons at L. W. Beecher, my grade school. I never learned to read or write music properly, but, either through my mother's commentary or something hardwired into my brain, I could visualize the notes in my mind's eye. When I sang, those notes were there, playing on the screen of my imagination.

Dad sang, too, by the way, but did it to combat his raucous children. Whenever we were traveling in the car and the kids became too loud or disruptive, my father belted out his brassy Ethel Merman rendition of "When you're smiling, when you're smiling, the whole world smiles with you. . . ."

This was Dad's peaceful yet persuasive method for telling us to shut the hell up. If we continued to fight or yell, Dad would sing so loudly and with such enthusiasm that we had no choice but to quiet down for fear of going deaf or insane or both.

My mother was more passionate about music. She had an extensive record collection of show tunes, and like many women of her era, she was a big fan of the dashing Mario Lanza, an operatic tenor who became a movie star. Mom had a good strong voice, and she was always taking singing lessons in hopes of performing one day. She also dreamed of making it as a songwriter. She never made it, but if you wanted to practice armchair psychology and say that I am living out my mother's dream, complete with my excursions into opera, go right ahead.

The first time I can remember someone commenting on my singing voice was when I was around the age of ten. It was my mother who heard me singing along with the radio and said, "You have a very good voice, Michael." It was my first good review.

Time after time, those closest to me, and strangers, too, noted that my singing voice sounded nothing like that of a skinny white kid. It took me years to grow into my voice, and my parents always supported and encouraged me.

Mom has been the biggest long-term supporter in my musical career. She still shows up at my concerts when they are within a hundred-mile radius of her home.

She and my father always supported our musical pursuits, even when they struggled to support us financially. Orrin may be the only aspiring drummer to receive his first drum kit one cymbal, one drumstick, and one drum at a time. He claims it took a year or so before he had a full set.

Chords and Discords

My father died about seven years before I made it big as an artist, which saddened me because he had always encouraged me as much with my singing as with my playing baseball and running track. With his booming voice, he was a great cheerleader at my games. The same held true with my singing. He'd always say the same thing after hearing me perform. He'd stick out that big Jay Leno chin and say: "Son, you're gonna be big, *big, BIG!*"

He always gave me three "bigs" in just that way, and that's how I hear him in my mind even today.

My father's faith in my talent helped me believe in myself. He and my mother were divorced and still combatants when they called a truce and teamed up to buy me my first guitar, a one-hundred-dollar Kay. I'd opted for the saxophone as my grade school band choice because I loved the rasp of that instrument, but there weren't many sax players in rock bands other than the Dave Clark Five back then. I never really learned to play my rented sax, but that raspy sound seemed to find its way into my singing voice.

My friend Johnny taught me my first three guitar chords, and I returned the favor by turning him on to his first joint. (It was considered a public service in those days, following the Beatles lyrics and hippie mantra that went: "I'd love to turn you on.")

I taught Johnny the proper procedures and techniques for inhaling, cautioning him not to suck in too much on his maiden toke. He performed admirably, though he bogarted the joint. That was my fault. I hadn't included the lesson on pot etiquette. Still, Johnny was not impressed with the experience.

"I don't feel anything," he said.

Disappointed, he went home.

He called me upon arriving.

"People were staring and following me all the way home," he said. "I could hear them talking about me."

I found it hysterical, given that he "couldn't feel anything" from the pot when he left the house. I talked him down.

Johnny and all my friends came to regard my mother as "the cool mom" because she didn't buy into the reefer-madness mentality of most parents, though there were limits to her tolerance. Her coolness quotient in our eyes was established one day when she burst into my bedroom during a serious joint-rolling, pot-smoking session involving six or seven of my buddies, band members, and a couple of our girlfriends. None of us was more than sixteen years old. We had rolled massive joints using as many as eight sheets of rolling paper to create doobies the size of Cuban cigars.

When the bedroom door flew open and my mother appeared, my friends freaked out. Everyone scrambled to hide the rolling papers, the bags of pot, and the joints. Our keyboard player was so frantic he plucked a burning joint from his mouth and put it in his shirt pocket, where it nearly smoked a nipple. Mom had to wait for the smoke to clear before she could identify all the suspects. She squinted down for a second or two before finding my face in the stoned crowd. Then she threw out an arm and opened her hand to reveal three of our giant joints in her palm.

Buzz kill!

Before any of my suddenly de-mellowed friends could speak or flee, my mother issued her decree: "Stop leaving these around the house!"

She then tossed the three joints into my lap, turned, and walked out, slamming the door on our small band of astonished scofflaws.

"Michael, man, I can't believe your mom didn't bust us!"

If anyone else's parents had caught us with the pot, there would have been serious hell to pay, so I felt a certain pride in my mom's go-with-the-flow attitude. She didn't encourage our marijuana use, but she felt we were doing what was typical for the times. Mom also preferred that we smoke at home rather than in public, so she didn't want to drive us out of the house.

I appreciated her attitude, but I took all the (hemp) rope she gave me and ran with it.

Chapter Three

Band of Brothers

When members of my generation reflect on the sixties, they often speak of a powerful sense of liberation, of boundaries disappearing and rules being broken. For some, this meant wandering the planet. For others, it meant experimenting sexually, smoking pot, or flouting the school dress code by growing long hair and wearing blue jeans.

The Bolotin brothers did all that and more. We ran wild.

Again, I followed Orrin's lead. Tall, charming, witty, and very funny, Orrin was perfectly cast as a Greenwich Village hippie heart-throb. He had a string of beautiful admirers, some of them older than he and many of them wealthy, including fashion models, actresses, flight attendants, and at least one Playboy Club bunny. (Her name was Lolita, and she took him home from a party and kept him.)

I first went to Greenwich Village to visit my brother, but I quickly joined the circus. In those Age of Aquarius days, the Village was like a rock festival every day of the week. Clubs that had featured jazz, folk, and poetry readings transitioned to the venues of choice for artists like Bob Dylan, Judy Collins, the Mamas & the Papas, Joni Mitchell, James Taylor, Carole King, Carly Simon, Roger McGuinn, Joan Baez, Richie Havens, John Prine, and Melanie. Many of them lived in the Village, too. I may have run into them, talked to them, heard them perform, or even befriended them back then, but the fog of those years will likely never lift.

I do recall that in those exuberant times the Village was so overrun with hippies, musicians, and kindred free spirits that straighter-laced tourists were piling onto double-decker tour buses and paying to ride through its streets to observe longhairs in the wild. For the male voyeurs aboard the tour buses—and teenage boys wandering the streets—I'm sure the biggest attraction were the females, who tended to wear gauzy tops and no bras.

Orrin went native in the Village, and I wasn't far behind. Our mother was probably grateful to have a few days of peace and quiet in the apartment. My father berated her for letting me roam for days at a time, but what was she going to do, kick me out of the house because I was never home? My mother always considered herself an artist and a songwriter, and she was attracted to the Village and its creative energy, too. She also thought that my brother and his friends were there to watch over me, so that gave her some comfort. Really, though, she had no idea where I was, what I was doing, or how far I had strayed beyond the fringe.

My vagabond ways began around the age of twelve in those days of crashing with friends, friends of friends, and total strangers, mostly in New Haven and Greenwich Village, where some young hippies we knew had sublet an apartment. We had shelter, and we foraged for food or panhandled for change on MacDougal Street.

One major draw to the Village for me was the presence of my teen crush, Cory Morrison. She was one of those irresistible hippie girls, blonde and blue-eyed with a dazzling smile. Cory was closer to Orrin's age, and, though she claimed to "adore" me, I suspect she merely tolerated me as sort of a tagalong little brother who made her laugh. I worked hard at making her laugh, but I had convinced myself that I could win her heart once I grew taller and had some facial hair.

Cory had dropped out of high school and immersed herself in the music and mayhem of Greenwich Village. She lived in some rich hippie's studio apartment with seven or eight other girls. I was the only boy allowed in this wild girls' camp. They thought I was harmless because I was younger than all of them. I may have been relatively harmless, but I wasn't blind. Believe me, I hung out with them as much as possible. For fun we'd throw eggs at people from the roof of their building. The neighbors weren't amused when the cops showed up and went door-to-door in search of the flying omelet pranksters.

Cory was also my grifter partner in the Village. She'd come with me when I panhandled for pizza money. I'd collar wealthy-looking women on the street and tell them that I needed money so I could send my sister home on the train to our sick mother. Cory was a good actress, so we ate a lot of free pizza. I always reveled in the fact that Cory told me I was her favorite Bolton brother. Orrin usually got all the girls back then.

I gave her photos of me and wrote on the back, "I love you and not like my mother and not like my sister, but YOU!" Unfortunately for me, Cory's fondness was more sisterly. She never gave me more than a kiss on the cheek, but she did help pierce my ear with a sewing needle and ice cube one night, marking another big step in my quest to conform to nonconformity. She was certainly a major attraction for me and a reason to hang out in the Village, where every night was an adventure.

I was young and indestructible until I wasn't. One night I was hanging out in front of Cory's apartment when a police squad car with two officers in it pulled up. One asked me what I was doing.

I told him I was staying with some friends. Something about that reply inspired the other officer to get out of the car and pat me down. When he turned to say something to his partner, it dawned on me that there were three little pills in my pants pocket. Someone had just given them to me, and I had no idea what they were, but I was fairly certain they weren't baby aspirin. The police officers departed, but I feared they might return, so I quickly downed the three little pills.

The next thing I knew, I was on another planet.

Friends found me wandering the streets in a daze. Fortunately, they showed an astonishing level of concern and responsibility by refusing to leave me in a gutter on Bleecker Street. Instead, they kept pouring coffee down my throat and walking me all night and into the morning. I don't remember much beyond some flashing colors and a series of restaurants speeding by on wheels. My friends reported that I was very amusing except when I was nonresponsive and nearly comatose. The scariest part occurred when I ran into my mother on the street just as the brain-bending drugs kicked in. She was in the Village visiting a friend. I told her I was just hanging out, doing fine, and that I'd be home in a couple of days. Little did she know that even as we spoke a purple haze was descending upon her son.

The next day, I ran into some people who'd encountered me during my unplanned trip into the cosmos. In honor of my state of mind they'd given me a new nickname: "Spaceman." Looking back, I'm thankful I didn't wind up in a hospital or a grave that night.

The Village wasn't all peace, brother. More than once my peace sign was returned with a pointed weapon and: "Gimme all your money, hippie asshole." New York's finest muggers, thieves, and thugs saw the hippies as fair game. Given my age, slight build, and penchant for wandering the streets in an addled state of mind, I must have seemed the fairest of all. Bad guys threatened me and, on more than one occasion, pointed lethal weapons at me.

One night a friend and I were walking around the East Village, which wasn't yet Trump territory, when two thugs grabbed me and put a large knife to my scrawny neck, which had yet to attract its first hickey. The mugger threatening to slice my Adam's apple explained with great sincerity that he wanted all of my money. I emptied my pockets to show him that I had all of four dollars. For a moment I thought he might cut my throat just for wasting his precious crime time.

That was a very up-close-and-personal brush with violent death in the Village. I also had more of a communal near-death experience in the same neighborhood a year or so later. There were seven or eight of us at an impromptu party on East Fourteenth Street. I can't even remember if I knew the resident of the apartment or had just wandered in with some nomadic hippie friends looking for a party. We were chattering away when the door flew open and in walked two guys who definitely were not from the hippie tribe. These weren't flower children, unless you are talking about the flowers displayed at funeral homes and cemeteries. They were in bad suits that fit too tightly, but it's not like anyone would ever tell them that. I don't want to stereotype anyone, but they appeared to be distinguished graduates from the wiseguys school of bone breaking and body dumping.

When they came in the door, there was a distinct mood swing. We went from stoned to scared shitless before the lock clicked back in place. The two party-crashers grabbed our panicked host and shoved him into a back room. They slammed the door, and the ensuing conversation was heated and loud.

Someone in our group suggested that the guy who lived there owed money to the wrong people and they'd sent a strong-arm collection service. In our little sector of the apartment, conversation grew hushed. I'm sure I was not the only person trying to decide whether a mad dash for the door would be a wise move or a dead end, with *dead* being the critical word.

A few other fretful souls talked about making a run for it, but no one could summon the courage to actually bolt for the door. The predominant fear was that if the bad guys shot or beat our host, we'd all become witnesses and maybe collateral damage. We mulled this over while the yelling in the back room went on for about an hour. Then the shouting subsided and our host walked out, looking much the worse for the wear. He tried to calm us, but he looked terrified: "Everything is okay, but you all have to leave now."

We did not let the door hit our terrified hippie asses on the way out.

Other New Haven guys my age were looking forward to their first year in high school and getting their driver's licenses. I lived in an alternate universe. There was no normal in my life. No routine. The temptation is to call those years a rite of passage, but really I was a lost boy. There was no passage for most of the people I was running with. They weren't preparing for careers or working on their dreams. They were getting high as much as possible with whatever drugs were available. Some of them were hard-core and dangerous to be around, and quite a few of them didn't make it.

My love of music, my family and friends, and definitely some form of divine intervention saved me. My voice was a gift, people said, and performing obviously was my greatest joy, but I could not express that gift or experience that joy if getting high continued to be the focus of my existence.

BAND OF BROTHERS

Aside from Orrin, his record collection, and local musicians, my major musical influences in those wilding years were the Friedland brothers, Marc and Ribs, whose dad, Bob, owned Quality Plumbing Supply. Our parents and grandparents had been friends. My grandfather Izzy Gubin was a plumber, too, so their family knew him through business. We had bowling bonds, too. My father and I were avid bowlers and so were the Friedlands, whom we often saw at the local lanes. We didn't become close friends until I was twelve years old. We first bonded over music at a teen party given by Jimmy Rozen, who was then a member of my first band, the Inmates. I walked into a room at the Rozen house during the party and was astonished to see Marc, whom I'd known only as a big bowler, playing a guitar while he held it on top of his head. I'd never seen anyone—at least no one who lived in my own zip code—pull off that Jimi Hendrix feat.

That's when I learned that Marc had given up his ambitions to become a professional bowler. He'd gone to a big concert where he realized there were many more hot girls following rock bands than bowlers. Since then, he'd become as obsessed with music as I was. Marc had been taking guitar lessons for a year, but he was a natural who learned to play any instrument you put in his hands.

Without "Marky Doodle," my youth would have been far less joyful. He was my confidant, my brother in music, and by my side during nearly a decade of our shared struggle to make it in music. The sound track of those years features Marc playing bass, guitar, and keyboards—and always playing them incredibly well. One of my favorite photographs shows Marc and me just after we'd opened for Leon Russell at a concert. He has a heavy black beard and long, thick, black hair, and we look like we just came off a pirate ship, or maybe an Amish carriage race. Marky Doodle Hamburger stuck with me through thin and thin—the very lean years—and I couldn't have asked for a better friend. I often wondered in those years how anyone could always seem so happy—even without the assistance of his bong pipe. Marc found humor in every situation.

Mellow to the bone, Marc is also among the most talented and versatile musicians I've ever played with. He still performs now and then, and I surprised him at a club in Los Angeles a few years ago. He astounded me that night because he was playing one of the most difficult instruments to master, the pedal steel guitar. He said he'd just decided to teach himself how to play it, and as always, he was great.

First Marc and then Ribs, too, became my adopted brothers, bandmates, bodyguards, and partners in adventure. Marc is two years older than me. Ribs is seven years older, which may explain why I always thought of him as this huge guy and my boyhood bodyguard, even though he never grew to be more than five foot nine inches tall. Never known by his proper name, Richard, except by his parents, Ribs was a rebel who most of all rebelled from the idea of joining his father's successful plumbing supply business. He wanted to make it in the music industry instead.

Ribs, whose nickname derived from his skeletal torso as a child, had molded a physique more like that of a pipe fitter than a band manager—and that was a good thing for me. My long hair and bag-of-bones body seemed to attract the wrong sort of attention. For some, the sixties may summon memories of people saying, "Peace, brother." For others it may be, "Make love, not war." But for those of us who were the first to grow out our crew cuts, the oft-heard comment was "Are you a boy or a girl?" Or the drive-by classic, which people would yell as they rolled down their car windows: "Get a haircut, faggot!"

Ribs, a martial arts student and weight lifter, became my defender against those taunts, whether they were hurled at me around New Haven or in diners, truck stops, or clubs when our band was on the road. Whenever some yahoo would target me, gentle Ribs transformed into his raging beast of an alter ego, "Rito the Madman." He'd scream profanities and threaten severe bodily harm to my tormentors.

Ribs also is fond of reminding me that the first time he saw me at the bowling alley, "I thought you were a girl myself." He got over that. While Marc became my guitar teacher and bandmate, Ribs offered his services as my manager. He was one of my first true believers not related by blood. When I met the Friedlands I already had my first band, the Inmates, but we soon joined forces and formed a band with an existing group and called ourselves the Coconut Conspiracy. But I'm not sure I ever performed with that band because Marc picked his "other" best buddy, Bobby "Goody" Goodman, to be the lead singer.

When I protested, Marc kicked me out of the band! At the age of twelve, I truly feared that my rock 'n' roll career had ended, but in the sixties a new rock group formed every two-point-five seconds somewhere in the United States. New Haven was a hothouse for start-up garage bands. Along with the Shags, the town's most successful group in the late 1950s and early 1960s may have been the Five Satins, a black doo-wop group whose biggest hit was "In the Still of the Night."

We were all inspired by hometown musicians and even more by what we listened to on the airwaves, courtesy of the trailblazing radio deejays led by New York's top jocks, including Cousin Brucie (who later became a good friend) and Murray the K. New Haven's own WELI radio station was one of the region's first all-rock-format stations, offering the popular *Jukebox Saturday Night*. The rock 'n' roll radio pioneers of the 1960s and 1970s usually took requests and played a wide range of music that included Motown, R & B, funk and soul, Memphis and Chicago blues, Southern rock, folk rock, California soft rock, country rock, the Beach Boys, antiwar protest music, psychedelic rock, and pop.

We had plenty of live music, too, thanks to all the college bars around the Yale campus and the New Haven Arena, which managed to bring in many of the biggest bands in the 1960s, although our hometown concert venue will forever be remembered for canceling a 1964 Rolling Stones concert due to lack of ticket sales. The Arena's other claim to rock shame was a 1967 Doors concert. One of New Haven's finest police officers came upon a couple going at it in a bathroom shower stall before the concert. The cop ordered them to leave, not realizing that the male was the lead singer for the Doors. Jim Morrison told the lawman to "eat it."

The cop brandished a can of Mace and repeated his order, saying, "Last chance."

Morrison's retort, which went down in rock 'n' roll history, was "Last chance to eat it!"

The cop sprayed his Mace and Morrison went down, delaying the concert for an hour. Once the Doors did take the stage, Morrison went off on a rant, berating New Haven's men in blue with obscenities, which provoked them to drag his ass offstage, arrest him, and haul him off to jail. A riot ensued, leading to the arrest of thirteen others. Charges were eventually dropped, but Morrison immortalized the event in the song "Peace Frog" on the Doors' classic 1970 *Morrison Hotel* album. The lyrics included the phrase "blood in the streets in the town of New Haven."

Bloodied but unbowed, the New Haven Arena survived to hold many more concerts that I attended, including the rescheduled Stones concert, finally held in 1965. I went with friend and fellow longhair Johnny, who, like me, dared to publicly declare himself a fan of both the Beatles and the Stones, which was rare because fans tended to split on them just as they did on the Yankees and Red Sox in our part of the world.

During that concert Mick Jagger threw his tambourine into the crowd, and Johnny snatched it out of the air. Before he could celebrate, a woman charged him, grabbed the tambourine, and chomped down on his hand until he let go of it.

While the Stones rocked onstage with "(I Can't Get No) Satis-faction," Johnny turned to me with a horrified look and screamed, "She bit me, man!"

Ah, sweet, sweet rock 'n' roll. Apparently concerned parents and cultural critics were right. It had turned us all into savages!

Chapter Four

Coming of Age

Music was everything to us. We were immersed in it, listening to the radio, the record player, or to live performances in clubs and concerts. Being in a band made me feel part of all that was going on around us. Making music and singing won me acceptance in an older, cooler crowd, and there were other fringe benefits. Girls started showing interest in me after I became the singer in a rock band. A lot of guys joined bands to get girls, but I wasn't one of them. I honestly had no clue that playing in a band would make me somehow more attractive to the opposite sex.

Not that I complained when that blessed bit of magic worked. My first experience of sex actually involving another person took place in an apartment on the Yale University campus, where I was never a scholar but often a visitor. Our first encounter was at a friend's place, a typical '60s den of sin with black-light posters, Day-Glo decor, and walls of stereo speakers.

I don't think we planned to do the deed. I didn't even know

what "the deed" was. We were just messing around, teasing, kissing, and suddenly, wondrous female nakedness was unleashed all over the place. She shed her clothes so quickly my eyes had trouble focusing. I had to take a moment. Was this really a living, breathing girl? If so, this was the greatest gift I'd ever received, though I really didn't have a clue what to do next. She was two years older, a couple of inches taller than me, and beautiful.

Nature took its course. I was thankful my parts fit her parts. Afterward, I thought, *Wow, no wonder everyone makes such a big deal about this!*

Unlike Santa, the tooth fairy, and the Easter bunny, sex was real. Soon other girls were more than willing to get naked with me. I was stunned at my luck. I'll be forever grateful that My First was a patient, kind, gifted, and enthusiastic instructor. Once she'd introduced me to the glories of sex, I realized what I'd been missing in my first precious thirteen years of life. I had to make up for lost time. So I immediately asked when we could do it again.

We were never a couple, but we coupled off and on for the next two or three years. And yes, I'm fairly certain that being in a band and losing my virginity were related incidents, and I didn't hate that part of my life at all. Sometimes I'd sneak her into our house while my mother was sleeping. Most nights I could have opened our doors to the Yale Precision Marching Band and Mom would not have stirred. She was exhausted from working as a secretary while trying to wrangle three teens bent on breaking every parental rule and crossing every boundary.

Turn On, Tune In, Drop Out

Somehow, around this time I convinced my parents that my career as a rock star was so promising I really didn't require any further public *ejication*. I never became a high school dropout, technically, but only because I never dropped in. My contention was that record company scouts were circling and I needed to practice with the band. To my everlasting shock and awe, my parents did not reject the idea out of hand. Instead, they countered with a tutor to homeschool me.

My guess is that the high school board kicked in to help pay for the tutor rather than have to deal with my rebellious ways. Still, the poor guy hired for the job of teaching me high school freshman courses at home never had a chance. He quickly realized that my focus was on an entirely different three Rs (rock 'n' roll and reefer) than those mandated by the state of Connecticut.

I did all of the homework my tutor assigned and earned As and Bs, but there were more than a few times that my homeschooling was more like homefooling. Sometimes, my designated homeschooler couldn't get in the front door of my home. We'd moved from the big house with the big yard on Boulevard, first to a little apartment and then to the lower half of a two-family flat on Elm Street, which is where all hell broke loose—from my parents' perspective, that is.

With Mom working long hours and Dad relegated to the visiting team, we lived in the designated parent-free smoke zone for all my bandmates, buddies, and our girlfriends. By the time the tutor came calling each morning, I was often too stoned to hear the doorbell. Marc Friedland and other co-conspirators frequently joined me in hiding behind the couch, giggling between hits on a joint, while the tortured tutor stood on the porch. I reasoned that I couldn't let him in because the entire house reeked of marijuana smoke. Many times we watched out the window, tears of laughter running down our faces, as he returned to his car and drove away in surrender.

Thus ended my formal education. I was about to enter a much bigger classroom in the world of music, a course of study that continues today. I also embarked on a lifelong effort to educate myself by reading English literature and philosophy, which would continue to inspire and enrich my passion for writing. I probably have enough hours in English literature to qualify for a degree by now.

I certainly recommend that people get as much formal education as they desire. I read a lot of great writers and poets on my own, and that helped my songwriting a great deal. I tried to study music so I could read it, but even that took too much time away from songwriting and performing. I am proud of what I achieved without a formal education because I immersed myself in what proved essential for my life's work. At a very young age, I began putting in twelve- to fourteen-hour days, honing my talents as a songwriter, producer, and performer. Still, the abrupt end of my schooling also meant there was no fallback from music, other than hard labor or washing dishes. I went all in.

My Moment

I believed singing was my destiny, especially after I had my first "moment" onstage. In 1967, the Nomads were playing the Exit, a college bar on the Yale campus in New Haven. Something happened to me that night while performing a raw B. B. King song, "I Got a Mind to Give Up Living," which was also recorded by the Paul Butterfield Blues Band and many others.

This big, slow blues song is very demanding to sing and, at fourteen years old, I was still finding my voice, trying to figure out who I was as a performer. Up to that point, I'd thought of myself more as a band member than a true singer, but that night my perception shifted. A minute or so into the song, the bar banter hushed. Suddenly I could hear my voice clearly. Startled, I looked out through the haze of smoke and realized that the college students and locals, all of them much older than I was, were actually listening to me. I could see the girls and women moving with the music. *Whoa!*

This powerful feeling came over me, better than any high I'd ever experienced. The audience was connecting to my music and to me. I felt powerful, appreciated, and grateful to my audience for listening, so I let it rip, wailing with all the vocal strength I could muster. When the music stopped, everyone in the place jumped up, cheering and applauding.

It was the first time we'd ever brought down the house. I'd been more accustomed to indifference and even the occasional "Get that kid out of here." So I was stunned by this response. And in that moment, I was hooked for life. Forever compelled and powerfully driven, I'd found my purpose.

COMING OF AGE

Just as my formal education was ending at the age of fourteen, I signed up for a different sort of class. Once again, I followed Orrin down this path. He'd been into martial arts for a while and he'd taught me some moves. I loved the kicks especially, and I thought they might come in handy. I was taking some flak for having long hair, since crew cuts were still the more socially acceptable style. I figured that Ribs couldn't always be there to defend me whenever some bozo threatened to cut my hair or kiss me, so learning self-defense seemed like a smart move.

Orrin introduced me to his instructor, Bill Haughwout, a thirty-year-old guy who owned the Connecticut Karate Association's dojo above our favorite source of music, Cutler's Record Shop in downtown New Haven. Bill was a stand-up citizen and a serious martial arts master who trained the local cops in self-defense. He also worked with underprivileged kids to build their self-esteem and confidence through martial arts. This was a few years before Bruce Lee's movie series—and long before the Teenage Mutant Ninja Turtles—incited a boom in the martial arts in the United States. Bill's dojo was ahead of its time, and considered one of the most advanced along the East Coast.

In the typical Hollywood scenario, two long-haired, pot-smoking musician brothers who signed up for karate classes with a hard-nosed, clean-living, martial arts sensei would be whipped into becoming disciplined, respectful, productive members of society and future presidents of the chamber of commerce. In the Bolotin real-life scenario, things didn't work out that way. Bill drank our Kool-Aid. He grew his hair long, got a divorce, and became the roadie for our band.

Seriously, when we first met Bill, he was a pillar of the community, with a wife, a house, two dogs, and an aquarium. Within a few months of hanging with our band and our bongs, even Bill's fish bailed on him. Our dojo master moved over to the dark side— the *sensei-milla* side, if you know your weed buds. Bill's dojo even became our rehearsal hall a couple of nights a week. He embraced the sixties lifestyle once his divorce came through. At one point, he started dating a really cute girl whom I had once dated. That was a little strange even for me, especially given that she and I had once rendezvoused in the basement of the Jewish Community Center when our band played there. I always hoped that Bill didn't find out about my earlier dalliance with the girl who became his girlfriend. I feared he might take it out on me during a sparring session and with one kick make my demise look like "an accident." Fortunately, we remained friends, and my bandmates and I were glad to hang out at his house, which was an adult-free zone. The fun was dampened, though, when no-neck Gino showed up. He wore black shirts and white ties and had no interest in the martial arts, the music, or the parties.

Gino was somebody somebody sent. Bill had apparently borrowed money from a student who had "connections." When our dojo master failed to make prompt repayment, Gino, the muscle, was dispatched. I don't know if Gino ever collected what Bill owed, but he went away after a week or so. He did seem to enjoy listening to our practice sessions. I like to think he was our first wiseguy fan.

SPARRING PARTNER

My best friend and sparring partner at the New Haven Karate Club was Bruce "Bree" Belford. His father was a prominent local lawyer and liberal. He and Mrs. Belford always welcomed us into their huge home. When I married a hometown girl, the ceremony was in the Belfords' backyard. An excellent student and a friend to everyone he met, Bree wasn't a musician, but we both became vegetarians at a young age and also shared an interest in Eastern philosophy and religions and, of course, martial arts.

Bree wasn't a big guy, but his martial arts skills brought him big respect. He was among the top students at our dojo, and I had benefited from sparring with our teacher, a third-degree black belt with shins made of iron. Bree and I were highly competitive, so we always sought each other out as sparring partners. We are close friends to this day, even though Bree lives in Australia and we see each other only a couple of times a year. Our friendship grew beyond the dojo in part because he was one of those rare people I trusted instantly, someone with integrity, someone whom I could talk to about anything and he would get it.

Even better, Bree could take a punch and a kick. Bree is Cato Fong to my Inspector Clouseau, as in the Pink Panther movies.

Like them, we enjoy springing surprise attacks on each other any-where and at any time. Sometimes it's just a brief burst or flurry of punches and kicks while the elevator is between floors or we're waiting for a cab. Other times, we go at each other for longer peri-ods, trading insults, shots, and blocks for fifteen minutes or more until the battle dissolves into exhaustion and laughter.

We lived with our girlfriends for a time in an apartment on Stanley Street in New Haven, and it was there that we began this ritual of whaling on each other in spontaneous assaults. Neither one of us could walk in the door without the other jumping out from behind the couch or a door, or out of the closet or pouncing down from the kitchen counter. We would then bash each other with high-speed punches, kicks, and blocks. If one of us woke up in the morning and sleepily came down to get a drink from the refrigerator, the odds were that the other one would be wait-ing and lurking somewhere, then lunge into an ambush, yelling "Haaiiiiiiiiyaaaaa," and the pummeling would begin yet again.

I particularly enjoyed waiting for Bree to come home from the grocery store carrying two or three bags of food, trying not to spill anything as he opened the door. I'd spring on him with a series of kicks and punches, ripping open the bags and sending heads of lettuce and bean sprouts flying across the room. Occasionally, my girlfriend, Maureen, or his girlfriend, Gypsy, would get caught in the fast-and-furious cross fire as collateral damage. The girls did not seem to find it as amusing as the boys.

Our rabid sparring often spilled out into the streets or erupted in movie theaters, restaurants, and other locations generally not receptive to what we regarded as part play-fighting, part training, part practical joking, and—since we were very competitive guys—always an attempt to land a good kick or punch just for bragging rights.

I have to confess that even today, Bree and I beat the crap out of each other at every opportunity. After my most recent trip to Australia for a 2012 symphony concert tour, I returned home with most of the skin on my shins shredded and bruised, courtesy of Dr. Bree Belford. I'm sure many of his patients wondered why the backs of their physician's forearms and his elbows were bruised and bloodied. I shouldn't be surprised that Bree knocks people out for a living in his anesthesiology practice. He's been trying to knock my ass out for years (without success, so far). We still greet each other with karate punches, blocks, and kicks. We say good-bye with flurries of the same. And in between, whether it's in a fine restaurant, a hotel elevator, or backstage at a concert, we take every opportunity to inflict bodily harm upon each other.

As we've gotten a little older, I've expected that Bree might back down a little. He has a booming medical practice and his hands are sort of important in his line of work. But no, my good buddy just keeps coming at me like a human weed-whacker. He's not exactly the underdog in this fight. I have had a lot of martial arts training. I spent hours upon hours sparring with Bill all through my teen years, but with all my travel and work as a performer, I never made the time to do all that is required to earn a black belt. Bree is a sixth-degree black belt in karate and a first-degree black belt in aikido.

In a 2012 dinner get-together, Bree brought backup—his friend William Cheung, who is a Wing Chun kung fu grand master and was an early instructor of Bruce Lee. During our meal, the gracious and fit seventy-two-year-old Chinese physician explained some of his kung fu techniques and philosophies, which only fired up our friendly fight club.

Jabs and kicks ensued over and under the table. Bree's fiancée, Pia, was with us, and she was not entirely amused: "You act like a grown-up until Michael comes to town—then you both act like children." (Which, I must say, is quite gratifying for both of us to hear. We just reverted back to living on Stanley Street as teenagers forty years ago.) We were really going at it that night. We were so busy trying to block and strike that we were oblivious to all the commotion we were causing in the restaurant. We started out sparring sideways, since we were seated next to each other, but then we pushed our chairs back from the table and went at it face-to-face, throwing shots faster and faster. We were laughing the whole time, but I think some of the other diners must have wondered if they'd walked onto a Jackie Chan movie set.

The restaurant manager approached my tour security guy, who was sitting a few tables away, and suggested that he might want to intercede, but he knew Bree and I were just playing. Fortunately, our kung fu grand master dinner partner also got the joke. He coached us and urged us on. Then, after dinner, Bree and I continued the sparring like middle-aged ninjas in the hotel elevator, with William Cheung standing between us. The grand master, who is still no one to mess with, amused himself by occasionally blocking our shots with a shrug of his shoulders.

By the time we reached our floor, we all stumbled out giggling like schoolboys, but only two of us continued trading shots down the hallway, laughing and limping all the way.

My Doggone Trip to California

In 1967, my other best hometown buddy, my musical sidekick and guitar hero Marc Friedland, lured me away from my first band, the Nomads, into a new group. This rock band was a reconstituted version of a group called George's Boys. Our drummer, Bob, was one of the original George's Boys, so he brought the name with him. Most people, including my father, assumed the band was named after my dad, but it was just a coincidence. Of course I never told my dad that. He was too big a fan and supporter. If it made Dad happy to think we named the group after him, that was fine with me.

George's Boys became a popular band around the local bars and Yale campus parties. But we never moved much beyond the hometown circuit because the lead singer—me—announced that he was quitting to embark on a personal quest. I wish I had some noble purpose to explain this decision, but in truth, I had a mental meltdown because my mother gave away my dog, Dog. (He was a mutt, but not stupid. If you said, "Nice Dog," for example, he perked right up.)

Mom gave Dog away because she said I wasn't taking proper care of him. Imagine that. I suppose food, water, an occasional walk, or basically any sense of responsibility whatsoever would have been nice. Eventually I made up for it in what became a life full of tremendous responsibility. I may not have exactly doted on the mutt, but for some reason the loss of him sent me into the doldrums. To recover, I decided to hitchhike across the country to California, where I planned to jump into the loving arms of the woman of my dreams, Cory Morrison, who was then living in Berkeley. Actually, just being in her vicinity was enough for me. I was not discouraged by certain harsh realities: I had no money, no real idea of how to get to Berkeley, and no claim on Cory, as she had never expressed anything other than a big-sister sort of fondness for me.

Maybe I was still angry about my parents' divorce and angry at the world. High levels of THC in my bloodstream and raging hormones may have played a role. Everyone has a male or female Cory Morrison at some point in life—an enchanting, unattainable, yet unforgettable object of desire. This wasn't lust. My first groupie was lust. I seriously wanted to marry Cory, join a commune with her, and spend my life playing guitar and singing while basking in her sweet glow.

Cory was five years older than me. She had a boyfriend, but I was sure I could win her heart. She'd stolen mine and taken it to Berkeley after she was kicked out of high school for daring to say that her history book was only one interpretation of events. Cory was right, of course, but the principal didn't see it that way.

After moving to Berkeley, she'd made the mistake of telling me to come visit anytime. She didn't mean it, but that didn't matter to me.

"I'm quitting the band and hitchhiking to Berkeley to see Cory," I announced to Ribs and the guys in the band. I figured they'd just find another singer and continue without me. Instead, Ribs and Bob announced they'd come along.

"If you leave there's no band, so we might as well go, too," Ribs said.

I told my mom I was hitchhiking to California.

She said, "That's ridiculous, you are not hitchhiking to California."

So, naturally, I hitchhiked to California.

By that time, she was used to my disappearing for extended periods. Most of the time I was hanging out with Orrin or other friends in the Village, or staying at the Friedlands' house, where the parents were stricter but the food was plentiful. The Friedlands always seemed to have a full pantry and they were extremely generous and welcoming. Looking back, I am especially amazed at how they opened their home to me and even allowed us to have band practice there. I'd like to take this opportunity also to set the record straight on something that occurred at the Friedlands' house: The ashes of charcoaled weed and seeds Mrs. Friedland kept finding in her fur coat pocket were not mine. They belonged to our friend Tom, who often took refuge in a basement storage room to smoke his pot in a pipe. Unfortunately, Alice Friedland stored her beloved fur coat in that same room. I had visions of her attending some social function, sticking her hand into her coat pocket, and coming up with illicit residue clinging to her hand and wedged under her manicured nails: "Good to see you, Mr. Mayor, please forgive the burned remnants from my pocket."

I feel so much better after clearing the air on that.

Now back to the story of our hitchhiking trek to California: All I knew was that we had to get on Route 66 somewhere in the Midwest and follow it to California. This was the sixties. Nobody had a plan. Or a map. We just went with the flow. We walked out to the nearest highway and stuck out our thumbs.

It was October. We were wearing light jackets. We had a grand total of twenty dollars between us, none of it belonging to me. There were consequences, naturally.

We damn near froze riding in the backs of pickup trucks or sleeping in ditches and under bridges. The trip took six days, and for half of them I was fairly certain I was dying of exposure and starvation. At night, I would find a bush to wrap myself around in between other bushes, which was the only thing that stopped the wind from continuously assaulting my face and body. My body shivered so hard some nights that I thought they'd find parts of me scattered all over in the morning. Ribs still had short hair at that point, and Bob's wasn't nearly as long as mine. They quickly figured out that if I stood beside the highway alone with my thumb out, the truck drivers would figure I was a girl and pull over. Their ruse was more than a little insulting, but damn if it didn't work. Ribs made sure to sit between the driver and me so the trucker couldn't make a grab for me. I wasn't allowed to talk for fear the driver would realize I wasn't a girl and throw us all back out on the road.

The highway was not a friendly place to be without a vehicle. More than once, we had to run for our lives because of hostile rednecks, predators, or perverts. I had nightmares of ending up as an ingredient in some serial killer's Hitchhiker Stew. Our twenty-dollar grubstake didn't last long, considering there were three of us and we were starving. Our salvation came when a family of good Samaritan "church people" picked us up one night somewhere in the heartland, took us to their warm home, and fed us until we fell blissfully asleep.

Another time we lucked out when Ribs spied a family checking out of their roadside motel room at 5 a.m. As soon as their car pulled away, we tried the door to their room and it was open. We went in, cranked up the heat, took hot showers, and slept under the covers until the maid came in four hours later and kicked us out.

You might find it hard to believe that alert lawmen in every state were eager to check us out. Most seemed to think we were juvenile runaways or escaped convicts. Ribs and Bob were over eighteen. I had Marc's driver's license, which put me at sixteen. Luckily, driver's licenses didn't have photos back then. Most cops just questioned us, checked us for drugs—we couldn't afford any on this trip—and let us go.

There was one notable exception. We were somewhere in an old neighborhood of Saint Louis, and the next thing we knew they were hauling us into their station. They said they were going to throw us in jail unless we cooperated in "an investigation." The cops wanted us to hang out in a strip mall known for its drug dealers. Our mission, should we decide to accept it, was to find out who the dealers were and rat them out. If we did not play along, they vowed to lock us up for vagrancy, or for violating the Clean Air Act.

We said we'd cooperate, mostly because we were freakin' starving and they bought us fast food. Their plan also was for us to be seen hanging out with an undercover cop, to give him credibility. He was a tough sell. He looked like a kid trick-or-treating as Teen Wolf, or Serpico having a bad hair day. Even we could barely contain our laughter every time we'd look over at his enormous black wig. But we pretended to go along with the plan. They dropped us off at the strip mall in a scary neighborhood and promised to return in a few hours. What ensued wasn't exactly a drug raid.

We eventually ditched Teen Wolf and ran to the roadside, where we hitched a ride back to Route 66 and hauled ass out of town.

We encountered other law officers but managed to avoid arrest through the rest of Missouri, Kansas, Oklahoma, and Texas. In New Mexico, another highway patrolman hauled us in to the station to make sure we weren't on the FBI's Most Wanted list. Once he confirmed our lack of criminal expertise, he was nice enough to drop us off on the highway so we could continue our trek through Arizona and into California, where we met up with another lawman in downtown L.A. He announced within about two minutes that he was hauling us back to headquarters and calling my parents because I was a minor far, far from home. He put us in the backseat of his squad car and slammed the door.

We thought, *This is it? We've come all this way just to get busted and sent home?*

The cop was in the front seat, talking on the radio, when another LAPD squad car pulled up behind us with its lights flashing. He jumped out and took instructions from the other cop. The next thing we knew, he threw open the back door and told us to get out. Apparently, there were more serious criminals afoot. We gladly climbed out and waved farewell as the two squads took off with sirens blaring.

We took this as a sign that karma was on our side, finally. We set out for Berkeley, and about ten hours later, we were knocking on the door of Cory's apartment. She seemed moderately thrilled to see us. Her live-in boyfriend wasn't nearly as enthused. Soon, though, he realized I wasn't much of a threat. Cory had room for only one guest on the couch, so Ribs and Bob had to find shelter with other friends. We stayed a couple of days, but it became clear that Cory wasn't going to ditch her boyfriend, quit college, and run off with me to a commune. So Ribs, Bob, and I hit the road again, my love for Cory still unreciprocated.

PLAYING FOR JOY

When we returned to New Haven, George's Boys re-formed as a new band named Joy, featuring Marc on bass guitar, Fred Bova on lead guitar, Bob on drums, and me on rhythm guitar. We performed at every opportunity, gradually moving up from high school dances and teen parties to Yale mixers, clubs, and college bars, which was interesting, since we were all underage. We could play but not drink, even when people sent up shots for us.

That was okay, because beer and shots were not our favorite intoxicants anyway. Some of us managed to keep a buzz going during our breaks by dashing out to our converted Wonder Bread delivery truck, which was adorned in psychedelic colors and trippy drawings of a giant sun with glowing rays, stars, moons, wizards, and rainbows rendered by our drummer, Bob, and hippie artist Brad Johannsen, who became a noted illustrator of posters and album and book covers, especially science-fiction novels.

Our truck's bold exterior screamed, "Officer, pull this vehicle over—stoned hippie musicians inside!" But that didn't stop me from using it as a rolling den of sin and vice. The truck's Wonder Bread origins were appropriate, since I was usually fully baked when riding in it. Once safely locked inside with friends and maybe a few fans, some of us would light up or fire up the bong and do our best to smoke the glass so no one could see in. We'd be in a blissful, silent stupor until the entire vehicle would seem to be exploding. It would take a while for us to realize that it was Ribs yelling and banging on the windows and doors: "You're supposed to be starting your next set!"

Back then, being stoned was part of my performance. Long-term career planning wasn't a priority for the artists or the record companies. Yet despite occasional lapses due to mind-altering drugs, Joy developed a strong following at hot clubs like the Yale hangout Hungry Charlie's, later known as Caleb's Tavern and then, most famously, as Toad's Place. The hometown crowd was always supportive, and Toad's also attracted other musicians. I was stunned during a set break one night there when David Lee Roth walked up, put a hand on my shoulder, and said, "Man, you've got a serious set of pipes there." He then proceeded to tell me a very sick joke, which I will not—and cannot—repeat here.

The first night we played Hungry Charlie's, we drew such a crowd they ran out of beer glasses. We were proud of that, though not so happy when we figured out they'd shorted us on our paycheck, which was supposed to be based on a "piece of the door," or the night's receipts. Still, we couldn't complain, because they kept inviting us back to play more gigs, once they stocked up on beer glasses.

California Dreamin'

Soon we were spreading Joy through all the Havens (New, North, West, and East) and beyond, into Branford and Hartford. Our fan base kept growing. Ribs always told me I was better than anyone on the radio. I thought he was nuts. Other friends of friends who knew somebody in the music industry were telling us that we should write more of our own songs if we wanted to get a recording contract. This encouragement inspired my unilateral decision to pack our guitars, drums, amps, and other gear into the Wonder Bread truck and head to Northern California in the summer of '68.

This was the summer after the Summer of Love, a historic period of creativity in rock and hippie history, but the Bay Area, and in particular the San Francisco neighborhood of Haight-Ashbury, was still very much a happenin' place. Janis Joplin of Big Brother and the Holding Company, the Grateful Dead, Jefferson Airplane, Sly & the Family Stone, and other psychedelic rock acts were based there. I can't fully explain why we had to leave Connecticut to refine our music, but then I can't explain, or remember, most of my teenage years.

I reasoned that if we wanted to "make it" in the music business, there was a lot more going on in the Bay Area than in New Haven. The other members of Joy weren't all that hard to convince. Our parents were another matter.

Somehow, I conned my mother into signing a letter making Ribs my temporary guardian, since I was still too young to travel without adult supervision. Marc was seeing a therapist who decided this trip would be good for him. His parents followed the doctor's orders and let both brothers go. Given that their family was in the plumbing supply business, I'm sure it was a wrenching experience (sorry). However we wrangled our freedom, we were soon on the road again, returning to California. This time instead of risking our lives as hitchhikers, we took our chances aboard our own hippie hallucin-o-van with a funky stick shift and a hit-or-miss clutch, which made driving it a trip unto itself. That constant grinding you heard along Route 66 many years ago was Joy in transit. We'd travel by day, clutch willing, and smoke up the interior at night, often parked in cow pastures or vacant lots.

Once again, I'm not sure how we made it. I can remember waking up in the back and discovering our designated driver asleep at the wheel on more than one occasion. Hell, they even let me drive, and I was only fourteen years old. Somewhere in Nebraska, Ribs checked us into a motel. Bob and I drove in search of some burgers (I was still in my pre-veggie days) and pulled over at what appeared to be the local version of a fast-food joint. As soon as we walked in, I felt like an alien being. We were obviously the first long-haired hippies to have ever dared enter this establishment. Before Bob and I could say, "We come in peace, brothers," the Nebraskans were all over our hippie faggot commie asses. They chased us into the parking lot, apparently fearful that we would infest their community or kidnap their women in the otherworldly Wonder Bread truck.

The local police stopped by not so much to enforce peace but to "confirm that you are not considering stopping anywhere near here ever again. We don't want your kind around here."

We fled the Cornhusker State for the much friendlier brotherly love of the Bay Area, and searched for an affordable space with room to live, write music, and practice for eight hours a day. Our lack of funds ruled out anything in San Francisco, so we ended up in a sketchy neighborhood in Oakland. The only thing we could find in our price range and with enough room to serve as a rehearsal hall was a loft space above a Laundromat in East Oakland. When we moved in, we had no idea that we were just a short distance from the headquarters of the Black Panther Party. Nonviolent protest was not the Panthers' thing. They seemed to be perpetually fighting gun battles with lawmen in the streets. We arrived just a few months after the Panthers clashed with local cops and lost one of their own. It was around this time that the FBI's J. Edgar Hoover denounced our hometown revolutionaries as "the greatest threat to the internal security of this country."

Despite the urban warfare in our community, we had no shortage of visitors to our Oakland crash pad. Along with four band members, our manager, Ribs, and his girlfriend, Denise, we were joined by a steady stream of drop-ins and long-term guests, some of whom ended up sleeping in the building's boiler room. We called our Oakland dive "a seventeenth-century loony bin," which was appropriate given the fact that it was occupied by a horde of pot-smoking teenage rockers and an ever-changing cast of friends.

We paid the rent and fed ourselves on the Bolotin beggar plan. Nearly every day Ribs or Marc would panhandle for cash to buy gas so they could drive me to the Berkeley campus in the Wonder Bread truck. The first challenge was to get our not-so-magic bus started, because its battery was roached. Once they had gas money, the Friedlands would use their mother's AAA card, call out their road rangers, and have them fire up our ride. Every now and then we'd just push-start it down a hill, but there were obvious hazards to doing that.

Once I was dropped off on campus, I'd find a shady spot, pull out my guitar, put out a tip box, and perform for whatever pocket change came my way. Long before I made hit recordings of "Dock of the Bay" and "Georgia," I sang those same songs for nickels, dimes, and quarters to pay for our meals. Since Marc and I weren't yet vegetarians, those meals consisted of grilled hamburgers, Hostess Zingers, and soft custard. Ribs, however, was already eating what appeared to be bark and grass.

When we weren't grubbing for meal money, we were rehearsing and writing new material. Ribs was convinced that we were on the path to greatness. He often told us we had it all—the look, the sound, and the music—and that we were "ahead of our time." I was harder to convince. My perfectionist's drive had kicked in, and I was constantly pushing the band to practice and refine its performances. I refused to take gigs because I didn't think we were where we needed to be.

I was so relentless that our drummer, Bob Brockway, practiced until his hands and feet bled. He was intense, too, ripping off such a fast, tight roll of rim shots that he'd break the wires that held the snares on his snare drum. That happened so often he had to buy heavy-duty deep-sea fishing line to hold them in place. Fred Bova, the guitar player, worked almost continuously inventing new and strange sounds by rewiring the guitar and the amp. Marc was already a flawless bass player, but he practiced so hard his fingers went numb. My throat grew raw from all the singing, but I was my own harshest critic.

It was my perfectionism, and maybe my fear as well, that drove me. Whenever Ribs or the others in the band pushed to take a gig somewhere, I dragged my feet, driving them to near revolt. The only live performance we did was opening for the talented blues singer Tracy Nelson and her Mother Earth band at a Sausalito club called the Ark. Tracy went on to win Grammy nominations for performances with Willie Nelson in 1974 and with Marcia Ball and Irma Thomas in 1998, but our concert with her band drew less than a hundred people.

I kept pushing everyone, including myself, to get better. I was the youngest member, but as the lead singer and songwriter, I had clout and I used it. When I decided that we needed to leave Oakland and return to New Haven to make our first demo record and to try to get a recording contract, the others in Joy followed, muttering mutiny and cursing my name under their breaths.

BACK HOME TO NEW HAVEN

We loaded up the van and returned to Connecticut in December 1968. There, we rented a big house at 555 Amity Road in Woodbridge that became known as the "Joy House." We probably should have called it the "Bubby Ida House," because the rent was paid for with money given to the Friedlands by their grandmother. Actually, Bubby Ida subsidized a lot of what the brothers and I did in those days. Mostly she gave money to Marc, not because he was her favorite grandson but because of guilt.

When Marc was six years old, he was running around the house like a typical crazed kid waiting for his favorite cartoon, *Heckle and Jeckle*, to come on. Bubby Ida was washing a window in the living room and somehow, just as Marc ran beneath that same window outside, the glass broke. Marc looked up at the sound of the crash and a big shard of glass hit him and sliced his forehead with a deep gash that required seventy-two stitches.

Marc eventually recovered, but Bubby Ida never did. She was forever saddled with guilt and remorse, blaming herself for the scar every time she saw her grandson.

"From that point on, Bubby Ida felt that she had to give me every spare penny that came her way," Marc said. "It was her way to make things right with the world."

Bubby Ida, like my own grandmothers, was a very loving, warm woman who even signed over her welfare checks to Marc, and I think gave us food stamps, too. She was in many ways a typical grandmother. Jewish, black, Irish, or otherwise, grandmothers always want to make sure everyone has a warm bed and enough to eat.

With her help, the Joy House provided all that and more. We worked hard on our music, and our weekend parties drew friends and strangers from up and down the East Coast. People I swear I've never met still tell me they "lived" with us on weekends at that house. I'm sure they did. The Joy House was so big, so crowded with visitors, and so fogged with the residue of reefer madness, I probably never saw them.

From Demo to Dojo to Deal

I'd pushed the band to return to New Haven because I thought we could cut a demo for an affordable price at the same place the Shags had recorded, Syncron Studios in Wallingford, which later became known as Trod Nossel Productions and is still in business. Ribs scraped together the money for producing a demo, so after we'd settled into the Joy House back home in Connecticut, we spent several days at Syncron cutting a demo tape with two songs I'd written in Oakland: "It's About That Time" and "This Man." I had not a clue what I was doing in the studio, but everyone seemed to like my crazy songs and we rehearsed them well. The studio's engineer walked us through the entire process in a few hours, and before we knew it, we'd made a recording.

Once we had the demos down, Ribs fired up the magical mystical tour bus and set off to lay siege upon every record company in New York City. He refused to leave until they listened, so most gave in just to get Ribs out of the office. By night he slept in the truck and by day he did everything short of offering sexual favors or taking hostages to convince record company executives to listen to our demo and offer us a contract.

I'm not really sure about the sexual favors part, but Ribs was very determined. I know he camped out in the office at CBS's Epic Records. The receptionist kept telling him the person he needed to see was busy, but Ribs refused to give up, bless him. That was Ribs. He believed in us and fought for us. After waiting all day and into the night, he finally collared someone and played the demo. We must have impressed the guy. A few weeks later an Epic producer, Ken Cooper, asked where he could hear us perform. We set up a session in our old martial arts studio hangout.

We'd been rehearsing eight hours a day in Oakland and we were eager to perform for someone, anyone, but it was especially sweet to play for a producer for a major record company. Epic was launched as a jazz, pop, and classical label by CBS the same year I was born. When the rock 'n' roll wave hit, Epic quickly became home to some of the top acts, including Jeff Beck, the Hollies, the Yardbirds, and the Dave Clark Five. I was a fan of all of those groups, so it was both exciting and intimidating to see their records on the wall.

RECORD DEAL NO. 1

Ken Cooper came to the dojo audition with his girlfriend. We played four or five original songs. Ken was very complimentary. He said my voice was "distinctive" and he liked the songs I'd written. He offered the band a recording contract on the spot. I was fifteen years old, and, believe me, I didn't have to "talk to my people" about making a decision. Well, actually I did have to ask my mom because I was still a minor. A few weeks later, a recording contract for two singles arrived. I didn't bother to read the pages and pages of legal mumbo jumbo. I signed on the dotted line, and so did my mother as my legal guardian.

It was 1969. Getting the Epic contract seemed like a sure sign that I was about to fulfill my father's big, *big*, *BIG!* prediction for my musical career. History, *Billboard* magazine, and Wikipedia will note, however, that my timetable turned out to be off by just a bit.

Eighteen long and frustrating years would pass before I finally had my first hit.

Credit: Epic Record Company

Chapter Five

The Epic Struggle

E pic Records' Ken Cooper promised us a bonus of $2,000 for signing the recording contract. The poverty-stricken members of Joy and our manager, Ribs, were thrilled. Even with a five-way split, this was a windfall.

Imagine our excitement when the check arrived and with it came an extra "0."

Some soon-to-be-terminated clerk in accounting had goofed, making it out for $20,000 instead of $2,000.

A heated and lengthy ethical discussion ensued. The band members and our manager debated whether we should cash the check or do the right thing: call Ken and tell him about the mistake. Some of the guys argued that it wasn't a mistake. They felt we should have been paid $20,000. They'd heard that amount was more with the norm for a signing bonus for bands.

The debate and arguing went on for three or four days. Ribs and Marc asked their parents, and, of course, they told us we should call Ken and report the mistake. In the end, that's what we did because no one wanted to tick off Epic before the band had a chance to put out a record.

Naturally, Ken said it was a mistake. Epic canceled the big boy check and sent us its little sister. Each member of the band received $400, which still amounted to a huge payday for each of us, me in particular. Since the Wonder Bread van had finally expired, Marc used his share to buy an old ambulance that he called "the Enterprise." He transformed the emergency vehicle for accident victims into our band transport, and, as I recall, there was some sexual healing that went on in that ambulance when we were its owners.

With my vast financial windfall, I bought my first serious guitar, a red Rickenbacker just like the one George Harrison played. It was mere coincidence that our first single featured a "B" side track written by a couple of other Beatles. Ken Cooper had the final say on the songs on the record. He decided the "A" side should feature a song I'd written back in the Oakland Laundromat loft. It was called "Bop Bah," and it was a breakup song with the lyrics: "Help me to understand exactly where you're goin'. / Help me to understand just what it's like to be knowin'...."

Ken apparently selected that track because it was our only original up-tempo song and the closest thing to mainstream pop rock in our repertoire.

While "Bop Bah" was a decent song and people were responding well to it, some of the guys in the band argued that it wasn't our strongest. They thought this particular song did not fit our desired image as a soulful blues rock and pop band. Our contract also called for each single to have a "B" side, and Ken Cooper chose that song for us, too. We weren't happy about this choice, either, since it wasn't our original song. That's not to say Lennon and McCartney weren't great songwriters, but "It's for You" wasn't really our kind of sound. They'd written it for their friend British pop singer Cilla Black, who released her version in 1964. The Beatles never did their own recording of the song, but Three Dog Night recorded an a cappella version for their 1969 debut album.

Again, we didn't want to tick off our record company during our first dance with them, so we went with the flow. We worked hard in the studio to give them a couple of different versions of "Bop Bah" with varied lengths and drum effects. Of course they put our least favorite version on the record. They also printed the wrong name on the label, calling it "Bah Bah Bah," which sounded like either a lamb's lament or a solo from *Scrooge the Musical*.

The regrets and embarrassments did not end there. I was still using my true family name then, but Epic managed to spell it wrong, as "Bolotkin," in the songwriting credit on the label. In fact, the only things right on the label of our first single were "Epic" and "produced by Ken Cooper." Still, our friends and family were excited when the record came out, so we didn't want to be "kill-Joys" and tell them that it was the wrong name on the wrong version of the wrong song.

This did seem like a bad omen for our first record, but we felt better when our local rock radio station, WNHC, jumped on the song and gave us a lot of airplay. Our first single premiered at No. 60 on the New Haven station's hit chart. Members of the Joy fan base suspected that our hometown sales may have been boosted by a certain Cutler's Music Shop salesperson named Kathy, who happened to be dating a certain lead singer of a certain band at that time. She was a very sweet and supportive young lady, but despite her efforts, "Bah Bah Bah" went bust after a couple of weeks and dropped off the charts with little fanfare beyond our hometown's city limits.

Ken Cooper did set us up with a good gig after our record came out. In November of 1969, we played the Electric Circus in the East Village. This was a very happening place, one of the wildest in New York City. Billed as "hallucinogenic and hedonistic," it had featured performances by the Allman Brothers, Sly & the Family Stone, the Velvet Underground, and the Doors, among other groups somewhat more renowned than Joy. I stood on that hallowed stage that night and felt both thrilled and panicked because we were there, but I didn't feel we were ready to be playing where the greatest had gone before.

The other positive memory I've had over the years to help counter the otherwise "Bah Bah Bah" bad experience is that while we were recording the song, a veteran sound engineer at Epic pulled me aside and said, "You have that thing in your voice, that thing that it takes to make it big as a singer." His words of encouragement meant a great deal to me, because he was a professional who'd heard many singers and bands. I put his comment in my confidence bank. I would need it.

Our contract with Epic called for us to record and release two singles, each with "A" and "B" sides, but after the quick death of our first effort, our record company seemed to lose interest. Epic also lost Ken Cooper, who suddenly was "no longer with us." We soldiered on and recorded another two songs with our new producer, Sandy Linzer, who also was a very successful songwriter.

For this record we put down two original songs. The "A" side featured "Going Back to New Haven," written by Tom Pollard; and the "B" side had "Cookie Man," contributed by Sandy. The record was never released, so the world was robbed of the chance to hear me singing some sweet harmonies with brother Orrin, who joined us for that session.

RECORD DEAL NO. 1: DOA

After they treated our second record like an ugly stepchild, Epic's silence was deafening. We felt like orphans who'd been adopted by

Daddy Warbucks only to be tossed back out onto the street. Joy went from playing a big-time venue, the Electric Circus in Greenwich Village, to doing sets for our hometown friends at the auditorium of the New Haven Jewish Community Center. The latter venue also provided the stage for my one and only venture as a stand-up comedian.

Once again, Marc Friedland was my co-conspirator.

One of our favorite pastimes was to create various comedy routines. Neither of us can remember exactly what inspired this particular event, but when we smoked pot, Marc and I were convinced we were the world's funniest people. In fact we were—to each other. So I guess we decided to share our *high-larity* with the rest of the world, or at least those within driving distance of the New Haven Jewish Community Center.

Marc recalls that our audience consisted of fewer than a dozen people, and it's likely half of them were relatives, members of the center's custodial crew, or friends. We decided it would be funny to share our impressions of Jack Abramowitz, a Friedland family friend with a distinctive style of speech and a penchant for cigars. I'd never actually met the guy, so my impression was actually my imitation of Marc and Ribs imitating him. They said Jack often bragged about his son Alan, and we made fun of that. We also told a long story involving red and green tomatoes that we thought was extremely funny.

The audience did not concur. Thus ended my one and only foray into stand-up comedy. Since then I've come to know many professional comedians, including my friend the late Rodney Dangerfield. I did a cameo in his 1997 movie *Meet Wally Sparks*, and after I demonstrated my impersonation of him Rodney said, "You do me better than I do me."

NOT MY LUCKIEST OF TIMES

I woke up in my Joy House bedroom in a daze one day in August of '69. Usually there was live or recorded music blaring, but on that day there was nothing but silence. I was home alone. I grabbed the phone and called around, but I couldn't find my bandmates, my brother, or any other friends or girlfriends.

I discovered that while I was sleeping like Rip van Winkle, everyone I knew had headed to a dairy farm 130 miles away in upstate New York. It seemed that the rest of the world had decided to have a party—a three-day music festival—and I'd missed the memo. Later, some friends claimed they called and tried to wake me but couldn't, and so I became forever known as the guy who was too stoned for Woodstock.

If I could have dragged myself out of bed, I might have been hanging out with Orrin and other friends when the Woodstock documentary cameras caught them dancing at the front of the stage for the legendary Carlos Santana performance of "Soul Sacrifice." You can see them clearly in the film. (Hint: Orrin is *not* the bare-ass-naked guy dancing with a live sheep the size of a Labrador in his arms.)

Apparently, this wasn't exactly my time. Soon after I missed out on the experience of Woodstock, I met a girl I really liked. I was pursuing her, but it turned out she was more into another guy. On top of that, within a year of our signing with Epic, I received a "Dear Michael" letter. Some Harvard law grad probably put the wording together—"You are free to sign with other labels"—but it sounded to me like a teenager lamely trying to dump her boyfriend without hurting his feelings by announcing: "You are now free to date other girls!"

I was confused, disappointed, and discouraged. Yet I was

determined to get back into the recording studio. We'd been so close twice. I wasn't about to give up. After all, I was Bullet Bolotin's boy. So I kept driving toward my goal, but I had to build a new band to do it. After Epic gave Joy the kiss-off, Marc and Ribs decided that the music business was too crazy for them. They moved to Los Angeles and opened Nature's Door, a twenty-four-hour vegetarian restaurant named after a song I'd written. I could never blame another artist for throwing in the towel and saying "enough" because a career in music is so unpredictable. I would face many more tough years myself.

While they were dishing up tofu and brown rice in West Hollywood, I put together a new band in New Haven. I rounded up a few other musician friends—Fred Bova (lead guitar), Hilly Michaels (drums), and Glenn Selwitz (bass guitar)—and we went to work learning new songs I'd written. Since money was tighter than ever, we recorded a new demo on a reel-to-reel tape recorder set up in my apartment. We put three songs on the demo: "I Work for Freedom," "The Fire Keeps Burnin'," and "Running Away from the Night Time."

We had the demo ready for prime time in May 1971, and by then the Friedland brothers were back. Nature's Door had closed, which freed up Marc to rejoin the band and set loose Ribs to once again serve as my manager and pitchman. I sent Ribs the new demo and either he really liked it or just needed something to do because he was out of work; either way, he offered to take the new Joy demo around to record companies and music publishers in Los Angeles and Hollywood. Thanks to Ribs and his persistence, we landed a production deal with Dimension Music, run by Michael Z. Gordon and Steven Lewis. This deal allowed Dimension to place the album with a major label.

RECORD DEAL No. 2

Dimension Music helped us secure a recording contract—for an album, not just a single—with Pentagram Records. Pentagram was a low-budget record company based in L.A. One of the owners was a great recording engineer and mixer named Al Schmitt, whom I would work with many times over the years. We were extremely excited and equally nervous about this new record deal. We didn't want to blow it this time. I was determined, and fully committed to writing, recording, and delivering the most compelling music possible.

We decided to work on this new record in Southern California. Ribs and Marc were living in Venice, and my mother had moved out to L.A. to finally devote herself to writing songs while also working as a secretary at Universal Studios, where she typed television show scripts and saved us copies to read so we'd all know ahead of time what was happening on our favorite shows. She enjoyed meeting the actors and actresses. One of her favorites was the smooth-talking charmer Telly Savalas, star of *Kojak*, whom I would hear more about nearly twenty years later when I began dating his stepdaughter.

When the band and I moved out to California in 1971, I was in my first serious relationship. I had met Maureen, an Irish girl who would become my wife four years later, while she was working at Cutler's Record Shop. Like many record stores of that time, Cutler's also had a "head shop" section that featured rolling papers, pipes, Day-Glo posters, black lights, and all the other essential hippie accoutrements. Maureen worked there and she was everyone's sweetheart—a warm, kind, and friendly soul who was fun to be around. Marc and Ribs and all the guys in my bands loved her.

I never had to work at getting girls. I was the lead singer in a rock band and girls were throwing themselves at me, but I was never interested in dating them for more than a couple of weeks. With Maureen it was different. When she and I started "going steady," and I embarked upon my first real relationship—which would become one of the most important relationships of my entire life—I had a lot to learn.

Perhaps seeing my mom and dad split gave me a sense of insecurity or fear of abandonment. I was a teenager, in the midst of new love, and for those reasons I was holding on tight.

CRAZY KIDS

I rode out to California aboard Marc's converted school bus, dubbed "Oogy Ahhgy," in the summer of '71. Nobody seems to know where they came up with that name, but it might have been the noise the six of us made while trying to push-start the damned thing, which weighed more than a loaded garbage truck. We often had to push it more than fifty feet to get the thing started. Aside from that, this was the smoothest cross-country trip we'd had. There were actual bunks aboard the bus, which was all done up with an interior that resembled a Peter Max poster.

Maureen and I eventually settled into an apartment in Van Nuys. It had hot and cold running water, air-conditioning, and a third occupant: Marc Friedland, who slept in the second bedroom and helped us cover the rent while working on new songs with me. Shortly after he settled in with us, Marc found his first-ever serious girlfriend. She was a nice Jewish girl named Wendy Abdul. Marc was twenty; Wendy was seventeen and still lived with her parents and sister in Van Nuys. She couldn't go out much because both of her parents worked and she had to take care of her little sister, who was only nine years old.

The little sister's name was Paula, and she was a cute little thing. Maureen and I often went to Wendy's with Marc to hang

out. Paula, the adorable, nine-year-old Brownie, was always dancing and singing around the house, bugging me to play the guitar or
play board games with her. I enjoyed teasing her and I would call
her a "little brat."

On *Jimmy Kimmel Live!* in 2011, that same cute kid, now grown
up, talked about those days and noted that she was often frustrated
because I refused to pay much attention to her. She said I was
more interested in practicing guitar and rehearsing with my band
members, who lived in her building. She also said that I was nice
enough to sing her to sleep.

Paula told Jimmy that one day when I was babysitting her with
Marc, she was jumping on the couch and somehow managed to
get a pencil jammed into her leg. She claimed I showed complete
disinterest but finally drove her to the hospital, but honestly, I
only vaguely recall the incident. My story is that she poked herself
with the pencil so we'd take her out for ice cream by way of the
emergency room. Unfortunately, we lost touch with each other
when things between Marc and Wendy didn't work out after a
couple of years.

In the 1980s I heard that Paula was making a name for herself
as a choreographer for the Laker Girls cheerleaders and for music
videos by members of the Jackson family. My songwriting career
took off around the same time, and I decided to track down Paula
when I was preparing to do a music video for the first album featuring my own pop songs.

"Paula, this is Michael Bolton," I said.

She didn't seem to recognize my voice at first and she thought
someone was playing a prank on her. Then she thought a minute
and said: "*It is not!*"

"Who else would call you a little brat?" I replied.

"Oh my God, it *is* you!"

We later met for dinner with her sister and talked about old times. I also convinced Paula to work out the basic choreography for my "Wait on Love" music video, co-written and produced by Jonathan Cain of the band Journey. If you've seen that video, you might not be able to recognize the young bass player because of his high-rise flattop haircut, but it is Randy Jackson, who would work with Paula on another stage many years later. (Randy and I had fun working together and have long talked about putting together another rock band and going on tour—we might just do it one of these days.)

I still see Paula from time to time in my travels. We had a great time at the 2012 White Nights Festival in Saint Petersburg, Russia, which brings together performers from around the world. We visited a children's hospital together, and then, during a talent contest at the festival, we laughed our asses off talking about old times and how crazy our lives have been since we first met. I love catching up with her. Even though she has become a very successful entertainer on so many levels, she's still the sweet, down-to-earth, unpretentious, and cool person I've known for so long—and is no longer a little brat at all.

Joy 2.0

When Marc moved in with Maureen and me in the late summer of 1971, we focused on writing songs for our Pentagram album. Then we began rehearsing with a new, expanded version of our band. Our practice studio was aboard Marc's Oogy Ahhgy school bus, which he kept parked at the apartment complex on Coldwater Canyon managed by my mother and her boyfriend, Bill Segal. It was good to have them as landlords since we were often—make that always—behind on our rent. Joy 2.0 included Michael Hillman (aka Hilly Michaels) on drums and percussion, Glenn Selwitz on bass guitar, Marc Friedland on piano and organ, and my brother, Orrin, who was back from one of his exotic adventures, sharing lead and backing vocals with me as well as some guitar. We recorded ten songs.

RECORD DEAL NO. 2: PENTAGRAM BECOMES PENTA-GONE

We worked to perfect the recordings. I drove everyone, including myself, relentlessly. My hunger to make it in music was ferocious. I often carried around this intense feeling that I had to perform at the highest level of my abilities, and I demanded the same of the others in my band. One of the inner messages that played over and over in my head was, *You never know if you'll get another chance. You have to seize this opportunity because it might be your last.*

In this instance, as in many others, I was adamant that we do all we could to make this album a hit. To my consternation, it was another miss. As soon as we emerged from the recording studio with our songs ready for the album, we were informed that Pentagram had gone out of business, which seemed to happen a lot to record companies I signed with in those days.

My bandmates were as despondent as I was at this setback. We did have one brief glimmer of hope when the guys at Dimension set us up to write and record songs for the sound track of a low-budget scary movie. They could give us only a $500 advance to split seven ways, and they could pay for only four songs. They had to pay our musicians union dues, and they couldn't afford to do that and finance an entire album at the same time. We recorded these songs: "Running Away from the Nighttime," which I wrote and sang lead vocals on; "Where Do We Go from Here," with words and music by Michael Z. Gordon of Dimension; "Our Town," with words and music by Larry Quinn; and an instrumental called "Cowboy's Theme," of undetermined origins.

The songs were for the little-known 1971 movie called *November Children*, which was later re-released as *Nightmare County* and then re-re-released as *Nightmare of Death*. Good luck trying to find a copy of the movie: like our record, it disappeared almost as soon as it was released. As excited as we were to be involved in making music for a movie, this was, sadly, not our foray into blockbuster film sound tracks.

Blood, Sweat & Bolotin

After our disappointing Pentagram and moviemaking experiences we were feeling down and out. Yet every time depression threatened to slap me down, something would happen to give me hope.

In 1972, drummer Bobby Colomby called and asked me if I'd like to discuss joining Blood, Sweat & Tears, the Grammy-winning rock-jazz fusion band formed four years earlier by Bobby and Al Kooper in Greenwich Village. The band had gone through a series of personnel changes. While Al was a noted songwriter, musician, and producer who'd worked with Bob Dylan and Mike Bloomfield, BS&T had their biggest commercial success with his replacement, David Clayton Thomas, a tremendous lead singer.

After four stellar years with the band, David decided to move on to a solo career, so Bobby asked me to come to his home to discuss joining BS&T. There was still some dissension in the band over whether they wanted to be more of a pop-rock or a jazz-rock fusion group. Bobby and I talked for a few hours at his home, but in the end, nothing came of our discussions. Another near miss racked up. BS&T went through a couple of different lead singers before David Clayton Thomas returned three years later. Bobby now manages Chris Botti, who performed on my *GEMS* album.

These were lean days, in more ways than one. My finances

were slim and I was slimmer. I'd been a vegetarian since the age of eighteen and that had something to do with my fat-free frame, but there wasn't much bread on our table, either. Today, my daughters still joke that I'm really a "junk-food vegetarian," because I tend to graze on Pringles and similar snacks. Back then, in the Lean & Mean Times, my bandmates and I would pile aboard Marc Friedland's Oogy Ahhgy and go for gorgings at Pizza Hut's 99-cent "All You Can Eat" lunch buffet. It wasn't health food, but it was cheap.

Finally, I had to find a day job—or two—just to pay the rent. Beyond music my credentials were not impressive. Most people my age were just finishing their senior year in high school. I'd skipped every year. Then again, my first real-world nine-to-five job attempts didn't exactly require a higher education. When I was fifteen and basically homeless (I did live on and off with my grandparents), a friend of mine helped me get a job at his father's Splash car wash near the Westville Amity Shopping Center. My job was to wipe down the cars. I wiped out instead. The boss fired me a few days into the job for lacking the proper drying technique. He said that I rubbed both customers and their cars the wrong way.

My next non–rock star career move was to work as a waiter in a vegetarian restaurant. I figured the fringe benefits would be better there than at the car wash, but again I lacked certain essential skills. The owner fired me after his family came in for dinner one night and his sister ordered a veggie burger. I was on the sandwich line so I whipped it up superfast. When his sister complained that there seemed to be no actual veggie burger in the veggie burger sandwich, the owner told her to keep biting. She'd nearly finished it before determining that the superfast sandwich artist—me— had neglected one key ingredient. The veggie burger itself.

In my previous job at another vegetarian restaurant when I was living in L.A., I distinguished myself there by dumping salad dressing all over a customer when I became distracted by a group of models in miniskirts being seated at a nearby table. I wasn't cut out for the service industry, apparently. Of course, most of the waiters and waitresses in L.A. really are actors and actresses waiting for a break. That may not have been my dream, but I did get to try it on for a bit part.

Our Band in Blume

While we were in L.A., a friend of ours hooked us up with his father, who was a casting director. He tipped us off one day that a movie crew was looking for extras. The pay was thirty dollars a day, so we went for it, which is how Marc, Ribs, Tom Pollard, and yours truly came to be the real stars (at least in our mothers' minds) of the 1973 movie *Blume in Love*, which also featured George Segal, Susan Anspach, Marsha Mason, Shelley Winters, and Kris Kristofferson.

I made it into two scenes because I brought a change of clothes, hoping they wouldn't realize I'd already been in one scene. I was hoping to double my money. Our big scene in the movie takes place, fittingly, in an unemployment line. The scene was shot at the public welfare office in West Los Angeles. I'm shown sitting and reading a book and the others are standing in the line. My role was more of a stretch than theirs, but I thought we all gave masterful performances thanks to our many years of perfecting our unemployed postures and expressions.

Tom and I filmed another scene that didn't make it into the movie, probably because they would have had to pay us more and give us screen credits. I'd brought along my guitar to practice and write some material during breaks in filming. Tom, who had a beautiful voice, was singing and harmonizing with me and the director decided to shoot us. Though the scene was lost on the cutting-room floor, I did get one good review. While we were practicing a song Tom wrote, Kris Kristofferson walked by, listened for a second or two, and, walking away, he said: "I wish I had a voice like that."

I was surprised and grateful for the compliment from the great singer and songwriter, and oddly enough, this was the first in a series of similar brief encounters I would have with Kris over the years. Though we never became friends or even had an extended conversation, he has cropped up at interesting times in my life, almost like some sort of herald of things to come. In this first instance, it was as if Kris Kristofferson were sent by the music gods to give me enough hope to keep striving.

My next Kris encounter of a strange kind was only about ten months later. I was working again as a waiter, this time at H.E.L.P. (Health through Education, Learning & Peace), which owner Warren Stagg, a holistic healer and spiritualist, claimed was the first organic vegetarian restaurant and spiritual center in the U.S. The restaurant, which also served as the setting for a scene in *Blume in Love* (with Warren playing a waiter), was more like a hippie dinner club.

Marc Friedland had worked in the kitchen and the adjoining grocery from time to time. I was living in North Hollywood and commuting to and from work on a sorry-as-shit red Vespa with a broken accelerator cable that I had to operate by tying a shoestring to it that I pulled to go faster and let go of to slow down. The brakes had surrendered after I lost control on an oil patch and nearly went ass over elbows to the bottom of a canyon.

Kristofferson, who'd been in H.E.L.P.'s scene in *Blume*, walked into the restaurant one day as a civilian with his beautiful wife, the singer Rita Coolidge. I served them and reminded Kris that we'd met on the *Blume* set. He said they were back in town working on a record and I told him I was working on a demo. He was very genuine and kind, wishing me good luck, and he gave me a five-dollar tip, which was a lot of money back then for a starving hippie musician. Still, I appreciated his encouragement much more than I appreciated the money.

Chapter Six

Mad Dogs & Mites

M aureen left California and returned to Connecticut to find a job, so I moved in with the Friedlands and a small pack of other vegetarian hippies in a commune. Calling it that might be a stretch. The roadside dump more closely resembled a hobo camp for the homeless. Known as the "People Farm," it was not at all as idyllic as that name may imply. Most pigs had better living quarters. I'm just glad we didn't realize at the time that Charles Manson and his murderous harem lived nearby.

Seventeen humans and an equal number of domesticated animals and wild beasts lived on the forested small parcel of land just off Grandview Drive along Topanga Canyon. Marc and I shared an old metal trailer. The others lived in a motley mix of makeshift shelters; everything from tepee tents to plywood shacks, ramshackle old cabins, and crudely constructed tree houses.

Ribs had somehow claimed a lower-level apartment in the only true house with electricity and plumbing. The main house had the only refrigerator and bathroom on the premises. Ribs was very strict in guarding both, but especially the bathroom. The plumbing for it ran through his apartment's walls, and if someone flushed it sounded like a tsunami or Niagara Falls descending upon him. At one time, Ribs limited use of the bathroom to pregnant women, but even they could use it only during rainstorms. Otherwise, all residents were expected to use the great outdoors. After all, there were many strange characters living on the People Farm.

SHELTER IN A STORM

My band and I were all struggling to hang on to our dreams in the early '70s. One by one many of our musician friends were giving up because they couldn't support themselves or their families. I had my moments of doubt, but I didn't have a family to support, and without even a high school degree my options were limited. So I was more determined than ever to make it in the music business, but there was a lot less Joy—the band, that is. We'd worked hard to create the album for Pentagram, but the stress and strain and disappointment of another failed record deal resulted in the departure of everyone but Marc and me.

For a while we tried to recruit some new band members, and one of the drummers we auditioned was this tall, skinny, clean-cut blond guy who looked just like the actor Ed Begley Jr., because he would soon be the actor Ed Begley Jr. He was just twenty-three at the time of his audition and a very good drummer. Ed had been struggling to make it in show business, so he was considering all options. I remember Marc saying, "He's an excellent drummer, but he looks way too normal."

Oddly enough, Ed later served as the drummer for the performance of the "Gimme Some Money" video in This Is Spinal Tap.

Ed didn't get the chance to play with Joy. We never really reformed that band again, and shortly after auditioning for us in

1972, he was mugged and stabbed by teenage members of an L.A. street gang. He nearly died, but eventually recovered and went on to a great career without any help from us.

Our band was all but disbanded, down to two members, but Ribs continued to knock on doors around L.A., trying to secure a record deal. Thanks to his efforts, Marc and I were called in for auditions from time to time. Marc played piano, and I sang and played acoustic guitar. One of those auditions was for Joe Cy, a young producer with Shelter Records, the company founded by songwriter and rock piano genius Leon Russell and his business partner Denny Cordell, who was a successful record producer for the Moody Blues, Procol Harum, Tom Petty & the Heartbreakers, Phoebe Snow, and Joe Cocker, among others.

We performed in the studio with Joe listening in the control room. He later told us that Denny was working next door in another studio and he'd been impressed. It's a good thing I didn't know that, or I would have been even more nervous. After we auditioned that day, Marc and I left with no promises from Joe. Only later did we hear that Denny had been listening in and as soon as we left he asked Joe, "Who was that kid singing for you?" Denny told Joe that he'd like to hear me again, so Joe asked us to come back for a second audition for the boss.

After the second meeting Denny was very complimentary, and a couple of weeks later Joe called Ribs and asked if I could fill in as Leon's opening act for three concert dates on a big national tour. This was a huge break on several levels. Leon was a highly respected music industry insider, a songwriting session player turned main act, and a musician's musician whose circle of friends and admirers ranged from the Beatles, Eric Clapton, and Elton John to Joe Cocker and Willie Nelson.

I asked Joe Cy if I could have Marc play piano and accompany me on the tour and he agreed. We weren't exactly prepared for this gig, but how could we turn it down? Once we agreed to do it, Marc and I had to hustle to put together enough songs to play a thirty-minute set for the biggest crowds we'd ever been in front of—nearly ten thousand people—for shows in Philadelphia, Chicago, and Detroit. Did I mention the first concert was, like...the next night?

Marc and I scrambled, putting together our set list on the flight to the Philly concert at the Spectrum on July 27, 1972. Denny Cordell had not mentioned a word about actually paying us for these three concerts (I think we both got checks for $150 at the end of our tour), but we were thrilled—and more than a little scared—to be invited. Our flight out to Philly was the first time either of us had flown first class, and that treatment continued throughout the mini-tour. We'd always dreamed of being rock stars, but we'd never actually enjoyed the lifestyle of limos, great hotels, and all expenses paid.

We also experienced what it's like to be the opening act for a performer like Leon Russell, whose fans were the rowdiest I'd ever encountered. One critic wrote that "Joy exited joylessly" and I don't doubt that our nerves got the best of us, at least in the first show. Marc and Ribs's parents made a recording of that concert, and, when I listen to it now, the crowd sounds more supportive and appreciative than we remember. Back then they seemed downright hostile, but maybe that was my fear screaming "You guys suck!"

Marc and I had convinced Leon's road manager to get us a rental car so we wouldn't be stuck at our hotel all day prior to the concert. We may have been playing rock stars on that tour, but we were still blue-collar hippies, so instead of hanging out by the pool, Marc and I went bowling. We were having so much fun we lost track of time and cut it way too close getting back to the hotel. Our late arrival threw off the entire timetable for the concert and resulted in a late start for Leon, which didn't earn us any points with the main act.

Serving as Leon Russell's opening act put me on the big stage for the first time, and I quickly learned that the warm-up role has unique challenges. Marc and I were performing as many in the audience were still showing up and finding their seats and sometimes yelling out: "Who the hell are these guys?" It was humbling, but somewhat of a rite of passage for any band or artist to try to win over an audience that hadn't come to see us. I'd think back to that experience twenty-five years later, when I sold out the Spectrum as the headliner, and again at the Pine Knob Music Theater in Clarkston, Michigan—the home turf of Bob Seger, for whom I had opened in 1983. We sold out for six nights with a new name as my opening act: Celine Dion. Even if I wasn't the main act in 1972, that appearance did give me my first taste of what it's like to play for a packed house of ten thousand or more. An even better reward was getting to know the great and passionate musicians and Shelter Records people working with Leon. Many of them complimented me after our sets, and that was pretty spectacular because they'd worked with the best of the best.

Shelter Records picked up on the good vibe, and shortly after our time with the tour ended they offered me a production deal to record some songs with the option for them to give me a contract. It was a production deal that could turn into a record deal in ninety days. Again, this wasn't a major recording contract, but it was very encouraging to be hooked up with this respected group. The Shelter Records guys weren't "suits"; they were serious music industry people, but as far as I could see, the emphasis with them was always on the music first and then the business, and that was very gratifying. Even better, as part of the production deal, Shelter producer Joe Cy asked me to put some songs together and then record them on a demo at Leon Russell's studio inside his Tulsa home.

Imagine being twenty years old, living hand to mouth, with two pairs of jeans and a couple of T-shirts to your name and hardly enough cash for a taxi to the airport. But when you get on the plane to Tulsa, your seat is in first class. There is a limo waiting for you upon arrival, and it takes you to the biggest mansion you've ever seen. And there to greet you are many of the best rock musicians in the world—people who worked in the studio or toured with Leon, Eric Clapton, George Harrison, and the Rolling Stones.

I was thrilled beyond words at the prospect of just working in the same studio. Once again, my hopes were raised. If Shelter Records thought I was ready to play alongside their studio musicians and artists, then maybe, just maybe, my fortunes were turning.

I called Marc, who had all but given up on ever making a living in a band. He'd moved back into his parents' home in New Haven and was teaching guitar lessons to half the teen population. It wasn't difficult to tear him away from a couple thousand kids eager to learn "Stairway to Heaven" so he could help me work on the new songs for Tulsa.

Leon Russell's mansion had once been a synagogue, which seemed perfect for me, the wandering Jew troubadour. The house stood on a grassy hill surrounded by Rolls-Royces and other exotic vehicles driven by Leon and his *Mad Dogs & Englishmen* friends. (Leon had been the musical director for a raucous 48-city, 30-musician Joe Cocker tour nicknamed that by Denny Cordell. It fostered both a hit live album and a hit concert movie of the same title.)

Leon had another recording studio in an old Tulsa church, but his home studio was not lacking. The studio's equipment included the first Mellotron I'd ever seen. This expensive piece of equipment, modeled on the Laff Box used to put prerecorded laughter into TV and radio programs, had a keyboard that played prerecorded strings and other orchestral instruments. The Moody Blues and the Beatles were among the first bands to use Mello-trons, which, despite their heavy weight, became a staple for pro-gressive and hard rock bands.

Once we went to work in Leon Russell's studio, there was no doubt that Marc and I were in the company of giants. Our stu-dio band included the great bass player Carl Radle and guitarist Wayne Perkins, along with other top-level musicians who'd played on Clapton's "I Shot the Sheriff," his hit version of Bob Marley's reggae song. I'd liked it, but reggae was new to me. When the guys in the studio kicked into their Marley riffs during our recording session for "It's a Hard Life," Marc and I thought they were messing with us because we'd never heard real reggae. Marc thought it was "some kind of calypso music."

We both realized we'd entered a musical universe that extended far beyond the rock, blues, and soul of our world. I have this vivid memory of one morning sitting on a kitchen counter at Leon's house talking to other musicians and the singer Phoebe Snow, whom Denny Cordell had just signed for Shelter Records after hearing her perform at the Bitter End in Greenwich Vil-lage. Within two years, she recorded "Poetry Man" and became a star. Phoebe would become a friend of mine and perform at my Michael Bolton Charities events for many years. She shifted her focus to becoming a fantastic, loving mother and passed away far too young a few years ago. She had a phenomenal, soulful voice. As we drank coffee, Leon strolled in, and it was just surreal to be there with him and the others whom I'd seen in concerts or listened to on records. I was a little worried when he walked in, because I'd picked up his guitar and was playing it without asking permission. He didn't seem to notice. He and the other amazing musicians roaming around the grand old house and filling every room treated me not like some outsider or amateur but as someone who belonged in their circle. Their praise and acceptance of me were like drops of water to a man wandering the desert.

I knew I wasn't there yet, but just being around those great musicians in Leon's studio helped me hold on to the feeling that their levels of success were within my reach. I was so inspired that one morning I got up early, grabbed my acoustic guitar, and went to a park near our hotel. There, in just a couple of hours, I wrote a song called "Dream While You Can," which we put on the demo. We decided on four songs altogether, two originals ("Dream While You Can" and "Your Love's Much Too Strong") and two selected by Joe Cy ("It's a Hard Life" and "I'm Riding Home").

ITCHIN' FOR A RECORD DEAL

There were moments of pure bliss in Leon's studio, and moments of pure terror, too, especially when Marc confessed to me that he'd brought more into Leon's house than his duffel bag of clothes and his sheet music. We were in our hotel room alone when I noticed him madly scratching himself like a flea-bitten dog. It looked like he was trying to tear his skin off with his fingernails.

"What the hell's itching you, Marc?"

"I don't know whether I got into some poison ivy or a mound of fire ants, or some sort of rash," he said, whipping off his shirt. "But I've been taking baths and showers twice a day trying to get rid of this itching, and it only gets worse."

His bare shoulders, chest, and back were covered in tiny red spots that looked like the measles—or something worse.

"Whatever this is, it's driving me freakin' crazy, Michael," he said.

I was afraid Marc's nasty-ass mites would crawl from his bed to mine, and we both lived in terror that his scabies would somehow infect Leon and his band of all-stars, since Marc had been playing Leon's guitar and the studio piano during our sessions. If any of those people are reading this book, please accept this as the reason "Itchy" Friedland and I tended not to mingle much after the first day. We were both intimidated and at least one of us was infectious, too.

When Marc returned home, his doctor told him he'd have to wait two weeks for an appointment. "By that time, I will have burned off all the skin on my body to stop the itching, so there wouldn't be any reason to come in," Marc replied.

The doctor saw him the next day, confirmed it was scabies, and gave Marc a salve treatment to relieve his agony before he skinned himself alive.

BROTHERLY INTERVENTION

Once we had the demo cut, Marc and I left Leon's Tulsa estate, returned to our lives of relative poverty, and waited to hear if Shelter Records liked the songs enough to exercise their option and sign me to a recording contract. I waited and waited and waited, and then just as the six-month contract was about to expire they notified me that, once again, I was free to pursue other deals.

This time the loss of a potential record deal didn't burn quite so badly. I felt good about my experience with Leon Russell and the Shelter team. They told me to keep working on my own songs and refining my singing so I'd be ready when the next opportunity came. Joe Cy, in particular, assured me that it was only a matter of time before we were working together on a record. I was beginning to wonder if I'd ever actually have a record released, but in this case, Joe was on the mark—if not on the money. He and I would reunite for another album, but it would not be with Shelter.

By the summer of 1974, my loyal road buddies Marc and Ribs Friedland decided to go their own ways. They'd hung in with me through all of my teenage years as one record deal—or potential deal—after another came and went. They were both older than me, and they had other responsibilities to look after. Marc married and moved to Fallbrook, California, to teach guitar and sell instruments while performing now and then. Ribs, who had dedicated about ten years of his life to promoting my career, threw in the towel. I could hardly blame him.

My fires were still burning, stoked by encouragement from people like Leon Russell, Denny Cordell, and Joe Cy, but at twenty-one years of age, I'd already been fighting this battle for six years. I had the Tulsa demo to market myself to record companies, but I don't know what I would have done at that point if my brother, Orrin, the man of many hats, hadn't appeared out of nowhere and offered to serve as my co-manager along with Alan Klatzkin. Known as "Klatty," or "GMK" (Good Man, Klatzkin), he had worked alongside my girlfriend, Maureen, at Cutler's Record Shop in downtown New Haven, where his family owned Charm's Locksmiths. I've always appreciated how his fantastic parents and entire family embraced me.

Klatty was friends with the Friedlands as well as with my brother, who had just returned from one of his longest global adventures. Orrin had gone to India, but somehow he'd ended up in Afghanistan, which was enjoying a peaceful monarchy until my brother showed up. Orrin said he and a business partner were preparing to open a café in Kabul when a disgruntled cousin of the king staged a coup, spoiling the business environment. Orrin's café partner was thrown in jail for some reason, but my brother escaped back to India, where he fended for himself on the streets for nearly a year before making it home.

Orrin is more than six feet tall, but he weighed only about 120 pounds upon his return. Half of that weight may have come from his heavy Afghan-esque beard and shoulder-length hair, but even after cleaning up he seemed like my brother from another planet.

Gone was the mellow fellow who preferred lounging with the ladies while pulling the sweet smoke of the finest weed from a hookah pipe. Orrin had discovered a guru and embraced meditation in India, and once he recovered from nearly starving to death, he set about promoting my demo with messianic intensity and focus.

Orrin's middle name should have been "Resourceful." He has many talents and a wealth of knowledge. He had worked as a door-to-door salesman selling tear gas canisters, and he had once published his own magazine. Orrin has great taste, too. He was the best-dressed hippie in the Village, and I marveled at his ability to transform every apartment he'd ever had into a chic bachelor pad. He once lived above a car repair garage, but his loft was decorated with rich imported carpets from around the world, so it looked more like Lawrence of Arabia's crib.

Orrin felt that my singing voice was a blend of Joe Cocker and Ray Charles, and he took it as an outrageous insult to the Bolotin family name that no record company had successfully marketed my music. He made it his mission to change that.

RECORD DEAL No. 3

Orrin also inherited our father's competitive drive, and he saw the emergence of disco music in the mid-'70s as an affront to his beloved blues-rock and R & B music. My music, he said, was his weapon against the disco onslaught. Orrin put together a management and publishing agreement to promote my singing and my songwriting, and then he and Klatty took the Tulsa demo around to every record company he could find. At each stop, he introduced himself as "Orrin Mitchell" to hide our family ties, though even with his beard we looked and sounded very much alike. I'm not sure he fooled anyone, but he did succeed in landing me a sweet recording contract at RCA.

Orrin played my Tulsa demo for RCA representative Stephen Holden (who later became a rock and then film critic for the *New York Times*), and he said he loved "Dream While You Can," the song I'd written in that Tulsa park. Stephen then convinced his boss, Mike Berniker, a senior vice president at RCA who had produced Barbra Streisand's first three albums, to sign me to a solo deal.

I'd hardly had time to digest that amazing development when I received an invitation to meet with the most respected record company executive in the business, Clive Davis. A Harvard Law School graduate turned music impresario, Clive had been a talent magnet during his six years as president of Columbia Records. His roster included Janis Joplin; Carlos Santana; Chicago; Bruce Springsteen; Billy Joel; Blood, Sweat & Tears; Pink Floyd; Simon & Garfunkel; the Byrds; Earth, Wind & Fire; and Aerosmith, among other top acts.

Clive called me about a year after leaving Columbia and told me he was in the process of rounding up talent for a new record label he'd created, which would later become Arista Records. I've always considered him to be the master of both the business aspects of the music industry and the artist development side. Clive could identify talent, and he knew how to nurture and develop it so that the artist could mature and achieve longevity. He has always been especially wonderful working with young artists because he loves music and listens to it constantly. There've been several times over the years when I've witnessed this. Clive and I often stay at the same hotel in Los Angeles, and more than once I've heard music blaring from a room and discovered Clive is the occupant. I've been known to pound on the door and demand he turn down the music. He always invites me in to hear "this amazing new artist." I know how musicians must feel to have Clive's support. After so much struggling and disappointment—two failed record deals, two failed production deals, and the fresh rejection by Shelter

Records—I was beyond ecstatic back in late 1974, when both RCA and Clive Davis had me on their radar.

When Clive called we were still negotiating my contract with RCA. The talks were going well but there were no guarantees at that point, even though the executives at RCA seemed to be excited. Still, I could not pass up the opportunity to audition for Clive. Orrin and I went to his office and after listening to my demo, Clive said he heard something "commercially viable" in my voice. He then asked me to put a band together so we could do a live showcase performance to give him a better idea of my range and stage presence. We promised to do that quickly, though we had not a clue how we could pull it off.

When we left that day I felt incredible validation and not a little vindication. If Clive had offered me a record deal then and there, I probably would have signed it. But over the next few days, the negotiations with RCA rapidly progressed. My brother continued to push aggressively for a bigger deal and a longer commitment from RCA during contract negotiations. Orrin was a natural-born salesman, sort of a hippie hustler in a gauze shirt and bell-bottom jeans with a peace sign on his pocket. He didn't seem to be intimidated about playing hardball in negotiations with top executives at RCA. He kept pushing for more than one album and bigger promotional and marketing budgets. Even Klatty warned Orrin to ease up some in the way he argued about the deal with RCA vice president Mike Berniker. Berniker kept telling Orrin there was a fixed budget that he had no control over, but Orrin was tenacious.

My brother wanted to ensure that RCA was committed to giving me a real shot. Still, I grew nervous when RCA refused to budge and Berniker warned Orrin that he would not be intimidated. Near the end, I was very worried that Orrin had pushed too hard, but RCA shocked us both by proposing a contract for not one but two albums. This deal for an unproven artist was beyond remarkable. Even better, they promised the first album would be produced by Joe Cy, who'd been my champion at Shelter Records, and my second album would be produced by Jack Richardson, the Canadian music professor turned record man, who created hits for the Guess Who, Bob Seger, Alice Cooper, Badfinger, and Poco, among others.

Clive Davis and I are friends to this day. I revere him as one of the classiest men in the music business, and I respect his dedication to artists and music. As much as signing with him appealed to me, he hadn't actually offered a contract, and there was no guarantee he would invite me to join Arista's fold at all, let alone for a two-album deal like the one we secured with RCA. Orrin; my attorney, Bob Epstein; and other advisers talked it through with me and we decided to go with RCA. We thanked Clive for his precious time and his extraordinary support, and then I signed on the dotted line with the other guys.

And so, after a couple of swings and misses and more than a few bitter disappointments, I finally recorded an album that was actually released and sold in record stores for public consumption. The album, which featured some great musicians, including saxophonist David Sanborn, was creatively titled *Michael Bolotin* and featured psychedelic waves of color surrounding a picture of my face with my eyes shut. Despite the cover shot, that album was a huge smash, a total megahit—with all my relatives on both sides and some of the guys who remembered me as the badass in Hebrew school.

The rest of the world pretty much ignored my blues-rock triumph.

No, I take that back. *Rolling Stone* gave me a very kind review: "His soulful songwriting and strong backup provide a striking debut." Even with that sterling recommendation from the leading rock music magazine in the free world, my album sold like not-so-hotcakes fresh from the Chernobyl bakery. Eventually, this first effort with RCA sold about ten thousand albums, which was barely enough to keep the record company interested in me. The one light of hope was that the songs I wrote for it generated a little praise and interest in the music industry.

Still, we all had dreamed that this would be my big break, and it wasn't even close. I felt terrible, not only because a major record company had done all it promised in supporting the project but also because I was no longer flying solo. Maureen and I had been living together off and on for a couple of years. We both returned to New Haven in late 1974 and were married while the album was being completed. Fortunately, I proved better at making a baby than a record that year. Two months after the *Michael Bolotin* album was released, beautiful Isa was born, on August 3.

It was no longer just about me and a wife getting by. The pressure to produce a successful album on this second try with RCA was already intense, and Isa's birth made me all the more determined to succeed. It was a scary time. Maureen worked as many jobs as she could manage, but I felt the need to step up as a provider, which meant stepping up as a recording artist. I also figured RCA would not be inclined to offer me a third chance if this record was not a hit.

Maureen and Isa rode along when I drove up to Toronto for the recording sessions with Jack Richardson, a successful and strong-willed producer who intimidated me. It was comforting to have my girls to return to after each session because I was very, very insecure in the studio at that stage of my career. He was too big a producer to let an unproven talent take control of the project, and the truth was I didn't know the first thing about making a great album. To his credit, Jack patiently welcomed the new material I wrote for the album, and we recorded some of those songs as well as some others we agreed upon.

This album was released in 1976, and again, I was supported by some of the best R & B and blues musicians in the business, including blues fiddle master Papa John Creach, who performed with Jefferson Airplane and Jefferson Starship. This more soulful R & B meets blues-rock album was called *Every Day of My Life*.

RCA sent me out on a publicity tour to radio stations in Connecticut, Philadelphia, and New York to help deejays put a face with my name, my voice, and the album, which was a very important part of an artist's role. Even with those promotional efforts, *Every Day of My Life* faded quickly from sight, and the days that followed became even more difficult.

Two & Out

After my two albums went nowhere, RCA showed zero interest in allowing me to go for strike three. I was determined to keep moving ahead despite this setback. Stephen Holden, who'd brought me into the fold at RCA, went on to have an outstanding career as a journalist and critic with *Rolling Stone*, the *New York Times*, the *New Yorker*, and other publications. A couple of years after he left RCA, he wrote a fictional book about the music industry called *Triple Platinum*, in which he described the environment as "cutthroat."

"Cutthroat" may be putting it mildly. Dreamers are rudely awakened, and the business is not for the faint of heart, as hearts are broken one after another. Few musicians get the opportunity to make even one record. I'd made four by the age of twenty-five, and they'd gone nowhere. I might not make it as a musician, but then what? I had a wife and a daughter. Those new responsibilities weighed like cargo containers on my back.

Within four years, Maureen and I had two more beautiful daughters, Holly and Taryn. During most of that period from 1975 to 1979, I struggled to keep them sheltered, fed, and clothed. We'd lived for a couple of years in Bree Belford's family home, a huge old house that his father rented out after getting a divorce and moving into a commune. Maureen and I were married in the backyard and Isa was born there, but eventually Mr. Belford sold the house. We had to find another apartment, and our new landlord wasn't as benevolent. After that, eviction was a constant threat. I had rent checks bounce. It tore at me that our kids wore hand-me-downs. Many nights the only thing to eat in the refrigerator was frozen broccoli.

I managed to keep a roof overhead only by working odd jobs here and there and performing wherever anyone would let me play. Maureen was also working hard to raise our three small daughters while holding down a job when she could to bring in income and help make ends meet. I'm told that it helps to think of difficult times as character-building experiences that will make you stronger and wiser. But man, when I'd wake up in the morning to hear my babies crying and there wasn't enough money for diapers or baby food, let alone for a decent meal, it took more optimism than I could muster to believe, *This will all turn out for the good.* I wanted to feel hopeful, but mostly I felt desperate.

Chapter Seven

Higher Stakes

Slowly, it dawned on me in my late teens that drugs were not adding as much to my life as they were taking away. Missing Woodstock was bad enough, but the stakes began to rise when I noticed that smoking pot was affecting the power and tone of my singing voice and endangering my dream. I've seen photographs of iconic artists with a glass of booze in one hand and a cigarette in the other. For some a drink or a smoke might help them relax for a performance, but your body has to deal with the effects of the drugs, and sooner or later, the impact is negative.

Most people who grew up in the Woodstock culture will say, if you can remember it, you weren't there. Some of the greatest artists we've known have been able to perform at an amazing level under the influence, but drugs and alcohol eventually killed them. These magnificent artists—including Jimi Hendrix, Janis Joplin, and Jim Morrison, like Billie Holiday before them and Amy Winehouse after them—were so gifted, yet I can't help but wonder how much greater their extended careers could have been.

I don't pretend to know the burdens and demons any individual wrestles with, and I would never judge. It simply saddens me that their presence on earth with us was cut short. Their lives ended at such young ages, when they were seemingly nowhere near their ultimate potential. There's no way for us to ever know the depth and breadth that their work could have attained over a lifetime.

When I started to realize that being high was a threat to everything I loved, everything changed. The gift of song and music is precious to me. I had to honor that gift. It became clear that I could no longer get stoned and expect to perform at the level necessary to succeed. I knew that not only did I want to be great but I also wanted to be around for a long time, and to be at my best I needed to be fully present in every way.

The Turning Point

I was a child of the sixties' experimental culture that we all explored back then. Although I was fiercely independent, it was easy to get swept up in cultural waves. In some cases, there were great benefits to be found in those waves.

Enter the guru Maharaj Ji, the Indian teenager who led me out of the darkness and into the light, and into a much healthier and saner lifestyle. It was just a few years before I got married and started a family. My cosmic brother, Orrin, once again was among the first of our American generation to embrace the teachings of Indian gurus, whom he discovered in his travels abroad. Maharaj Ji expanded his mission into the United States in the 1970s and, before we married, Maureen and I joined our friends who'd become regular visitors at his ashram on Whitney Avenue in New Haven.

Maharaj Ji was four years younger than I was, but he'd been attracting followers around the world since childhood. When I first learned of him, he was known as a "Perfect Master," as was his father. His teachings were called "the Knowledge," which was a form of meditation that allowed one to become connected to the infinite. I felt confirmation in having the Knowledge revealed to me. It validated everything I'd read or been taught in school or had learned from the Bible. Maharaj Ji's teachings seemed to be directing people to the same spiritual place as the major faiths. I don't believe anyone should force spiritual beliefs on others. Khalil Gibran advises us to not say, "I have found the path of the soul," but instead to say, "I have found the soul walking upon my path."

My spiritual inquiry might have all started while I was up in Berkeley, when a girl gave me a booklet called *Sermon on the Mount*. There I was, a long-haired hippie Jew, reading about Christ and finding that more of his teachings resonated with me than did the lessons I learned in synagogue.

By the time we began studying the Knowledge, the Beatles had already found their guru, Maharishi Mahesh Yogi, and embraced Transcendental Meditation, or TM (not to be confused with TMZ). Many young people were looking for similar ways to tap into a more spiritual, tranquil, and contemplative lifestyle.

Our guru, who is now known as Prem Rawat, held that "peace, enlightenment, love, and wisdom reside within each of us." The Knowledge taught by him and his followers consisted of meditation techniques that allowed one to access those elements within. The Knowledge came without the social structure found in most churches and faiths. There was no Bible, no Koran, and no commandments to follow, though there were elements of Hindu, Buddhist, Muslim, and Christian faiths in his teachings.

Maureen and I went to the New Haven ashram and took the introductory course before we were married. We were asked to keep an open mind and to give the teachings a chance. Each of us was given our own techniques for meditating anytime, anywhere. I had studied other religions over the years because I needed a spiritual element in my life, something to speak to and ease my soul.

The Knowledge was the greatest awakening for me. It felt like the key to everything I'd read about in my search for some sort of spiritual connection that provides true peace. All religions I'd studied seemed to be talking about the same thing: becoming one with your creator. This guru taught that the Knowledge was the key. Once you have that key, you always have access to your true home and a sense of true peace. The Knowledge fast-tracks you to a place where you can be wiser and not reactive. Whatever your hair trigger is, when you consistently meditate you are calmer and you make decisions not out of anger or fear but from a more peaceful state of mind. You become more of an observer, and that allows you to be more compassionate instead of being a victim or getting caught up in the stress and drama around you.

I still meditate to quiet my mind. The goal is to slow the activity of your brain in a way that allows you to actually hear, sense, feel, and experience what is known as the "primordial vibration," or your spirit, which is your true essence beyond your body. We were taught that we are all part of something greater than ourselves, and that there is always a divine presence in our midst. We acknowledged that spiritual presence at every meal by meditating quietly before eating.

Meditation is still my path to inner peace during difficult times, when stress threatens to send me into a raging panic. I go there automatically now. It's like diving into a pool of calm. The longer you stay immersed in a meditative state, the less likely you are to be reactive because you feel threatened or intimidated or angry. The Knowledge reinforced my efforts to look inward for strength. It became very clear to me that this was a life choice. I wanted to aim inward through meditation instead of dealing with stress by drinking or getting high.

One of my favorite memories of going to the ashram in New Haven was being asked to sing by the other members. At first I preferred not to, because I was still trying to focus on learning to meditate properly, but as I became at home with the Knowledge, the more I found peace and comfort in singing the devotionals. I found some of the soul of it all in those sessions because singing wasn't about entertaining anyone. It was about feeling inspired and inspiring others, which isn't far from what I try to do onstage, except no one at the ashram threw panties at me. Seriously, meditation helped me stay on course even as I struggled in my musical career.

RECORD DEAL NO. 4

Nearly two years after my second solo album with RCA fell like a tree in the desert—with no one listening—my career took an abrupt U-turn, thanks to a call from Phil Lorito, who was managing me then. He connected me to Steve Weiss, an attorney for artists and bands including Bad Company and Led Zeppelin. Steve sent a limo to bring me to his home on Long Island. He'd heard my two solo records with RCA and complimented me by telling me I was "a tremendous talent." But Steve thought I needed to be the lead singer in my own band instead of a solo act. I told him about Joy and our lack of success. Steve thought my new band should follow the pop-rock track taken by Foreigner and Journey.

I'd given away my roach clips and rolling papers, but my wardrobe was still Haight-Ashbury haute couture. The only pants I had that weren't jeans were corduroy. I wanted to look like a rock star when I showed up at his house because I thought Steve had the power to change my life. I walked into this palatial home rocking the cords and figuring my long hair gave me Zeppelin cred. I was prepared to pitch myself to him, but Steve was already stoked. He did the selling. I listened.

He'd already worked out a plan to put me back in a band, a rock band in the Journey mode. Steve envisioned me as the lead singer and songwriter for his new project, and he made me a believer. He was one of those bigger-than-life guys who seem to step out of movies and into reality.

His words, gestures, and claims seemed grandiose, except that he had the gold and platinum records on the wall to back them up.

"Everything you see here I have made from representing other bands, and believe me, when success happens there is plenty of money for everything," he said Weiss-ly.

I looked around his cavernous home, which may have served as the model for the future Hard Rock Hotels. There was at least one Rolls-Royce parked out front, with a driver in waiting. A coach and horses would not have surprised me.

I was not inclined to argue with a Long Island mansion-dwelling lawyer with platinum plaques lining his den walls, especially when he was talking about lining my own pockets with some of that gold. Steve was then part of the management team of Swan Song Records, which was founded by the members of Led Zeppelin to produce their own records, those of Bad Company, and other performers, including Dave Edmunds.

Steve promised that if I put together a strong band, he'd help me get a record deal either with Swan Song or with another company. He recommended his friend Phil Lorito as my manager for this new band. The group came together as Blackjack in the fall of 1978, with Sandy Genarro on drums, Bruce Kulick on guitar, Jimmy Haslip on bass, and me on vocals. Because of the talent we'd assembled, Blackjack had a much more hard rock, though not "heavy metal," sound than any of my previous bands. Bruce is a world-class rock guitarist, and I had to sing with all my power to be heard over his guitar and Sandy Genarro's thunderous percussion.

Steve Weiss lived up to his word once Blackjack was ready to rock. We were signed to a two-record deal with Polydor, a division of Polygram, and we released two albums: *Blackjack* in 1979, and *Worlds Apart* in 1980. The first album was produced by a true genius, the late Tom Dowd, who was the only nuclear physicist I've ever had as my record producer.

Tom was in his fifties when Blackjack recorded at Criteria, his Miami studio. Thirty years earlier, he had worked on the Manhattan Project, which produced the atomic bomb. A classical music lover, he changed his career course to more peaceful pursuits and became a revered record producer who worked with Ray Charles, Eric Clapton, Otis Redding, and Aretha Franklin, among other stars.

When Polygram execs learned that Tom Dowd was producing our record, they broke out the champagne and toasted our inevitable success. Having him on board was a major deal. I felt damned lucky just to be working with him. But Tom wanted us to take a little edge off our sound. I wasn't thrilled, but Tom's track record was so much better than mine at that point. He was a very expensive producer who had huge hits. He had just turned out a big one in Rod Stewart's "Do Ya Think I'm Sexy," which sold more than two million copies. Tom also packed heat with the record companies, who wanted to keep him happy. Polygram seemed confident in his approach with us. Any lingering doubts we had about Tom's strategy were washed away when we heard reports that other artists with the record company were pissed because Blackjack was getting so much promotion money that there was little left for them.

To this day, the irony in Tom's prophetic suggestion makes me smile. He wanted us to turn down Bruce's amp, declaring, "What do you think this is, KISS?" He only said it once, but we never forgot it. That was the sound Bruce was looking for and would fully realize several years later, when he became the lead guitarist for KISS.

Polygram did pull out the stops to promote Blackjack. Our record company even paid for music videos with each of the two singles released from the first album, "Love Me Tonight" and "Without Your Love." They also had us open one night for Ozzy Osbourne at Roberto Clemente Coliseum in San Juan, where I later performed with the Joe Perry Project. As soon as the tour ended, so did our relationship with Polydor and Polygram. There were a dozen or so top rock bands that fought the good fight and stayed on the record charts during the disco era, but Blackjack wasn't among them.

Record Deal No. 5: Crash & Burn

Shortly after Blackjack got the Poly-ax, Allen Jones asked me if I'd like to cut a record with his production company in Memphis. Allen had been a Stax Records producer and songwriter. He'd worked with Otis Redding and the Bar-Kays, and he'd won a Grammy for his contributions to the *Shaft* sound track. When he said he thought of me as "a white Otis Redding," he won me over. I flew to Memphis and recorded about ten songs with him and some amazing musicians at SoulTastic, but that production company was shut down by financial difficulties before the record could be released. Another record deal crashed and burned.

I had no problem getting record deals in the 1970s, but capitalizing on them with hit records, or any records at all, was definitely a challenge. I had some rough breaks, but today the environment is even more treacherous. Record companies now will sign groups or individuals to deals; and if they don't like the first four or five songs they record, they'll drop them after keeping them tied up for years. There is no going back to work to refine your act. They cut their losses and move on. As tough as it was for me, I would not trade my experiences for being a new artist in this current climate. I hear repeatedly that artists and bands are dropped one after another in the midst of recording. Just a few years ago, I watched an A and R person at a record company listening to CDs of songs she'd been waiting for from bands they'd signed. One by one she dropped them into the trash can, signaling the end of their record deals. I knew many of those whose names were on the CDs.

Orrin, Klatty, and Phil Lorito, who had signed on as my manager before the Polygram contract, had worked their asses off for me and I appreciated all they'd accomplished, but I needed to find a way to get more traction as an artist. I decided it was time to look for some veteran professional management.

The pressure of having virtually no income and rent checks bouncing and only enough food in the fridge for one more meal was sucking the life out of me. I couldn't handle being such a disappointment to my family. When I'd feel a wave of depression coming on I'd try to stay focused on building a career and being successful, but it was increasingly difficult.

I was really sick and tired of coming up short, and haunted by concerns that I was letting my family down. I had nightmares of being thrown out of our crappy little apartment and my girls having to live on the street while I sang and begged for spare change. My lack of formal education left me without anything resembling a Plan B, so I had to find a way to make a living as a singer, songwriter, or musician. There was just no other way. Besides, I had a friend who went to law school and abandoned his music career. He had written a couple of successful songs, but he never returned to it because the family law practice took all of his time. He always told me he wished he'd never developed a Plan B, because he would have stayed with what he loved, his music.

Dinner with Ted's Heads

In early 1981, a young junior manager named Louis Levin asked me to sign with a management company led by Steve Leber and

David Krebs. They had a reputation for developing new artists and seemed hungry, so I joined their roster of clients, which included Aerosmith, AC/DC, Def Leppard, Ted Nugent, and Joan Jett. Steve Leber wrote the check to buy out my management contract with Phil Lorito for about $20,000, which turned out to be a very sound investment for them and a very good move for me as well.

One of the first things my new managers did was take me to meet with their client Ted Nugent, who was looking for a lead singer for his band. They were about to make a record and go on tour. Joining another band wasn't my goal, but I'd just signed with Leber and Krebs so I agreed to go with David Krebs to Detroit, where Ted lived. The idea was to have dinner and hang out at Ted's place so we could get to know each other. I'd heard that Ted was an avid big-game hunter, and the walls of his home offered testimony to all the animals he'd bagged. I'd been in zoos with fewer species.

When dinner arrived, I realized no one had tipped off Ted that I wasn't so big on game myself. He noticed right away that I was eating everything but the meat course. There was no hiding from the hunter. I had to confess that I was a vegetarian.

"So what do you have on your walls, cabbage heads?" he asked, and we all broke out laughing.

The ice was officially broken. Despite our vastly different menu preferences, Ted, David Krebs, and I talked music and had a great evening. He could not have been a more gracious host, and my new management team was smart to see that there might be a fit, but my interests at that point were really to pursue a solo career and there was some support for that back at the home office.

A short time after we visited Ted's really excellent animal-head house, David was talking with some of his secretaries and other women staffers about the challenges of the business climate. He asked them if they thought there was one artist on their roster who could sell ten million albums.

One of their long-term staffers said, "Yes, Michael Bolotin."

David found that curious since I'd had all misses and no hits up to that point. Still, when David and Steve saw how their staff members responded to my singing, they became true believers. They dished out cash advances so I wouldn't have to worry so much about feeding my family. The cash helped, but it would be more than six years before I lived up to the ten-million-album-man billing. After all those years of struggling, my fortunes were about to take a favorable turn in a way that none of us had anticipated.

SHAKING THE MONEY TREE

I'd signed with the management firm of Leber and Krebs with the goal of getting a breakthrough record deal. While working on demos, we brought in some background singers for a session in the studio. On the day we'd set aside for them, they were running late. I was told that they were stuck at a "jingle house" but would be arriving soon. I'd never heard that term, so when the singers arrived, I asked what they'd been doing. One of them, Angela, explained that they were making "good money" singing for radio and television commercials.

I found that very interesting.

"Would you ever consider doing jingles?" Angela asked.

I guess she thought I was too proud to do commercial work. I might once have considered myself too much of an artist for that line of work, but any opportunity to earn extra income was enticing at that point.

I wasn't thinking "stigma." I was thinking "food for the family."

Louis Levin filled me in on the pros and cons of doing commercials, and he assured me that many singers on the charts had done jingles early in their careers. Some, including the R & B star Luther Vandross, continued to do them after they'd had hits.

Louis explained that singing jingles could be especially lucrative if the commercials a singer did "went national" and were
played repeatedly over extended periods. Jingle singers were paid
an up-front fee, and they also earned residuals every time their
commercials played. The challenge for many singers is that jingle
writers and producers—and their big-brand clients—often have
very specific and inflexible visions for how they want their commercials to sound. In other words, I would have to check my ego
at the door in exchange for the paychecks and residuals. Louis said
most jingle singers were making $50,000 to $70,000 a year, but the
top singers who were in constant demand could make $100,000 or
more with residuals just doing commercial jingles.

I thought about that for, oh, a minute before I had Louis make
some calls and line me up for auditions in an entirely new area of
the music industry.

Ego Checked!

If I had any reluctance about singing jingles, it disappeared when
I did a commercial session with singer Valerie Simpson, half of
the legendary performing and songwriting team of Ashford &
Simpson. She and her husband, Nick Ashford, had already written many of Motown's biggest hits, including "Ain't No Mountain
High Enough" and "Ain't Nothing Like the Real Thing," when she
began doing jingle work for Budweiser and the Hershey's candy
bars Mounds and Almond Joy, among other clients.

I'd been performing in clubs and bars, parties, and small concert venues since my early teens, and I was always cutting demos
for record companies. I thought I knew a lot about singing and
vocal techniques, but jingle singing proved to be a revelation on
several levels. Like most musicians and singers, I am not an early
riser, but if the jingle was being recorded in the studio at 9 a.m., I

had to be there and ready to sing or miss out on the paycheck. Usually there is no freestyling and no ad-libs unless the client requests them. The singer has thirty to sixty seconds to sell the hook of the jingle, which is the brand message created by the jingle writer under the direction of the advertising agency and the top executives of Coca-Cola, Budweiser, or whoever the client might be.

The singer must also deliver that message in whatever musical style the commercial calls for, whether it's rock, country, classical, pop, folk, blues, or polka. And while proper enunciation was never a big priority when I was singing rock and blues music, clients paying big money for these musical commercials want the viewers and listeners to understand every word of the message.

Once I established myself in the jingle world, most of the rules relaxed. I worked mostly with Susan Hamilton, known as the "Jingle Queen." Susan was a classically trained pianist and music lover who was president of HB&B Productions, a jingle-making machine. A great champion of singers, she gave me license to improvise more than most. She'd tell the advertising execs or clients that I was temperamental and might walk out if they tried to rein me in too much. The truth is, I was willing to sing jingles in Swahili if the big-paying advertisers wanted to hear it.

You would never hear me arguing that to be a successful singer you need to do commercial jingles, but it sure didn't hurt me. Commercial work has helped pay the bills—or paid all of them— for many of the top studio and session musicians, composers, and talented singers who otherwise might not have been able to make a living doing what they love. While some may not ever admit it publicly, there are more than a few jingle performers who went on to sell millions of records.

Richard Marx, whose father owned a renowned jingle company in Chicago, began singing for commercials as a boy before going on to a hugely successful career as a pop singer, songwriter, and record producer. (Richard is also one of the funniest people I know and a great friend.) Grammy-winning jazz singer Patti Austin, who later recorded one of my songs; the soulful singer and songwriter Marc Cohn; and, of course, the late Luther Vandross, who earned eight Grammys and sold more than twenty-five million records, all shook the jingle-house money tree.

Luther had an amazingly flexible voice with phenomenal pitch, and he had the ability to blend with other singers so that his vocals didn't overwhelm the others. He was already a major R & B star when I began doing jingles, but he continued to do them, too. His fans rarely noticed because he was singing background vocals, not lead vocals, so people couldn't usually pick out his voice. Commercial producers always wanted him to perform their jingles because his pitch was so great and his voice so flexible that Luther made their commercials sound better even when he was blending into a chorus of singers.

I'd see Luther often and we got along well. Then we had one of those odd moments that can easily occur in a chaotic business with strong personalities; one that is plagued by miscommunications and misunderstandings because we often see each other only while on the run from one appearance to the next.

Luther and I were backstage at Dick Clark's American Music Awards just after Luther had a monster hit with his *Power of Love* album, released in 1991. That album won every award in sight, and on this occasion Luther took home two awards in one night for favorite soul/R & B male artist and for favorite soul/R & B album. I went to Luther to congratulate him as one jingle survivor to another. I'd just told him how great the album's first single had been when his expression turned very sad.

"Yeah, but the new one is over already," he said. "They released the second single and it isn't happening."

I knew his record company team was really proud and excited

about this album so I asked a question that is typical in the business: "Who picked that single for release?"

Obviously, my innocent question hit a sore spot because Luther suddenly tensed up, glared at me, and jabbed a finger in my face, stating, "I don't particularly appreciate what you are saying!"

Just as Luther was doing that, Dick Clark came walking around the corner behind him. Dick's eyes met mine as he recognized that he'd stumbled onto a confrontation. The beloved television host of *American Bandstand*, my favorite childhood television show, then shot me a comical *Uh-oh, I'm outta here!* look—like a kid who'd wandered into a grown-up fight—and scooted back around the corner in a theatrical sort of 180-degree move, as if he'd walked into the ladies' room by accident. I will never forget that visual.

I won a couple of awards that night, too, but my misunderstanding with Luther put a damper on things. Later, Tommy Mottola explained that Luther was eager to push into the mega-platinum-album sales level and was determined to make every song a hit, so when the second single didn't take off, he was frustrated.

"Don't worry, Michael, it wasn't personal," Tommy said. "You just walked into a buzz saw."

Still, I didn't want my relationship with Luther to end that way. I was a big fan of his, too. We didn't meet up again until about two years later, when we both were asked to perform at a Richard Marx fund-raising event. I was in my dressing room when someone knocked on the door and pushed it open.

There stood Luther.

I flinched, fearing he might give me the finger again.

To my great relief, he gave me a warm greeting and told me he just wanted to say hello. I gave him a hug. There was never another cross word between us, and I was very grateful that our friendship was renewed. So was Dick Clark. I know because years later Dick and I joked about it. I teased that I wished I had a video of his reaction to put on his blooper reel.

JINGLE HOUSE ROCK

As I said, I did a lot of my commercial work with Susan Hamilton, who ran HB&B, one of the biggest "jingle houses" in New York City, from a brownstone on the Upper East Side. It was a crazy hive of creativity and really a fun place to work. HB&B's recording studios were like most, except, as the inside joke went, the music was all about "the Generals"—General Motors, General Foods, and General Electric.

My first gig was a commercial for Subaru cars, and once that was in the can, the opportunities began pouring in. The U.S. Army, too, drafted me for one of their celebrated marketing campaign commercials, *"Be all you can be."*

I did all sorts of commercials, but mostly I rode the beverage cart. I did a lot of Coke, Diet Coke, Cherry Coke, and Coca-Cola, not to mention Pepsi, 7-Up, and Budweiser (*"I'm a BubabaBud Man"*). In some cases, the client company would want different versions of the commercial or jingle for different parts of the country, so I might sing one version for the East Coast, one for the Midwest, and another for the Deep South.

I performed more than thirty commercials, so many that while recording one day I opened a drink cooler and it hit me that I'd sung a jingle for every form of liquid refreshment in the entire selection. When I was really cranking them out, I'd go to the mailbox at home and many days there would be a stack of checks—like gifts from the gods—piled a foot high. Some would be only for a buck ninety, but others would be for $900 and more, and they just kept on coming.

I'd also signed a songwriting deal with CBS Songs around this time and they were paying me a salary, so I suddenly had more income than ever before. You can imagine how it felt to finally have a decent source of income for the first time in my life. My commercial jingle earnings allowed me to move my family into a nice home in Stamford, Connecticut, closer to New York City to cut my commute. I also rented a New York City apartment in the Symphony House building on West Fifty-Sixth, because the jingle work and songwriting often went late into the night.

This line of work quickly became so lucrative that after a few months, I told my daughters, "Ladies, I'll be going into the city today to shake the money tree." There'd been times when I couldn't make a dime and I felt like a lousy husband and father. After nearly two decades of struggling and perseverance, it felt like I was living the American Dream.

The joy of finally being able to provide for my family really hit me while I was working on what turned out to be my favorite commercial of all. This one was for Kodak and it was called "Daddy's Little Girl." The commercial first aired during the Academy Awards show and became a classic, running over and over, and it is probably the only commercial I did that was also played by wedding bands across the country and around the world. I am very sentimental about this one as the father of three girls whose lifestyles benefited greatly from the success of this commercial.

That Kodak commercial was also one of the last jingles I did because my musical career was finally taking off in a couple of other directions. I'd had such tremendous, life-altering success with jingles that I never thought the day would come when I'd stop shaking the money tree, but in 1987 I was driving into New York City when one of my commercials came on the radio, followed by one of my hit records, followed by another of my jingles. I became worried that hearing my voice on both records and commercials would confuse radio station program directors and they'd say, "Isn't that the same guy?" I didn't want them putting me in a box as a jingle singer and not thinking of me as a solo performer who could have hits as an artist.

Then, around the same time, I was recording a solo album with producer Jonathan Cain, one of the key members of and primary songwriters for Journey and a rock-star producer as well. We were in his studio's waiting room and the television set was on. As luck would have it, a Sure deodorant commercial began blaring—and it was one in which I sang the jingle.

I cringed because Jonathan isn't a big fan of artists doing commercials. He'd gone into another room and I was hoping he couldn't hear the commercial, but my friend had very good ears.

"Bolton! Is that YOU singing on a deodorant commercial?" he demanded.

(Gulp!)

"Uh, yeah, but that was from back in the lean years. I don't do those anymore," I assured Jonathan.

I later told my manager, Louis Levin, to stop booking me as a jingle singer. He didn't argue, because by then we had other trees to shake.

PART II
The Rewards

Chapter Eight

The Talent I Didn't Know I Had

W hen looking back at my long climb, I'm reminded of Woody Allen's response when he was asked, "Do you believe in life after death?" His answer was, "I'm still trying to figure out if there's life before death!"

I'd made unsuccessful records as the lead singer in the band Joy, as the solo act Michael Bolotin, and as a member of Blackjack. Music industry professionals, including Denny Cordell, Leon Russell, and Clive Davis, had told me my voice could sell records, but so far, I'd come up short.

By the early 1980s, I was open to suggestions.

That marked a major change in my attitude—one that paid off in buckets. I was about to enter a decade in which opportunities flowed to me as never before.

My teens and most of my twenties were spent in determined pursuit of a career as a rock 'n' roll musician and singer. As a single guy I was all about the music and not the money. I was focused and driven, and adamant that I would sing the way I wanted to sing and play the way I wanted to play. I didn't think you could be a true artist and live and work any other way.

Most high-achieving people I've known, in any field, do not have "balanced" lives because their level of accomplishment requires such intense focus to attain and then build upon. Most have had to make sacrifices in other areas, especially in their relationships and, sometimes, in their health.

I see it with the professional golfers I meet in Pro-Am tournaments and I see it with the members of my touring band. To reach the top of your game and to take full advantage of the opportunities, you can't maintain the ideal work-family balance. Some of my touring band members have been traveling with me for nearly twenty years. Most have struggled personally due to the rigors of the road. They perform with joy and they love playing for audiences around the world, but I've seen it wreak havoc on their relationships.

Record producers, talent managers, and other type A professionals tend to take responsibility for every aspect of their work, and that leaves them little time for life outside the "office," the creative laboratories we call recording studios. Their schedules are dictated, often by factors beyond their control—including the hectic schedules of the busy and quirky artists they work with—so the needs of their families cannot always be accommodated.

High achievers in every field tend to be consumed by their passions. With me, it's not so much the idea that "winning is everything" as it is that losing—in my case, not making the most of my gifts—is intolerable. That is what drives me to perform to the highest possible standards, and to push those around me to do the same. I can't enjoy the garden until every weed is removed. I'm not okay with a recorded song that is good. I need it to be great. That's the reason I stay in the studio until I've done all I can possibly do to produce the best I am capable of doing. Working the hours that I work, whether touring or in the studio or writing songs, makes it very difficult, if not impossible, to be as great a friend, boyfriend, husband, or father as I would like to be.

It's the price I pay and often it weighs on my heart. I wish it weren't that way, but it seems to be the way things work in my world.

Failure can lead to success, sure, but you have to learn from your failures, give up on behaviors that haven't worked for you, and find more productive patterns. I realized I couldn't keep doing the same things over and over again, refusing to make changes, if I wanted to achieve better results.

I changed my entire approach to the music business in the 1980s. My name change was simply an indication that I was willing to make adjustments—sometimes major, sometimes minor—to stay on the path to my dream. My last name had always presented problems because people, from telephone operators to record label designers, didn't know how to pronounce or spell it. I'd spent enough time around advertising people by then to know the importance of "brand clarity," and mine was a little muddled due to the difficulty of my last name. I thought record companies and radio deejays might have an easier time with Bolton than Bolotin.

I wanted better results, so I changed my approach and reaped the benefits.

In 1982, my new management team, spearheaded by Louis Levin, David Krebs, and Steve Leber, took my demos to Columbia Records and convinced the president, Al Teller, to sign me to a recording contract as a solo artist. David set up the meeting with Teller, whom he'd known for a while, and he also brokered the deal with Columbia after taking my demos to them. At the same time, I entered into a publishing deal with CBS Songs to write for other artists. Louis negotiated the deal, making sure I had enough time to pursue my solo career as well.

My songwriting contract was for twelve complete songs or twenty-four co-written songs, so it was more of a side gig. I started my own publishing company, called ISHOT, named for Isa, Holly, and Taryn. People told me that the serious money was in music publishing, and I had dreams that income from songs I was writing would take care of my children and grandchildren. CBS Songs was confident I would keep delivering songs on a regular basis, and I did.

I'd had recording and publishing contracts before, and they had not resulted in any major hits or big paydays, so I knew there were no guarantees. Yet the success of my work in jingles and radio and television commercials had given me more confidence and more optimism than I'd ever had. Maybe things were finally beginning to turn my way.

Sadly, my biggest champion, the guy who'd always told me to keep charging, keep punching, and keep swinging away at life, was not around to see me finally earn some rewards for following his philosophy of self-determination. His doctor called one night and said simply, "I'm sorry, but your father is deceased."

Dad died in April 1981, at the age of sixty-nine, from lung and heart problems related to his long addiction to unfiltered cigarettes. His slow decline was painful to watch. He'd always been a powerful man, the former fullback who could snatch me up and hold me high over his head. In his later years, he survived both a stroke and quadruple-bypass heart surgery. Yet he seemed to shrink before my eyes, losing weight and muscle, so that he finally needed a cane to walk. Orrin, always the stylish son, found our dad a very fashionable walking stick.

I swear that sometimes I still hear that voice when I'm performing at concerts. I have this image of him forever in my mind from one such event just a few years before he died. I looked out and there was Dad in the third or fourth row, poking the guy in front of him with his cane, telling him, "Down in front! Down in front!" I watched as the guy turned around in irritation, prepared to pop whoever it was poking him. He turned and there was my dad, wagging the cane in his face and pointing at the stage, saying, "That's my son! My boy's up there! I wanna see him! Sit down! Sit down!"

I've long had this sense that my dad did see my success happen in a way. His constant assurances that I was going to make it left the impression that he'd looked into the future and confirmed that my day would come. I didn't realize how much I was driven to fulfill his vision and win his approval until shortly after his death. His sister, my aunt Harriet, called to console me. She talked about how proud he was of me and how he talked with such enthusiasm about my singing. My dad often was very loving, but he could be gruff and distant—especially if the Yankees were on television and he wanted to focus on the game. When Aunt Harriet talked about his feelings for me, she said, "He used to call you his Jesus." I lost it. I broke down and sobbed.

Later, my therapist would help me walk through the father-and-son issues that burden so many men. Dr. Rabiner told me that I hadn't found closure with my father's death even after many years because I was still striving for his approval, or, as he put it, "You are still carrying conquered land to his grave." In gentle tones, he also suggested that I still carried other baggage related to my childhood—the trauma of watching him ordered out of our home as a result of the divorce initiated by my mother. My father was a good man in so many ways, and I aspired to have those good qualities while letting go of less desirable attributes.

A friend once described his father as "just another geezer trying to get through life," and that may be an apt description of my own dad. He tried to do the right thing. He was proud and stuck in his ways, like most of us, but he didn't believe in stepping on people to get ahead. He had friends from every walk of life, and he practiced forgiveness in admirable measure. I have looked constantly at the opportunity to self-sculpt rather than allowing time and outside forces to make me what I don't want to be. Like a sculptor working with stone, I want to remove all that is less compassionate, less patient, and less present until I become the best of me.

We are all works in progress. Guides to self-improvement often advise you to think of what you want people to say about you at your funeral and live accordingly. In 2012, I joined the hundreds who attended a memorial service for a beloved music industry leader, Frances Preston, whom Kris Kristofferson called "the song-writer's guardian angel" during her long tenure (1986–2004) as the president of BMI, the song-licensing powerhouse. Frances was one of the many people who encouraged me and kept me going. She was always an inspiration to me. Frances was renowned, and often honored, for her tireless humanitarian work and dedication to charitable organizations, the arts and culture, and public service on government commissions. Her causes included leukemia, cancer, AIDS, and retinitis pigmentosa (blindness) research. Even though she had her own significant health problems over the years, she never said no to a fund-raiser. Time after time she displayed incredible strength and willpower just to reach the podium at an event—and she always electrified her audience with her intelligence and passion. I'm writing from the heart when I say that it was a deep personal honor, in 2010, to be chosen as the first person to receive a prestigious award named for my longtime friend—the Frances Williams Preston Lifetime Music Industry Award, given by the music industry's largest charity, the T. J. Martell Foundation, which supports cancer, leukemia, and AIDS research.

The phenomenal country star Vince Gill said at her memorial service that Frances blended "power with kindness, success with compassion." He said, "Some have called her the most powerful woman in the music business. Power doesn't look good on a lot of people, but Frances was kind." His description was so accurate and so touching that it prompted tears from nearly everyone in attendance, including Vince and me. I don't know how he made it through the song he sang to honor our friend, but Vince, like Frances, rose to the occasion and did Frances proud.

RECORD DEAL NO. 6: CLOSE BUT NO SEGER

I released two solo rock albums with Columbia. The first was recorded in 1982 and released in 1983. It featured my new and improved name as the album title, *Michael Bolton*. We recruited some serious musicians on that record, including Bruce Kulick, later of KISS, and on the synthesizer we had a master of funk by the name of George Clinton, who also sang some backing vocals. Columbia put serious marketing behind the album and its first single, "Fool's Game." The record company financed an accompanying music video for that song, and then sent me on a short tour, playing mostly rock clubs. Then we were invited to become the opening act for Bob Seger and the Silver Bullet Band, touring behind their hit album *The Distance* and the single "Shame on the Moon."

The Columbia marketing plan was bigger than any I'd ever had for a record release, and it came with a secret weapon—my wily hippie hustler of a brother. Orrin was a guerrilla marketer before the term was widely known. We had both worked at young ages on voter registration campaigns for our father and his Democratic Party team in New Haven, and Orrin seemed to have a street-wise genius for finding low-cost, stealthy ways to promote products. When I told him about my first Columbia record, the music video, and the Bob Seger tour, Orrin crafted a plan for pumping the album and the single to get more airplay on the radio. He presented the plan to Columbia and they bought into it, sending Orrin on the road with me for the tour. In each town on the tour, he would recruit attractive local girls to distribute flyers between my set and the Silver Bullet Band's set. The flyers invited fans to come to my hotel to meet me after the show.

They came in droves, much to my amazement. My savvy brother had refreshments ready for them, and while they waited for me to get there, he had each of them fill out cards with their names, addresses, schools, and phone numbers. Once I showed up, usually clad in rocker leather, I made a big entrance for the fans worked into a frenzy by Orrin. He cranked up the speakers and played a loop of my songs on a tape recorder. There was nothing subliminal about his approach. Only a lack of technology prevented him from stamping my recordings into their shiny foreheads.

By the end of the tour, Orrin had collected more than five thousand names from around the country, and he built that into my fan club and his guerrilla marketing team. (If I ever run for public office, and I won't, Orrin will definitely be working on the campaign strategy.) Later, Orrin used those names and addresses to promote my records around the country. He would contact the fans in our file in each town and have them swamp local radio stations with phone calls asking them to play my records.

The *Michael Bolton* album sales were boosted by the "Fool's Game" music video. It made the rotation on a new music video cable channel launched the previous August. MTV was playing three hundred songs a day. "Fool's Game" made the playlist against some heavy competition, including songs by Duran Duran, who had four videos in the mix. The monster was Michael Jackson's

Thriller album, including the video for the title song, released in November 1983, which set a new standard for music videos. I quickly learned the power of MTV and the rotation of music videos played over and over again. I also realized that MTV was having a definite impact on my life as well as my career.

Suddenly, I was on television singing in the midst of some very successful company, and, if it was mind-blowing for me, you can imagine what my little girls felt like. My middle daughter, Holly, who was only about six years old, freaked out at seeing her father decked out in leather and rocking on MTV. She couldn't reconcile the fact that her dad was the same guy as the singer sharing screen time with Michael Jackson, Lionel Richie, Billy Joel, Cyndi Lauper, and Marvin Gaye. Holly wouldn't speak to me for a couple of days because it was so strange for her.

It was strange for her daddy, too. Shortly after the MTV play began, I took the girls to the movie theater multiplex in West Haven. We were in the popcorn line and noticed people staring our way. Some came up to me and asked for autographs. The girls were all traumatized by the sudden attention.

"What's going on, Dad? What do they want?"

We developed a plan after that of sending someone in to buy the tickets and the popcorn and secure the seats with the girls. I came in only once the lights were dimmed.

Things were even a little crazier when I visited Taryn's school for "What Does Your Daddy Do? Day." I arrived at the school and was walking down the hallway when the bell ending the class period rang and suddenly I was mobbed by grade-schoolers and a few teachers, too. Finally Taryn's teacher pulled me into the safety of the classroom. I was always glad to give these talks for my daughters, who seemed to enjoy having me there. During one of these visits, I gave a little talk and had the teacher play my "Fool's

Game" video for the class. The father who came on after me shot me a look as if to say, "Thanks for that. Now I'm left here to talk to them about aluminum siding installation!"

THE MAGIC WINDOW

"Fool's Game" did so well on its release that I thought it would be my first smash hit, but it was more like a comet. The single burned brightly on launch, but flared out at No. 82 on Billboard's Hot 100 list, and fell to earth after three weeks on the charts. This was the first time one of my songs had climbed so high, and I learned there is a magic window on airplay. Record companies are willing to pump a new single only as long as there is upward momentum. If a song has been playing for ten or twelve weeks and the radio airplay doesn't continue to grow, they shut off the marketing money, pack up, and go home. That's the cold, cruel reality of the business.

The record company president, Al Teller, called to say he was sorry that was all they could do for "Fool's Game," but the company was still behind me and Al pledged to keep supporting us financially on the Seger tour. But for the first time in my life, I felt like my solo career had some real momentum.

The *Michael Bolton* album had performed better than any of my previous attempts. "Fool's Game" was my biggest charting single. There were rumors that I might actually earn some residual income from those recordings—another first! Having money in the bank can put a long-struggling artist in a much more optimistic frame of mind. Still, the reason I was feeling more confident about the future wasn't only that my singing career was faring better.

The stream of paychecks from my radio and television commercials had helped change our lives. I also was thrilled to have "Fool's Game" in the Hot 100, and seeing the video for that record on MTV was an experience beyond belief. But actually, the greatest thing happening in my career at this time was a song that I'd written for another artist.

That one song was about to change everything.

SONGWRITER

Songs have come to me from the time I learned my first chords. The lyrics and music didn't bond into a coherent melody until my guitar playing reached a certain level of proficiency, but once my fingers were skilled enough on the strings, the songs came tumbling out. The first songs were often efforts to express my feelings about the breaking apart of our family, and about girls, of course. I was thirteen years old when my first love song was fully formed, a sentimental, folksy composition called "Dreaming Dreams." You will never guess my source of inspiration. Cory Morrison was the muse, naturally! The first "older woman" of my dreams, Cory had dated Orrin (who charmed every attractive woman within a thousand-mile radius of New Haven), but she only regarded me fondly, as her zany sidekick.

My first songs were very personal. My approach to songwriting had always been as a form of self-expression, not a product to be sold to another performer. I've often said it was a talent I didn't know I had. I couldn't imagine anybody else would be interested in my songs. Since I had no formal training and couldn't read music, I considered myself a raw amateur. Patrick Henderson, a terrific pianist and songwriter with Leon Russell's band, was one of the first to encourage me to market my songs. While Marc and I were recording at Leon's studio, Patrick suggested that I team up with him to write for other performers as a way to generate income while working on my solo career. I respected Patrick, whose songs were recorded by artists such as Michael McDonald and the Pointer Sisters, and eventually we would write a number of successful songs together.

Other friends and fellow musicians had long urged me to try to sell the songs I'd written instead of filing them away for myself. The success of "Fool's Game," which I co-wrote with Mark Mangold, had also stirred interest in my songwriting skills and boosted my confidence in writing for others. At that time, Patrick Henderson was on staff at CBS Songs, and he suggested I write with him while working on my solo singing career. I had never co-written for other artists, and Patrick helped me. He knew CBS liked songwriters who could sing and sell their songs.

The next thing I knew, CBS Songs asked me to come to their office in Los Angeles to crank out more songs with Patrick and other writers. They sent me first-class plane tickets. They had a rental car waiting for me, which I drove to the very upscale Le Park Hotel. This was a new and strange development, and, like the whole jingle experience, I found it both exciting and a little scary. I felt the weight of the reality of what I was doing there in that hotel.

I'd always thought of myself as a rock singer, not a commercial songwriter. Yet now, a very serious music industry player was putting me on a plane and bringing me in to write commercial songs for its very serious clients.

Was I ready for this? Could I produce songs on demand? Would I be able to deliver?

They treated me like a king, or at least a prince. CBS Songs put me up in the grandest hotel room I'd ever seen. Seriously, I was like one of the Beverly Hillbillies who moved to California and discovered "a *cee*-ment pond" in the backyard. I called Maureen because I was so excited after walking into my room and discovering it was a suite, with another room in which I could just hang out and watch television.

I was stammering as I said, "There is a room that connects to the bedroom area, but it's like another room to itself." That's how excited and giddy I was—I didn't know the word *suite*. When I hung up I realized these people had flown me out there, rented me a car, and put me in that fancy room, and I had to deliver. I wasn't there on vacation. They were expecting me to come up with song ideas and finish them. Thankfully, I had Patrick to help me get over myself and into crafting a song. He helped me get comfortable with the process and we had a great start. After we worked together on our first song, I went back to my room to work on lyrics for the last few lines of the bridge to make sure the lyrics lived up to the melody.

As we worked, I learned the value of capturing a voice and the emotions, which later helped me in my own performances. One of the other early compositions I wrote with Patrick for CBS Songs was "I'm Still Thinking of You." We gave it to them and waited to hear back. Soon, CBS notified me that teen heartthrob Rex Smith had picked up the song, renaming it "Still Thinking of You" for his *Everlasting Love* album. Within a few weeks, several other artists recorded the same song, and three more of my songs were picked up.

Suddenly, I felt like I had something really valuable to offer as a songwriter, and apparently I wasn't alone. Within a few months I found myself in the New York offices of CBS Songs. I had already written five songs that were covered by at least one, but often more than one, artist. In New York, I met Deirdre O'Hara, a "songplugger," who later became a top executive of CBS Songs and then of BMG Rights Management. She paired me with songwriter Doug James, whose creations include "After You" by Dionne Warwick

THE SOUL OF IT ALL

and Odyssey's "Don't Tell Me, Tell Her." We met in Deirdre's office and after a quick introduction she led us to a room, ushered us in, and closed the door on us, saying, "Get to work."

Doug and I spent an hour or two joking around and getting to know each other before he sat down at the piano and we started tinkering with ideas for lyrics and music. I loved writing with Doug, who is one of the most decent human beings I've ever met. We shared the desire to tell compelling stories through songs, and to take no prisoners on the Top 40.

"I want to make sure it holds water," he'd say, meaning the song had to be resonant, believable, and real, with a tight composition. Doug is a great pianist who plays with sensitivity, and yet he could bring the song home with strong, aggressive playing as well. We'd usually start from scratch, or begin with a simple idea for a title or theme. We worked some pretty long hours to create songs we'd be proud of. Songs that all types of artists and the world at large could not resist. Our approach worked. Nearly every song we wrote was recorded by an artist, and in some cases by multiple artists.

The very first song we came up with in our initial session was a career changer for both of us; we wrote most of the song "How Am I Supposed to Live Without You" that day. We needed two more sessions to complete it because, as often happens, we had a tougher time with the second verse than the first. Once we felt the song was ready for a test run, we called in a few CBS Songs executives and staff members. I sang and Doug accompanied me. They loved it!

In fact, CBS executives snapped it up and gave the song an unusual debut. I never was told how it all came about, but they wrote our song into the script of a CBS network show, *Knots Landing*. The actress Lisa Hartman, whose character was a rock singer, performed it in a music video written into the plot. You can still find that segment on YouTube. How strange that my biggest hit—as both a singer and a songwriter—was first performed on a prime-time television soap opera. Stranger still is the fact that I would later have a long relationship with another of the actresses on *Knots Landing*.

"How Am I" wasn't performed on the public airwaves again until 1983, but once it was out there, millions upon millions heard it, and I'm told a few of them even sang along. Justin Timberlake's mother once told me that her son, who was born the year we wrote "How Am I," won his first local singing competition belting it out when he was about ten years old. I'm thrilled that Justin, a fellow member of the *SNL* Lonely Island club, chose to perform our song, though at that age he was probably singing about living without a pet that had wandered off.

When Justin was still a member of 'N Sync, he sang "This I Promise You," written by Richard Marx. I remember listening to that record, thinking: *I don't know what will happen with that boy band, but this kid will have a long career.* Since then, I've heard many rave not just about his talent but also about his strong work ethic and dedication. I once saw Justin perform a *Saturday Night Live* skit in which he did an impression of me and sang "How Am I Supposed to Live Without You," and he knocked both me and the song out of the park.

After we released that song to the CBS Songs executives, they shipped it off to Air Supply, the artists from Australia. They were looking for songs for a new album. This was a dream scenario for us. We were thrilled when word came that they wanted to record it, because they'd been on a roll, selling millions of records.

In the meantime, Deirdre had shared the song with the managers for Laura Branigan, who was coming off her big hit "Gloria." Deirdre emphasized that Laura had connected with the song and wanted to make it her own. We knew her record label was committed to her since she'd had such a big hit. Once a backup singer for Leonard Cohen, Laura had a five-octave range. She broke out as a solo artist in 1982 with the platinum single "Gloria"—which became a standard in disco clubs—and another number one hit, "Self Control." That same year, for her second album, Laura chose to record "How Am I Supposed to Live Without You," which was released as the second single. Her version climbed to No. 1 on Billboard's Adult Contemporary list and spent twenty-two weeks on the charts. (The song "Solitaire" was released as the album's first single and marked the first major hit for *its* lyrics writer, Diane Warren, who would later write scores of hit songs—including several with me. Later I teased her that "How Am I Supposed to Live Without You" would have been No. 1 on the Top 40 charts if the record company hadn't released Diane's song first.)

Laura sang "How Am I" as a pop ballad, very much as I'd performed it on the demo. I'd written quite a few love songs already, along with a ton of rock songs, so I was comfortable with them, even though I hadn't recorded any myself. People often ask if my songs are based upon personal experiences, and I believe they all are connected in some way. Most writers of songs, novels, or poems tap into their well of emotions and past and present experiences. The funny thing is that "How Am I," which probably has impacted my life more than any other song I've written, was not inspired by an event in my life. I wasn't going through a breakup when Doug and I wrote that heartbreaker, but we both knew what losing a relationship felt like.

Not every song comes directly and completely out of a life moment, but I have no doubt that moments from my life are in each song, whether it's just a situation I've observed, empathy I've felt for a friend, or something deeper within me in a place where I don't care to consciously go. Many times, a song will begin with just a phrase or a theme and then, in a sense, write itself while I ride along taking notes or running the tape recorder. I love the creative flow that occurs when songs reveal themselves and you feel as though other forces are at play. I've heard of other writers and artists being caught up in the flow. Doug and I certainly were fully engaged in our first series of songwriting sessions and in all that followed. We'd spend hours and hours in our little room playing off each other, testing riffs and lyrics. There were times when the maintenance crews threw us out so they could finish their work, but we wised up and began slipping cash to the security guards so we could work through the night to complete songs and polish the demos.

At some point, though, nearly every song becomes work. The wind isn't always in the sails. You aren't always coasting along. Even when you feel inspired, you have to stay focused and keep the song rooted in reality. The story must be believable and relatable and accessible. Doug and I seemed to have the right recipe with our very first song.

I was touring with Bob Seger and the Silver Bullet Band when Laura's recording of "How Am I Supposed to Live Without You" was playing on radio stations everywhere we traveled. The fact that a song I'd co-written was soaring up the charts lifted my spirits because, at the same time, my own single "Fool's Game" was losing steam. There was something else nagging me as well. Every night after I finished performing with my band, I listened to the headliner sing and I had to wonder whether there was room for me, another white rock and soul singer with a gritty voice, because Bob was so talented, already established, and cranking out one hit after another.

With all those doubts dogging me, you can imagine how I welcomed the success of Laura's recording of our song and all the good things it was bringing my way. Louis Levin called me every day, often several times a day, with requests from other artists and record companies looking for songs. Just knowing my name was out there and my songs were respected gave me hope and the strength to continue as a singer, too.

Laura's emotional performance of our song was beautiful, and her success with it was a game changer for me—a major boost for my songwriting career, which, like my jingle career, took off at a pace that left me wondering what I'd done to deserve it. Once again, I'd always been told that you were lucky if one of every ten songs you wrote was recorded by another artist. Doug James and I went on a fast roll with our songs. They were snatched up, one after the other, by top-echelon performers who didn't have to beg for material.

My songs were being picked up and even custom-ordered by the Pointer Sisters, Kenny Rogers, Thelma Houston, Bill Medley, and another former jingle singer, Patti Austin. I managed to stay focused and keep writing, because this sudden change in fortune had me really fired up.

I'd been banging on doors in the music industry since the age of fifteen, never expecting that one day they would fly open and welcome me in with such warmth and enthusiasm. Top executives, producers, and performers were calling me with requests to write for them or their artists. The industry I had been chasing all those years was now chasing me.

In truth, I'd been writing songs for nearly as long as I'd been singing them. I just never thought that I could make a living writing for other artists. I'd always thought I'd be known for *singing* rock songs, not writing them. As they say, "Men plan. God laughs." It is kind of funny that I could barely make a living as a rock singer but did so well singing jingles and writing songs for other artists. As it turned out, my work as a songwriter eventually helped open the door to my singing career and the realization of my dreams. I was bullheaded and focused for many years, determined to stick exactly to the path I'd mapped out to be a rock star. I generally refused to listen to suggestions or advice from anyone about diverting from that path. There is a lesson in that. There can be more than one path to a dream, and it's rarely a straight path that takes you there. My experience is that if you fully commit yourself to your dreams, the path and the destination are one and the same.

Chapter Nine

Songwriter Shangri-La

W riting songs came naturally to me. Giving them away was something I had to get used to.

The fact that my music was something I could create for other performers took a while to sink in. Being a songwriter was part of being a singer for me. I'd always done both; I'd just never thought of myself as someone who wrote compositions for other people to sing.

My mother recognized early on that while I expressed my opinions freely, my feelings were another matter. I tended to lock those up. I spent a big part of my childhood in closets. The songs poured out of me there. Writing songs has always provided me with a way to express what is in my heart or eating at my soul. Over time, I grasped that songwriting helps make me a more compelling singer because I'm more aware of all the components of the song. Actually, every detail involved in delivering the power, which is the emotion and the sentiment of the song, needs to be embraced and learned in order for an artist to become better at both writing and singing. The singer is the messenger and the song is the message.

When you write for other artists, you do demo recordings that lay out the blueprint for them and the record producers, and that process also helps you become more thoroughly engaged as a singer.

I've had vocal performances that I would just as soon forget—especially from the early days—but I have affection for every song I've written. They are like my children. I love every one of them in a unique way, even though I have a few hundred songs to love. From the time I first learned to play the guitar, I've composed songs. Some of the most peaceful and fulfilling moments of my childhood and teen years were spent in my closet or another solitary place, where I could put together words and music in peace. I'd go to a place in my mind where there was no time and no distractions, and I'd lose myself in the creative process.

I barely knew what chord changes were in the early days. I didn't have an inkling about the craft, really, because I was just beginning. I was insecure about playing in front of others until I was sure I could play without making a lot of mistakes. I do still seek out quiet, private spaces when I want to begin a song. In that space, I try to craft something that will truly resonate. I draw on my emotions and experiences and observations, so I have to be alone or working with a trusted co-writer to reach into all of those places and then express musically what emerges.

I usually begin writing songs alone but team with someone to complete them. I've found that it takes me longer to write one song by myself than to write four in collaboration. A good pianist or keyboard player can help me, because the voicings on a piano are more emotionally powerful for me. I'm a big fan of the songs that came out of Motown, as you probably know or certainly will when my next CD comes out.

For that album I also wrote an original song with my longtime friend and collaborator Lamont Dozier, a member of the incredibly prolific Motown songwriting team of Holland-Dozier-Holland, whose songs were recorded many times by many artists, and they often had a song hit No. 1 more than once because of that. This was not my first collaboration with Lamont. In 1997, Lamont, Ken "Babyface" Edmonds, and I co-wrote "Why Me" for my *All That Matters* album.

To date, Lamont has written and produced fifty-four No. 1 hit records on the Billboard charts. While widely known as a songwriting legend, he also has produced every No. 1 song that he's written. Incredibly, Lamont has written more than 1,000 published songs and probably another 5,000 that are not published. He writes new songs every day, completing only those that he feels reflect his best work. At Motown and on his own, he's been involved in the creation of hundreds of classics, including "Stop! In the Name of Love," "Reach Out I'll Be There," "Baby Love," "Heat Wave," "You Keep Me Hangin' On," "How Sweet It Is," and "Baby I Need Your Loving." That last song alone has been performed nine million times, according to Lamont.

This Rock and Roll Hall of Famer and Grammy winner signed on with Berry Gordy at Motown in 1962. Writing with him is both a humbling and an inspiring experience—and I'm not kidding about the humbling part. I thought I'd done pretty well writing more than two hundred songs, but Lamont has written more than ten times that, and so many of them have been hits it's mind-boggling. A historian at the Motown museum told me that the writing team of Holland-Dozier-Holland has had more number one hits than the Beatles, the Rolling Stones, and Elvis combined.

Working with Lamont is like attending a master class in songwriting. I was floored by his melodic instincts and the way he plays with lyrics with such great style and class. Lamont gave me a taste

of what it must have been like to work at Motown with songwriters of his skill. He and the other Motown writers created songs
that have been recorded, sung, and loved by generations of fans
around the world.

Lamont described "being in the zone" with his songwriting collaborators during those Motown years. One of their secrets was to
know when to get out of the way creatively when great lyrics and
melodies were revealing themselves. There is a real thrill experienced when a song begins to write itself and the lyrics and melodies fall into place. You believe there is a greater creative power at
work in those moments where you feel immersed in the soul of it
all. You become both a participant and an observer in that time
of creative flow. You come out of that spell feeling as though all
of your gifts and talents and energy have been fully expressed and
fulfilled.

SECRETS OF THE MOTOWN SOUND

Most of the Motown songs I'm familiar with were written on
keyboards, and there is a little additional element in the chords
of these songs that bears mentioning. When you listen to the
chord structures, the hooks sound simple, but there is always
something else going on that is a little tricky or clever, a variation
that is more complex. In listening to multiple tracks of original
Motown recordings, I noticed that some of the string arrange-
ments seem to be in an entirely different form than you'd expect—
more classical than pop, but they are truly part of the Motown
sound.

Then I found that in the keyboard parts of many Motown songs
there is an unusual combination of minors and majors. Now, in
my little corner of the songwriting world, you usually don't hear a

major and a minor chord played simultaneously because they tend to fight against each other. The notes conflict and if you play just the keyboard parts, the notes have a certain amount of dissonance that sounds unpleasant. Yet the Motown songwriters realized that underneath the more pleasant harmonies going on—the hooks that were delivering these songs—the dissonance isn't perceived as dissonance. It creates a kind of tension that makes the release of it more appealing and compelling. It's an interesting little element; not a trick, but a skill.

In "I Heard It Through the Grapevine," the chorus has a minor and a major going on. When we were starting to lay down the tracks for the song, which is on my latest CD, I asked my co-producer, Paul Mirkovich, if he noticed the wrong chord was being played. "It's not the wrong chord," he said. "That's how it is written."

It is almost like one guy didn't tell the other that he was playing an E-flat minor to the other's E-flat major. Normally you would fix that chord. But the Motown songwriters knew what they were doing, and it's not like they were trying to create an alternative sound that was out of the mainstream or not commercially viable. The songwriters from Motown were delivering hooks that were impossible to get out of your head, but underneath them they had some unusual and complex movements going on.

Paul is classically trained and can write out orchestra charts. But even he didn't realize how complex some Motown tracks are. Discovering elements like that in songs can't help but inspire me as a songwriter. I can't imitate what the writers did, but understanding their techniques makes me want to elevate my game. I've played golf and tennis with professionals, and they have the same impact on me. You just hope a little of their superior talent rubs off. When I hear Motown songs even today I get excited about the greater possibilities for my own songwriting.

Writing songs is a craft, and there is a process I follow with each one. I first find the initial spark or theme to be developed and then build on it. Songwriting 101: make each verse compelling enough to keep people engaged and listening and get them emotionally involved so they follow you into the chorus—but don't take too long doing it. My mantra is "Don't bore us, get to the chorus."

There also has to be a hook in the chorus that stays with the listener. The legendary Quincy Jones, who has worked with an incredible list of performers, including Duke Ellington, Ray Charles, Miles Davis, Frank Sinatra, and Michael Jackson, is the master of record production and creating memorable performances. His line on the topic of songwriting is among my favorites. When listening to a song without a strong chorus he'll stop the singer and say, "I'm offering a twenty-five-dollar reward for the hook. Can anyone find it?"

The "work" of songwriting is in mastering such details; building a great bridge (the middle eight bars, which set up the final chorus), telling a story in three minutes, and then conveying the power of the composition in a studio. Early on I wrestled with the pressures of composing to order for a specific artist. I locked up creatively at first. When I first began working with Doug James in the CBS Songs office, Deirdre O'Hara would check in with us from time to time and tell us what performers or bands were looking for songs and what kind of records they wanted and what the hottest producers were calling for. I found it difficult to sit down and write a song with one artist or act in mind. I tried to do it many times. I have a good ear for artists and their voices and vocal ranges, and I know instinctively if a song is suited for a certain artist, but I can't tailor-make a song for an artist to save my life. What works for me is to try and write a great song alone or with a collaborator, and determine which artists it is best suited for. I've often had great success in matching songs to artists, but not in writing with a particular artist in mind.

Fortunately, when I received a "custom" songwriting request for a huge star in 1987, I already had a perfect song in my pocket. The request was from the team working with a Grammy-winning goddess of pop music. Cher had taken five years off for an equally successful career as a movie star and now wanted me to write songs for the album that would reestablish her singing career.

The initial call came from legendary A and R executive John Kalodner, who was then with Geffen Records.

"Michael, Cher needs a comeback smash record," John said.

A rock star since the '60s, Cher was coming off a five-year stretch in which she'd proved herself also as a gifted actress. She'd been widely praised for her roles in *Mask* and *Silkwood*, for which she received an Oscar nomination (and would later win). Word was that she'd get another Academy Award nomination for her role in a movie due to come out at the end of 1987, *Moonstruck*.

Having conquered Hollywood, Cher signed with Geffen Records to make a roaring return as a singer. Geffen was assembling a team of songwriters, musicians, backup singers, and record producers to make it happen—fast. They wanted the album released just before *Moonstruck* opened in December, so they were shopping for hits in a hurry.

They chose three songs that I'd co-written—"I Found Someone," with Mark Mangold; "Working Girl," with Desmond Child (who would have five songs on the album); and "Hard Enough Getting Over You," with Doug James. Other songwriters whose songs made the cut were Diane Warren, Richie Sambora, and Jon Bon Jovi. Laura Branigan had recorded the first song, "I Found Someone," previously for her 1985 album *Hold Me*. She released it as a single and hit No. 25 on Billboard's Adult Contemporary chart in

1986. Laura also had performed it on *The Tonight Show* on New Year's Eve in 1985.

I didn't tell Cher about all of that at first. Songs are often picked up by several artists, but I wasn't sure Cher would want to perform a song recorded by another artist on her comeback album. Keeping the song's history to myself proved to be a good move. Cher loved it, and she released her version as the first single. It broke the Top 10 of the Hot 100 on the Billboard charts. Of course, Laura hadn't done a music video to support the song, while Cher made a smoking-hot video that was a finalist for the Best Female Video of the Year at the 1988 MTV Awards.

The high-dollar video also starred Cher's boyfriend, dancer Rob Camilletti. This was supposed to mark his debut as an actor but few people noticed him, through no fault of his own. Cher wore a black leather coat over a fishnet body stocking and thong for most of the video. Male viewers may not have realized she was even singing. Cher did not look like a typical forty-four-year-old mother of two children.

She walked into the studio one day in a white dress, which brought out a beautiful softness that I hadn't seen in her before. I blurted out, "You look really great today!"

Cher smiled at the compliment, but she also looked at me like, "What do you want?"—as though I was just flattering her and had an agenda. I realized that through the years many people likely tried to charm Cher in pursuit of their agendas, so I was mindful of that while working with her.

Cher is a force of nature, incredibly savvy and great fun to be around. I produced two tracks on the album. This project was a great experience. I recorded and arranged the music and selected all of the musicians and backup singers, as well as booking the session and producing Cher's vocal performance. This undertaking

My very good-looking parents, George and Helen Lila Bolotin.

George Louis Bolotin.

My mom had her hands full with me, Orrin, and Sandra. No wonder I always thought I was a short kid at 5'11.

I'm wondering if this is my new coat, or just a leftover from my sister.

Me, Sandra, and Orrin. I don't recognize this building...maybe this is where our parents dropped us off hoping some other family would pick us up!

Bree Belford's father's house on Alston Avenue, which I rented with Maureen, Orrin, and a couple other friends for about a year. Maureen and I had our wedding in the backyard.

Marc Friedland and me after opening for Leon Russell at the Spectrum in Philadelphia in 1972.

Isadore "Izzy" and
Rose Gubin.

Orrin,
the hippie
heartthrob.

Orrin, the
bodhisattva.

Trying to write songs for my next record deal. My mom, in the background, at our Coldwater Canyon, North Hollywood, home.

Bolotin Family Collection

Wayne Logan

Me with my mom and Orrin after one of my MBC fundraising events.

Mom still comes out to my shows and MBC fundraisers whenever she can.

Wayne Logan

Isa practicing controlling her dad at just a few months old.

Me trying my songs out on Isa, my biggest fan at the time.

Me and Isa having a heart to heart.

Anita Lomartra

The girls with lifelong family friend and our first nanny, Anita Lomartra.

Left to right:
Holly, Isa, Taryn.
My little angels...

Anita Lomartra

Left to right: Taryn, me, Holly, Isa. Still angels, but not so little!

At one, Gwen is too cute for words. And Millie is a hard act to follow!

Left to right: Holly, Taryn. When they got along, they got along beautifully!

Isa and me at an academic graduation.

Our trusted nanny Laura McKinley during the girls' teenage years. Here at Taryn's high school graduation.

Some of my first hits written for other artists:

"I Found Someone" by Cher

"Forever" by KISS

"How Am I Supposed to Live Without You"
by Laura Branigan

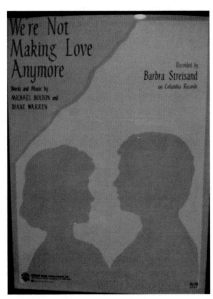

"We're Not Making Love Anymore"
by Barbra Streisand

With my good friend Rodney Dangerfield, who flew in to help raise money for "This Close" for cancer research.

There are no words to describe what playing guitar and singing with the one and only B. B. King was like on the televised Essence Awards at the Paramount Theater in New York City.

Singing "A Change Is Gonna Come" at Bill Clinton's first inauguration—one of the most powerful experiences I'll ever have! Fighter jets were flying in perfect unison above us and a new era (and did I mention eight years of our greatest prosperity?) would follow.

At the 17th Annual American Music Awards (at The Shrine Auditorium in L.A.) with the eternal and legendary teenager Dick Clark, who loved to kid around (and Louis Levin in the background).

was very exciting and more than a little intimidating, especially with "I Found Someone," because everyone felt certain our song would be a hit.

The high expectations made the days all the more intense and stressful. The project was a revelation from start to finish, including seeing up close what life was like for a multimedia star of her stature. Publicists, stylists, agents, managers, dressers, admen, photographers, magazine reporters, television reporters, and I think even perfume designers swarmed our studios, but I had a record to produce.

She is the most attractive conglomerate I've ever known. Our album was just the sound track to a stream of commercials, television appearances, concert tours, a major motion picture with serious Oscar buzz (Moonstruck), and an entire line of cosmetics.

Cher provided my first view of the highest level of celebrity and stardom. The disruptions distracted me at first, but she was a professional throughout our production. In the end, Cher proved to be so strong and in control that I just had to marvel at her. My goal was to deliver a hit record that would reach her existing audience and bring in new fans, too, and I felt that mission was accomplished. David Geffen called and thanked me for delivering the comeback record they'd wanted for her.

Even better, Cher sent me an autographed photo with this note: "Michael, I'm wearing white panties under my dress. Just kidding. I'm not wearing any."

She signed it, "The Daughter of the Devil." I think she was teasing me because apparently someone at the label had said she could be difficult to work with. I hadn't found her difficult at all. Cher was amazing. I just was so busy that we really didn't spend much time in the studio together, except to produce her vocals. I agreed without hesitation to work with her as a producer on a couple of songs for her next album.

WRITING FROM THE HEART

Teaming up with Cher, John Kalodner, and David Geffen was a step into the stratosphere of the entertainment business. I'd suddenly come a very, very long way after struggling a long time as an artist, waiting tables in a restaurant, and commuting on a rickety motor scooter with a shoestring for an accelerator. While putting in long hours on the first Cher album, I also was quietly coping with serious turmoil in my personal life. When I think about that time, I recall a moment in the recording studio in which I was telling myself, *You can't be thinking about your divorce while Cher is singing into the microphone right in front of you.*

Even more ironic, when I was recording "When a Man Loves a Woman" for my own album, my attorneys kept calling me as they prepared for my divorce. I don't recommend talking to your divorce lawyer before walking into the studio to sing a love song, but thankfully the music took me where I needed to go.

My struggles as a rock singer had been stressful on my marriage, but succeeding as a songwriter, jingle singer, record producer, and then ultimately as a pop R & B singer did nothing to save it. The financial strains on our relationship were all but eliminated with those successes, but in pursuing the opportunities that came with them, I was pulled farther and farther from home.

I felt blessed by my career success and I wanted to build upon it, which took a toll on my personal life. The long hours and travel left not nearly enough time for my family. As the child of divorced parents, I was aware of the lasting impact a split would have on our daughters. As I noted earlier, I have never figured out how to achieve a perfectly "balanced life" while working at the level I aspire to achieve and maintain, but later, when my girls moved in with me and traveled with me, we had some incredible times together.

During this difficult period, I wrote one of my few songs to come directly from my ongoing experience and emotions, and it proved to be one of my most successful collaborations. I wrote "We're Not Making Love Anymore" with the queen of songwriters, Diane Warren, who had become a good friend and collaborator. We'd both had our first hits on the same album with Laura Branigan five years earlier. Diane had sent seven more songs into the Top 10 since then. She was on a roll that still continues. The last time I checked, her songs were on albums and records that had sold more than 150 million copies and I'm proud to say that more than 50 million of those were mine. The success we had together helped her negotiate a very lucrative publishing agreement, so we both benefited from our collaborations.

Diane and I met after the Branigan album was released. A mutual friend introduced us, and we quickly realized that we had much in common beyond the source of our first hit songs. We began meeting for lunch whenever I was in Los Angeles. Then we bonded further during a ten-day glasnost trip to Moscow for a Songwriters Summit cultural exchange program with twenty-five top U.S. songwriters and artists, including Cyndi Lauper, Desmond Child, Barry Mann, and Mike Stoller.

Lunch and dinner with Diane were not for the faint of heart. She would sometimes bring one of her pet birds, usually a parrot named Butt Wings. I'd beg her not to bring the birds. They may have been parrots, but they acted like raptors. Or *crap*-tors.

Devilish Diane would hide her giant freaking parrot under her coat until we were seated and then she'd unleash it upon me and other unsuspecting diners. Within minutes, the raucous bird would be strutting on the white tablecloths at the Ivy in Beverly Hills.

"Diane, please!" I'd say.

"What?" she'd reply, pretending not to notice.

Diane was only slightly better behaved than her bird. She had a tendency to toss cutting comments and provocative observations like ninja stars across the room. Between Diane and Butt Wings, I never knew when we might get thrown out of a really nice restaurant. Usually Diane would temper her flamethrowing with a funny spin so people didn't know whether to laugh or to take offense, but they were almost always shocked.

She targeted me, too, but I returned fire. We had a contentious working relationship, so Diane took to introducing me to her friends as "my brother from hell." I countered by saying that working with Diane was a day at the beach—Normandy, 1944.

Whenever I think I might be winning my war with Warren, she pulls out one story that slays me every time. Shortly after my singing career took off, we were working in Santa Monica. We'd gone to lunch and we were sitting in my rental car in the parking lot talking before returning home. This woman came walking toward the car and I said to Diane, "She must want an autograph."

Instead, the woman, who was visibly irritated, said, "Can you please move your car? You are blocking mine!"

Diane never let me forget that story, and I deserved it.

Fortunately, we share a love for songwriting and, despite being loners by nature, we found ways to work together that produced some beautiful songs. I loved those moments when I'd see her antennae go up in a restaurant. A wicked smile would cross her face after she'd overheard something or had a creative flash. "I have a title," she'd say.

When we weren't throwing lightning bolts at each other, we wrote up a storm. If she came up with something she loved, Diane called me no matter what the hour. I was always eager to listen to her songs. She is a genius, with an unbelievable work ethic. She is also fiercely protective of her creations, like a Tiger Mom who follows her songs through every stage of their lives.

Most songwriters are very particular about how their songs are produced and recorded. We want the key notes and chords to be played as written so the song conveys the emotion we intended. Some demand to be present in the recording studio to make certain the original blueprint is followed. Often producers choose a song because they believe it will be a hit, but then they'll go with an arrangement that strays far from the songwriter's intent, which we feel makes it less likely to be the very "hit" they first heard and were drawn to. The producer can be slick or heavy-handed and overproduce a record, too, making it more about their own sound than the song itself. Maybe it's not a hit. Maybe it's simply a great song, but the full power of it will not be shared with the world. As my manager, Christina Kline, once said, producers can get so focused on the technical aspects and other sonic elements of a recording that these elements can overshadow or distract from the great song they have right in front of them. They can often miss "the soul of it." And I love that as a metaphor for what can spill over into all areas of our existence. I'm always wary of missing the soul of it all when my songs are recorded. I don't want the heart of it to be lost in the production process. The drum sound alone can distract from the lead vocal and alter the intention of the song. Too many effects on the lead vocal can bury the emotions expressed by the singer. The lyrics and melody are brought to life by the soul of the voice.

Once you've got the goods, the next phase is just as important. In my New Haven grammar school, L. W. Beecher, the teachers planted trees and had us tend to them by watering, fertilizing, staking, and fencing the seedlings to make sure they had the chance to live and thrive over a long life. I think about my songs, especially when they're released as singles, in that same way. You have to protect them in the initial stage of launch. Sometimes you have to fight like hell to make sure the record label and the promotion team are doing absolutely everything they can to make sure the song will survive on the radio. I've never met a songwriter who didn't want his or her creations to be huge hits embraced by millions of people. We're artists and we're competitive, too. Berry Gordy knew this when he created the Motown hit-making machine. His songwriters shared office space in Detroit at the house turned headquarters marked by a sign that read—and still reads—"Hitsville USA." Gordy put his songwriting teams under one roof, so he wouldn't have to motivate them. They drove one another because every one of them wanted to have the No. 1 hit record.

Lamont Dozier told me that Motown's songwriters would walk by one another's offices, hear great songs being cranked out, and run back to their rooms to come up with their own hits. The songwriter Barry Mann told me that all of the songwriters in the famed Brill Building in New York City would check one another's work and vacation schedules because they were afraid to be out of the office if everyone else was working. They finally resolved that problem by taking all of their vacations together—and going to the same place, he said.

It wasn't always peace, love, and understanding inside Motown's creative dens, either. Fittingly, another of Motown's biggest hits was "War." When you put creative, driven, and competitive songwriters together, there are bound to be some clashes. Holland, Dozier, and Holland had their share. Diane Warren and I did, too. Neither of us lacks for opinions, and we're not exactly shy about expressing them. I'm not saying we caused the Northridge Earthquake, but we were working together in Los Angeles when it rocked the city in 1994.

Have you heard the creative process described as "opening a vein"? Diane offered to cut my jugular several times. She is a tough customer, but Diane wouldn't be able to craft such gorgeous love songs if she didn't have a soft side, too.

Alone in a Manhattan apartment late one night, I tried to capture my emotional pain in a song. The title "We're Not Making Love Anymore" came to me and I wrote the first verse. Then I called Diane and played her a little of the song on keyboards I had set up in the apartment.

She was all over it in a flash, singing out more lyrics faster than I could write them down.

"So do you like it?" I said. "If you do, let's meet in L.A. on Friday and finish it."

Diane is not one to squander an inspired songwriting opportunity. We met in West Hollywood at the Sunset Marquis Hotel, which now caters to musicians by providing instruments and sound equipment for guests. I'd ordered a set of keyboards and we spent several days crafting the rest of the song.

Once we'd completed the song, Diane and I debated which artists to send it to. We felt "We're Not Making Love Anymore" deserved someone mature enough to sing it with the right kind of passion, which means the right voice as well as the right life experience. We agreed the perfect match would be Barbra Streisand, who possessed that rare combination of a Stradivarius-quality voice and a gift for storytelling in song. Of course, Streisand was at the top of every songwriter's list. Placing a new song in her hands was more difficult than arranging a personal audience with the pope.

Streisand had protective and hard-to-please producers who screened all the material sent to her. Luckily, we had a man on the inside. We reached out to Jay Landers, a member of Streisand's inner circle and one of my favorites in the music industry. Jay, who cast me as the recording artist for the *Hercules* theme song, "Go the Distance," was an A and R guy who always got it right. He had worked with Laura Branigan, too, and he has been executive producer on twenty-two Streisand albums at last count, as well as the music supervisor for most of her DVDs and concerts—and that's just where his résumé begins. He's been instrumental in the success of records for everyone from Frank Sinatra to James Taylor to Josh Groban, and he's produced sound tracks for many of Disney's greatest movies, including *Beauty and the Beast* and *Aladdin*.

Diane and I sent "We're Not Making Love Anymore" to Jay because we knew him and also because he has a great ear for hit songs. He agreed that the song was perfect for Barbra, so he handed it up the star chain to another heavy hitter—one who would become a major player in my own recording career—record producer and songwriter Walter Afanasieff. Like Jay, Walter has produced major movie sound tracks, including the one for *Titanic*. My album *Time, Love & Tenderness* marked Walter's explosive entrance into the world of pop music. He had been producing Kenny G, and I met him at one of Kenny's shows backstage, where Kenny suggested that Walter and I write together. The next thing I knew, Walter was in my hotel room with a truckload of high-tech gear and his keyboards. While we wrote, Walter was programming drums, bass, piano, and strings into his computers, basically building a record that sounded better than most of what you hear on the radio. I promptly made a call to Tommy Mottola to introduce him to Walter. Tommy then signed Walter to Sony and set him up in a state-of-the-art studio where he produced many major artists, Celine Dion and Mariah Carey among them.

Walter and Jay not only gave the song their blessing, they selected it to be Barbra's next single. They invited me to help produce the vocal session when she recorded it. I was honored beyond words at their invitation, but Streisand's production team was so tight and so experienced I didn't think they needed me in the studio throwing my two cents in. I preferred to let her

Grammy-winning producers do their jobs. I was more comfortable staying in the background, but close enough to send more songs to Barbra's team.

I had no doubt that Barbra would sing the hell out of "We're Not Making Love Anymore"—and not just because she is one of the world's greatest singers. I began writing the song from the heart during my divorce, and Barbra sang it from the heart in the studio. I was not at all shocked when her single immediately hit the Top 10 of the Adult Contemporary charts in 1989. She then made it the first song on her next album, A Collection: Greatest Hits & More, which went double platinum that same year.

History offers many examples in which emotional pain was the catalyst for artistic achievement, but I don't know if success has ever truly salved the wounded hearts of the creators. I can speak only for myself. As much as that song means to me—I'm proud and thankful to have co-written it—I'll never be able to hear it without associating it with a sad time in my life.

KISS and Tell

I've had many interesting experiences while working at the Sunset Marquis Hotel, my West Coast headquarters for many years. Another frequent guest was the distinguished actor Richard Harris, who once walked up and introduced himself to me while singing the lyric "How am I supposed to live without you." It was like having King Arthur or Oliver Cromwell (two of his biggest roles) serenading me.

You never know what stars you'll encounter at the Marquis. This landmark hotel, which opened in 1963 as the designated inn for the new Playboy West Coast headquarters nearby, is a Hollywood celebrity haunt that also serves as a creative hothouse for people in my business. Along with all the other amenities of a first-class hotel, the Marquis houses the noted NightBird Recording Studio in its basement.

I've often worked in my Marquis hotel room when writing songs, either alone or with a co-writer. Once the song is ready to be recorded on a demo, there are many studios in the immediate area, including the one in the basement. One of my favorite writing sessions at the Sunset was the one in which I crafted another made-to-order song for a group that might surprise you. One day at the hotel, I ran into my friend Bruce Kulick, who had co-founded the rock band Blackjack with me years earlier and had played on several albums with me.

This talented musician and songwriter had become the lead guitarist for KISS in 1984, after the band went through some personnel changes. By the time he arrived, they'd wiped off the face paint they had worn since the early 1970s. When I met up with Bruce at the Marquis, he mentioned that KISS co-founder Paul Stanley was also staying at the hotel, and that they'd talked about asking me to help Paul write a song for their new album.

The reconstituted KISS band was focused on recapturing the popularity and fan base they'd enjoyed earlier in their history. The new album was designed to trigger a comeback, so they were looking for at least one major hit song to crack the Top 40. They'd lined up one of the great rock producers, Bob Ezrin, who had worked on most of their biggest hits as well as those of Pink Floyd and Alice Cooper. Having a proven genius like Bob aboard was comforting, because there is nothing worse than creating a great song only to see it lose its soul due to inept production.

Bruce and I arranged for Paul to come to my room for a writing session. Paul and the other members of the original KISS were known for their wild antics onstage and off, but people in the business knew them to be very savvy, which explained the band's longevity. Paul is a great rock singer with a powerful set of pipes, excellent range, and a keen sense of melody, which is rare in a genre where singers often avoid it altogether to maintain an edge. He also impressed me with his business smarts and his sense of humor as we got to know each other. Paul is one of the funniest people I know. KISS was as much an entertainment empire as it was a rock band, and both Paul and Gene Simmons had been major forces in expanding their opportunities.

We talked about our careers and the direction Paul wanted to take KISS with the new album. We discovered that we shared the same twisted humor and shared "commitment issues" when it came to relationships. After a little "get to know you" banter, we settled down to write with a "give me hits or give me death" focus. As I recall, Paul offered an appealing melody for the verse to begin and it was quickly obvious that he understood the importance of thematic chords and vocal phrases. I came up with the opening melody of the chorus.

Neither of us was writing from an inspiration or personal experience, so we just followed the flow of the music and the melody as we worked out a song that we named "Forever." We completed it after one more session, as I recall. Paul and I both contributed lyrics and melody to the song that became KISS's biggest hit since "Beth." Our song appeared on the 1989 album *Hot in the Shade* and was released as a single in early 1990. It peaked at No. 8 on Billboard's Hot 100 and became KISS's first Top 40 single since 1979. The song was boosted by a music video that hit No. 1 on MTV's Most Requested Videos. The MTV play drove a big boost in their concert ticket sales, too.

I think we accomplished our mission quite well. Shortly after the release of the single, I saw KISS perform at the New Haven Coliseum in front of about ten thousand people. When they played "Forever," the fans in the darkened arena held lighters in the air, which gave me a great sense of satisfaction. After the show, I visited with Bruce, Paul, and the rest of the band and they seemed to be enjoying the fruits of a successful album and tour. I told them I hoped they'd be playing "Forever" forever.

I'm very fond of that song, and I believe in its message.

STEEL BARS AND DYLAN

In the fall of 1990, I found myself back at the Sunset Marquis, my emotions swirling, feeling more confident about my career, but distressed that just as I was better situated to support and care for my family I felt like I was losing them, and that my marriage was not going to be saved. At the same time, if I slowed down in my work, I feared sliding back financially and staring at more eviction notices.

I don't think you ever get the trauma of those darkest moments out of your system. And I don't want to. The struggle is a part of who you are, and what you find out you're made of. Still, I wouldn't wish it upon someone else, but if you do have to go through it, that's your journey.

My very intense focus is what prevented me from fully savoring the moments of victory. An artist puts his or her emotions on the canvas. I continued channeling my emotions into my work, booking myself in nonstop writing sessions, while also recording in the studio, touring as my own records took off, and doing interviews and photo shoots every spare moment. As a songwriter I was jumping between sessions with the most creative minds of the era, including Diane Warren, Desmond Child, Doug James, and the husband-and-wife team of Barry Mann and Cynthia Weil ("On Broadway," "Somewhere Out There," "You've Lost That Lovin' Feeling"). To have access to that level of talent, let alone to enjoy solid working relationships and mutual respect with these people, was something I never took for granted. Then some practical joker called and said Bob Dylan was interested in having a songwriting session with me.

Very funny. Bob Dylan wants to write songs with me? Next he'll be inviting me to become a Traveling Wilbury.

"Who is this, really?"

She gave her name again—Suzanne Mann—and said she worked with Dylan.

"Seriously, he'd like to work with you, and if you want to work with him, you'll have to come up here to his place in Malibu," she said.

My friends are category 4 pranksters. This sort of punking was not beyond Diane Warren, for sure. So I was still waiting for the punch line, but I played along.

"When would Bob like me to be there?"

"He'll be at this address in two days and he would love to get together," she said. "Do you have a pen?"

She gave the address that I knew to be Dylan's Malibu compound, home to his Shangri-La studio, where he recorded with Eric Clapton, the Band, and the Traveling Wilburys, the supergroup he'd formed a couple of years earlier with George Harrison, Tom Petty, and Roy Orbison.

After Dylan's rep said good-bye and hung up, I walked around my hotel room in a daze for a good ten minutes. I tried to get my head around what had just happened while my stomach did a break-dance in my belly. I had been told that Bob, who hadn't collaborated all that much in the past on his songs, was not one to spend weeks working with a new co-writer. "He's so busy with solo projects and the Traveling Wilburys tour that if he doesn't hear something he loves right away, you may never hear from him again—as in never," a friend said.

I didn't know whether that report was true or not, but it reached my core. I sure didn't want to find out by testing his patience. Feeling like a mere mortal about to be tested by the music gods, I started right in that night, working up fresh song ideas on my acoustic guitar in my hotel room so I'd have plenty of options ready for our meeting. My driving thought was that this was the artist whose songs had provided a good piece of the sound track of my life.

STALKING DYLAN

When I was a hippie wannabe roaming the streets of Greenwich Village, Bob Zimmerman was performing at Folk City, Café Wha?, the Gaslight Café, the Commons, and other bars and clubs. At thirteen, I was underage and couldn't get in officially, but I was known to stand outside, playing my guitar and hoping to attract a few nickels and dimes. Dylan was the first rock poet, the Shakespeare of activist folk pop. It also didn't escape me that he, like me, was the grandson of Soviet bloc Jewish immigrants; like me, he'd embraced rock 'n' roll, dropped out of school, and changed his name. (Don't worry, I won't push the comparisons any further.)

I'd been listening to his lyrics and studying his songs ever since the 1965 release of *Highway 61 Revisited*, always in awe. Just recently I was one of the longtime fans who appreciated the symmetry of Adele, the young superstar with the wondrous voice, making a global hit of Dylan's "Make You Feel My Love" just as he turned seventy. What a birthday gift and testimony to his enduring greatness and contemporary relevance.

So as I was driving along Malibu Beach in late 1990, I grew more and more nervous and excited the closer I came. After I pulled into his driveway and left the car, a fog, or maybe just a low cloud, settled in over the property atop a hill. One of his staff directed me to park near the garage that had become a music landmark after being converted into Dylan's Shangri-La studio.

"Bob will be here shortly," he said.

Expecting him to be on rock star time, I took my acoustic guitar from its case and began playing, fiddling around nervously, with my head down and eyes closed. Then I sensed someone standing directly over me. I looked up and it was Dylan.

I stammered something awkward about being thrilled to be there and a huge fan, and he asked a staffer to get us some coffee. He must have asked me what was going on in my life, or something about my family, because as the coffee arrived and we drank, I mentioned something about going through a divorce. Dylan put his hand on his head and said, "Yeah, that's draining stuff."

I don't really recall much of that conversation. I'd often sat and studied his lyrics on the liners of his albums in awe and so it was hard to process that I was sitting in his studio writing with him. Finally, after we'd chatted for about fifteen minutes, I blurted out that I'd worked up a few ideas that I thought he might like. I played the chorus chords that became the heart of our song. I didn't have any specific lyrics written, so I sang syllables and the notes I'd worked on at the hotel. I was lost in the moment, trying to hear the words suggested in the music, and suddenly Bob said, "Steel bars, I like that."

I didn't know if I'd said those words or if he'd just plucked them out of the air, but the image seemed right for a Dylan song and I was excited that the chorus was forming immediately. I sang them and the phrase "wrapped all around me" came to mind.

Bob added, "I've been your prisoner since the day you found me." We continued like that for about two hours. During an interlude, he started playing drums while I accompanied on guitar. Then he moved to the bass guitar.

We were looking for verses when he shouted out: "How about, 'Turn around, you're in my sleep'?" Again, perfectly "Dylan."

"Out-of-body experience" might not capture exactly the sensation that overtook me, but "surreal" definitely applies. There's a part of me that couldn't help but repeat over and over again, "Oh my God, this is Bob Dylan, it really is Bob Dylan," while another part of me was thinking, "Okay, you're here to work. You're here to get a song written," and then the other part of me would come back with, "It's Bob Dylan. He speaks like Bob Dylan, he looks like Bob Dylan, it *is* Bob Dylan." I have a feeling he gets that a lot.

No matter where we are positioned in the music culture, we are all fans at heart, which may be the reason music is such a healing and bonding force. I may have moved up a couple hundred rungs in the industry by then, but I could still lose it and regress into a totally awed guitar geek in the presence of Bob Dylan.

It was mind-boggling for me, but Dylan was so laid-back that his mood calmed mine. The process moved swiftly and comfortably as we worked out the lyrics and formed the melodies without any drama.

But then came a moment I had feared.

Bob Dylan suggested phrasing that didn't work for me.

"How about, 'It was your resistance; it was my persistence'?"

I thought: *Wow, I wish we could use that, but I think it has too many syllables for this place in the song. How do I tell Dylan his phrase doesn't fit?*

To my everlasting relief, I didn't have to give the thumbs-down to the Grand Master of Song.

"You know, Michael, that's too much, that's too much. There's probably too much going on there," he said.

I nodded gratefully, and we moved on. We'd worked five hours. By the time we called it a day we had nearly all the lyrics and about 70 percent of the song written. And I realized this was a moment of truth. Friends had warned me that if Dylan didn't think the song was going anywhere, I wouldn't be invited back to complete it. That's the way Bob rolled. Or didn't roll.

I understood, of course. Dylan's songwriting time was as valuable as Warren Buffett's investing advice. He couldn't afford to waste a minute. I was just hoping he was as enthusiastic about finishing the song as I was. I'd already had *Soul Provider* out and it had sold close to ten million copies, but no success could have diminished the importance of that moment for me. That week I was supposed to write with Diane Warren, Barry Mann, and Cynthia Weil, but I'd canceled their sessions to work with Bob. They all understood the importance of that decision.

"So Michael, when do you want to get together and finish this song?" he asked.

Music to my ears.

"I'll be available in a couple days if you can do it then," he added.

As Suzanne walked me to my car, she said, "Bob likes you."

Now I really felt like a schoolboy on a first date.

"What do you mean?" I asked.

"During one of the breaks, he said, 'Mike's a nice guy, isn't he?' And I said, 'Yeah, I'm telling you, he's a real nice guy,'" Suzanne said.

DYLAN-IZED

In the years leading up to that moment, I'd experienced nearly every form of rejection and humiliation the music business had in its arsenal: People throwing nasty shit in my street-corner tip jar while I sang and played for food. Boos and insults from drunks in bars. Rejected demos. Failed records. Canceled contracts.

None of that mattered anymore.

Bob Dylan had invited me back to his studio to finish a song.

Validation!

I'd been *Dylan-ized*. Seriously, no critic in the world could dent that armor. I'd been accepted into the rarest of circles in the music world, and no matter what anyone threw at me for the rest of my career, I would always have that moment when Bob Dylan said, "Come on back and let's write some more."

Not that I didn't fret for, oh, exactly forty-eight hours that Dylan might duck out, might have just been trying to let me down easily. I didn't take anything for granted. I called to make sure we were still on, and we were.

I called only once, but during the interim I did nearly reach for the phone exactly seventy-five times—an hour.

When I returned to Shangri-La, Bob welcomed me back and we got down to business. We worked another four hours, completing the bridge and the music, everything but some lyric lines. Bob said he had some Wilbury work, but he'd be in touch about the lyrics. I told him I was confident about the music and melodies and the bridge, but I had a lingering sense that two lines we had written didn't quite work.

Dylan said he'd think about them and get back to me.

"Steel Bars" was definitely a song I wanted to record myself, and as quickly as possible. So I told Walter Afanasieff that I had another song to play for him. Upon hearing thirty seconds of the work tape, he said, "Let's start recording it now," and literally, we did. We were working at the famed studio known as the Plant in Sausalito, California.

The one remaining question I had about the song as we prepared to make the recording were the two lines I'd talked about with Bob as we finished up. I thought he'd forgotten about them, but just as we were beginning the session, a staffer handed me a fax. It was from Dylan, who'd written ten alternative lines of lyrics for me, and a change in the bridge with a new line: "Time itself is so obscene."

I was blown away—grateful and relieved. When I got home to Connecticut, I showed my oldest daughter, Isa, who was then about fifteen, the fax from Dylan and his lyrics for our song. I wasn't sure she knew anything about Bob Dylan, but it proved to be one of the few moments in which her dad impressed her—or at least her father's co-writer impressed her.

"Dad, do you realize what an honor it is to have written with Bob Dylan?" she said.

I savored that moment.

I was proud and impressed to discover that Isa's range of knowledge of and preferences in music included a lot of Dylan songs. Years later she would ask me if I could get her tickets to the Metropolitan Opera to see Luciano Pavarotti and I did, along with backstage passes (though she didn't want to bother him by being another person to greet). My daughters have often amazed me with their awareness of and appreciation for diverse kinds of music.

"Steel Bars" was released as a single from my *Time, Love & Tenderness* album, and later it was featured on several of my greatest hits and "best of" compilations on CD and DVD. My "Dylan song" has probably been on nearly twenty million records sold around the world. You can be sure if Bob ever calls again, I'll be available.

GOING GAGA

Working with Bob Dylan had been a dream of mine because of his amazing lyrics and incredible influence on artists and writers around the world. Just a few years ago, I worked with another songwriter and singer who was just beginning to make her mark. I was taking a break from production on my *One World One Love* album in August of 2008 when my manager and my record company reps called to lobby me. They urged me to schedule a songwriting session with a hot young performer and songwriter who had an exotic real name—Stefani Joanne Angelina Germanotta—and a very unusual stage name—Lady Gaga.

I hadn't heard of Lady Gaga yet, but at that point neither had the rest of the world. That would soon change, of course.

My manager and the record company folks raved about her, saying she was a little-known singer who had once signed with Def Jam's L. A. Reid but been dropped. She had then signed another record deal and a publishing deal. After writing successful songs for other artists, Lady Gaga's singing talent was recognized and she was about to break through as an artist. She'd followed a path similar to my own, though she'd done it much faster.

I told them to send over some of her songs. One of the first I listened to was "Just Dance." The first verse and chorus convinced me that this girl was headed for a big launch. After meeting her, I knew she was headed for a big career, too. Fortunately she'd grown up with my music and loved it. It was a pleasure to write with her, and even better to hear her sing her ass off working on variations and different parts of the song we created. Sometimes younger songwriters will come in and want to open the whole big bag of studio tricks, but she was an exception. Gaga hit the notes like a pro as we crafted and revised the song, shaping it as we went, working from 8 p.m. until 6:30 in the morning.

In the early going, I told her that we needed to slay people with this song. She shot right back with what would become its title: "You murder my heart!"

Gaga was quick.

We worked through the night and into the morning in our first two sessions in L.A. As the song came together I felt certain that I was witnessing a superstar in the making. She had the energy of ten artists and an intense focus. She reminded me of a young Madonna, provocative and fearless, with extreme exuberance and sharp focus on the music. This young woman was committed to her art above all else.

When we discussed her upcoming first concert tour in detail, Lady Gaga described the production and it sounded to me like she'd need an elaborate hydraulic system for staging. I cautioned her that I've known many young artists who've been shocked at how expensive their tour productions turned out to be—and what a drain those costs can be on their earnings. I had to admire her reply. Lady Gaga said that she didn't care if the tour made money, she just wanted it to succeed as art.

I had no doubt that it would. At that point, her first album was due to hit stores in three months, and I was glad that our song would be done by then. I knew she was about to become a very busy young woman. After the huge release of *The Fame*, she belonged to the world.

Before that happened, we met for a third session to finish production of "Murder My Heart" in London. Songwriters and producers Michael Mani and Jordan Omley, known as the JAM, also contributed to the creation of the song. In the studio, Lady Gaga sang beautiful harmonies and answers. During the warm-up she riffed on a few of my hits and then performed some R & B ad-libs. Her voice and control were in the Christina Aguilera league and very impressive.

During that final session, we took a dinner break and I took Lady Gaga and her lovely mother to a restaurant. I could tell her mom was concerned that the record company had such high expectations for her daughter. I assured them both that there was no danger of overhyping Gaga's great gifts.

She is a singer-songwriter genius, and most veterans of the music industry will tell you the same thing about her. In a time when recording stars are created by television talent shows overnight, we may not see many performers with staying power, but Lady Gaga will be around a long time.

Gaga and I share a few secrets with many of those who hang around in the business for a long time. Neither one of us chose music as a career. Music chose us, and it became our passion. She has the same drive and focus. When you get your shot, you work your ass off and never look back unless it's for more fuel to drive you forward. I enjoyed watching Gaga lift off and felt like I had an inside peek at the engine of a driven artist who was going to earn the career she would create.

Like me, Lady Gaga began writing music and performing around the age of twelve. Music has always been at the core of our lives. When I listened to my first Beatles records, I found myself focused on the harmonies, and though I never learned how to read or write music, I could identify the notes. I could make out the elements in my head as if the notes were somehow already hardwired into my brain.

Another thing I discovered was that while I don't have perfect pitch, as my friend David Foster does, I'm close. (David is hard to beat. If a fly burps in a far corner of the room, he can tell you what note it was—and then if the note was a little bit flat or sharp. The fly would then be fired and removed from the studio.) The more I listened to the music playing around our house—whether it was my mom's operatic Mario Lanza records or Orrin's blues and rock music—the more I was driven to sing and write my own songs. There was never any question about whether I wanted to build a career around music, but, as many have discovered, making a living was another matter.

I began writing almost as soon as I discovered my singing voice. Based on the feedback I got, I became convinced that singing was my gift and the key to a music career. As it turned out, my songwriting was what really opened the door for me while also giving me insights into what it would take to have a long career doing what I loved. My success as a songwriter taught me that hit songs are the lifeblood of the industry, and that the life or death of an album is dependent upon having a primary song to launch it.

That lesson served me well when the success of my songs and my performances on their demos put me on a clear path to success as a singer—just not as the rock singer I'd always considered myself to be.

Chapter Ten

Feeding the Hunger

When the checks from my jingles and from my songwriting began to flow in a steady stream, we paid off bills, put some money in savings, and finally, for the first time in their lives, I took the girls to the Stamford Mall and let them go crazy buying whatever the hell their little hearts desired.

I guess the salesclerk in one clothing store hadn't seen many long-haired rocker dads because as she added up the damage from all the outfits and shoes piled on her counter, she said to my daughters, "I wish I had a cool big brother like you!"

It was so sweet and wonderful, that trip. For years, Isa had handed down her clothes to Holly, who handed them down to Taryn, who wore them until they didn't fit her anymore. We'd rarely gone to the mall because there just wasn't enough money to spare for shopping trips. But once my jingles were kicking back residuals and major artists were covering my songs, I wanted to make up for those hand-me-downs and discount-store clothes. I told them the only rule was that they had to buy things they would wear on a regular basis.

They were so excited. It was better than any Christmas they'd ever had, believe me. They were having the greatest time trying things on in the dressing room, laughing and screaming. I choked up a little just witnessing their joy. I thought, *This is how I've always wanted it to be.*

After that first trip there were many more, and even though I tried to establish some boundaries, I flunked in saying no to my girls. I had a lot of catching up to do.

Those were wonderful trips because I finally felt that all my striving was reaping rewards. The one area of my life that had not yet borne fruit was my singing career. My first album and single for Columbia faded fast after a promising launch. I feared that yet another record company would tell me, once again, that I was now free to "see other people."

My contract had an option for a second album. But it was not a guarantee.

Still, Columbia Records president Al Teller put his arm around my shoulder and essentially said, "We still believe in ya, kid."

Columbia allowed me to make that second album, another solo arena rocker titled *Everybody's Crazy*, which was released in 1985 with a music video for the title track. Hard rock radio stations gave the title single a decent run, and it was picked up for the sound track of the Rodney Dangerfield movie *Back to School* in 1986. Other than that, the second Columbia album was less successful than the first.

This is where Rod Serling, creator of the famed 1960s television series *The Twilight Zone*, appears in my dreams and says in grave tones:

Singer Michael Bolton landed his first record deal at the age of 15, his second at 18, his third at 21, his fourth at 25, his fifth at 26, and his sixth at 29.

Some of these recordings were never released. Some of the deals resulted in record releases but not major hits. Mr. Bolton recorded nine albums and two singles over eighteen years before his breakthrough to success came with his album The Hunger, which was certified double platinum in the United States.

Singing solo and with bands, the determined but luckless Mr. Bolton lost one recording deal after another. Then, after his fifth and sixth albums did not strike gold, the singer, who struggled for more than seventeen years while trying to make it as a rock 'n' roller, stepped into another dimension, a dimension not only of sight and sound, but of body, mind, and soul.

Yes, after many years of disappointment and heartbreak, rocker Michael Bolton journeyed into a wondrous land between the pit of man's fears and the summit of his knowledge.

He was finally leaving the Twilight Zone.

My Twilight Zone would soon end after nobody was crazy about Everybody's Crazy. By then I thought I knew the drill. I'd get a letter quoting poor sales numbers and they'd tell me to feel free to pursue other deals.

Al Teller, who had a Harvard MBA and two engineering degrees, was obviously a very smart man. He had moved up from president of Columbia to the head job at parent company CBS Records by this time. He called and graciously invited my manager, Louis Levin, and me to his office. I figured this would be the final reckoning. I reckoned wrong.

I had a hint of what was to come. On my way to his office, a memory flashed of something Al had said just prior to the release of Everybody's Crazy.

"Michael, there is a lot of buzz about this album, so it could do very well," he'd said. "But if it's not a hit, we'll have to meet and talk about the direction of your next record."

My NEXT record?

I'd heard some reports around the recording studio that Al liked my singing voice, but he was not so enthusiastic about my singing arena rock. I'd heard that before. Girls in my teen years often said they liked it better when I played the acoustic guitar and sang to them. Ribs and Marc were always trying to get me to do an acoustic set. "The ladies will love it," they'd say.

I saw myself as a rock singer, but it seemed Al Teller had something else in mind. As we drove to his office that day, I wondered whether he would be saying good-bye or whether he really did have some new direction in mind for my recording career.

I didn't have to wonder for long.

Al began the meeting by holding up a peculiar-looking device, which he explained was a CD player, and then he showed us a CD and explained that you could press a button on the player to go to different songs.

"This is the future of our business," he said. "Soon, fans won't be buying albums or cassettes. When the people making the CD players bring the price down, fans will only buy CDs."

Al was right about that, too.

I wasn't sure what that had to do with me in that moment, but I hoped it meant Al Teller thought I was part of Columbia's future, too.

"Michael, we're all aware here that your rock albums have not done well. You've had a couple songs do okay, but nothing has hit big," Al said. "On the other hand, Michael, we are very aware that your songwriting career has taken off. The Laura Branigan ballad, for starters, was beautiful, and that song will be around a long, long time. I don't have to tell you that.

"But what you may not know is this: I've been hearing from

a lot of people about the eight-track demos you make to get your songs recorded by other artists. People hear you singing with just a guitar or piano on those demos and they say, 'Who is this guy?' In fact, I'm told your demos are the hottest items in the building. Secretaries are trading them and buzzing about them. They aren't just excited about the songs, it's your voice. I know you like rock music and that type of production, but people love your voice, and it's been buried under a wall of sound. They can't hear you singing because of the layers of guitars and big drums pounding in your rock records. It's also clear that you should be singing the songs you are giving to other artists. You've got to stop giving away all of your hits!

"I'm about to tell you the best reason for keeping your songs to sing yourself. . . . The best reason is *the rest of your life*, Michael! You could have a long and great career singing those songs."

Al Teller was preaching to the choir at that point. (I can take a giant hint from the universe.) I was putting all my efforts as a singer into the rock albums and there were few rewards. At the same time, I found writing songs incredibly rewarding, and, in addition, when we completed a song I couldn't wait to record the demo myself. Simply writing the songs wasn't enough for me. Often songwriters will hire singers to do their demos. I loved doing my own. Singing the songs I'd just written had become so gratifying that I'd be chomping at the bit to step up to the microphone.

And so the timing of Al's meeting could not have been more perfect, and he could not have been more patient and generous. I'd done two albums for Columbia, then the world's biggest label, without creating a hit. In most scenarios, that second album would have been my last for Columbia, and maybe the last of my career. But Al had the vision and the courage to give me yet another opportunity. If it weren't for him, I might have missed the soul of it all concerning my career. I'd developed my voice to deliver the songs I was writing. I'd essentially trained myself to sing in a different style by doing the demos for my own songs. Because Al believed in me and because he had evidence from his office staff and could see their response to my demos, he concluded that I should move away from rock toward more of a pop and R & B style. I might never have tried that approach if he had not confronted me and pointed the way because he believed in me.

I don't have a tape recording of our meeting that day, so I can't give you Al's exact words, but that's the gist of what he said, to the best of my recollection. He was only saying what I'd been telling myself for a long time. I had fallen in love with the songwriting process, finding a title and creating a story around it. Often, I'd begin writing on a napkin in a restaurant and then join with a trusted friend and co-writer to expand on my original thoughts and stir each other's creativity. We always strive to move people with words and melodies that convey a specific emotion. The demos were the delivery device. Al's advice also reinforced what I'd been hearing from friends and others in the business about moving away from rock and embracing the R & B and pop music I had been giving away to other artists.

I'd been afraid to make the change from rock singing, even though it wasn't working. How many people make the same mistake? We all do it at times. We hang on to what is familiar and what we've always done in the past, even when it hasn't worked for us. I was very grateful to Al Teller for his honesty and even more grateful for his loyalty and support. He was giving me that rare gift, another chance. When I look at the music industry today, I am inclined to think that gift is even rarer now than it was back then. How many artists do you think would survive six failed record deals over nearly eighteen years?

Twilight Zone or not, I did step into another dimension of my career during that meeting. I'd become one of the hottest songwriters in the music industry, and the bulk of my songs that were picked up and turned into hits by other artists were not rock.

Teller was telling me the truth. Now I was ready to listen.

THE HUNGER ENDS

With support from the parent company's top guy, Columbia agreed to another album, called *The Hunger*, which would feature a different sound and feel. I'd done these more soulful songs before, but they were usually buried among harder rock songs and didn't get much attention. Now they were to be the focal point of this new album featuring my new sound.

That was the bull's-eye, and I honed in on it with more hunger than ever before. I went to work writing, performing, and producing songs for the album that we hoped would take me to a new level, by a route I'd never anticipated. Because of my success as a songwriter, I was able to call upon some of the best collaborators in the business, including Diane Warren, Jonathan Cain, Neal Schon of Journey, and Eric Kaz, who has written songs for Linda Ronstadt, Bonnie Raitt, and many others.

Jonathan Cain and I wrote the lyrics for *The Hunger*'s title song, and they definitely reflected my mood at the time: "As the hunger calls, then you run to the passion that takes you over. / No lookin' back. / The chance will never come again. / You risk it all, for your dream won't let you go."

Never before had I felt so intensely driven, so in the zone creatively, or so in control of my own album and my own destiny. I'd been given many, many chances—an incredible number when I reflected on them all. But I didn't see that there would ever be another opportunity to succeed as a singer if this album failed. The pressure was always on, but with this album it felt more like inspiration to me.

I was writing the songs, choosing my own collaborators, and singing in the studio with musicians of my choice. The top-notch producers were Jonathan Cain; Keith Diamond (who'd worked with Mick Jagger, Donna Summer, and Billy Ocean); and Susan Hamilton, the Jingle Queen who'd played a major role in my success in that field.

I was especially excited about the song I wrote with Eric Kaz because it was chosen to be the first single from the album. As Columbia released it, I could hardly contain my excitement. I was working day and night, often taking the last train to Milford out of Grand Central Terminal after working at the recording studio. I used the two-hour train commute to work more, prompting the conductor to finally ask, "Don't you ever stop working?" With my headphones on, I looked up, thought for a second, then smiled and nodded. "No."

I was in the final stages of working on the album one night in early 1987 when I walked into a commuter car for the train ride home and saw a familiar face; one that had inspired my very first original song, "Dreaming Dreams," and many that followed.

"Hello, Cory," I said to my boyhood muse.

"Why hello, Michael, what a great surprise," she said.

It came as no surprise that talking to Cory Morrison was just as easy for me at the age of thirty-three as it had been twenty years earlier. Her sweet spirit and her soulful blue eyes had always had that impact on me.

She'd been living in California, and though she'd heard about my marriage to Maureen, Cory was surprised to learn we had three daughters.

Cory, who had been through some hard times, was about to begin a marriage herself. She'd found a guy who she said was "very nice" and a straight arrow, unlike most of the old crowd we'd run with. We laughed about our "hippie" days in New Haven and

Greenwich Village. She hadn't realized that I'd written Laura Branigan's hit recording of "How Am I Supposed to Live Without You." I told her my songwriting successes had finally brought me into the highest levels of the music business and, suddenly, I had a world of opportunities.

After we'd talked through half of the commuting time, I finally got up the nerve to tell Cory I had something I wanted her to hear. I had the master recording of *The Hunger* on a cassette tape in my Walkman. I gave her my headphones and played "That's What Love Is All About" first, and watched as tears welled up in her eyes and streamed down her cheeks.

You can imagine what that did to me. It meant so much that she seemed proud of me and could see how far I'd come since I'd been her shadow all of those years. In that moment, I remembered how excited and light-headed I'd always felt in her presence, which may be what love truly is all about. There have been several women in my life who've had that effect on me. Cory was the first.

The Breakthrough

"That's What Love Is All About" was released as the first single from *The Hunger* and hit No. 3 on Billboard's Adult Contemporary chart and No. 19 on the Hot 100 in December 1987. Interestingly, that song had also made it to No. 62 on Billboard's R & B chart a couple of months earlier. There weren't a whole lot of white male singers on that particular chart, but apparently many fans who'd heard me sing only on the radio or their stereos thought I was black. Someone introduced me to Tina Turner around this time and the first words out of her mouth were "I thought you were a brother." I took that as a compliment.

That common misperception seemed to work in my favor initially with the release of the second single from *The Hunger*. That

Otis Redding R & B classic, written with singer, songwriter, and producer Steve Cropper, was the only cover song on the record, but it was one that was close to my heart. When I was a teenager adrift, playing for coins on the New Haven Green, on street corners in Greenwich Village, and in Berkeley Square, the one song always guaranteed to draw a crowd and bring in the cash was "(Sittin' On) The Dock of the Bay."

Later, when I played Yale frat parties, clubs, and bars with my first bands, our audience always responded with the most enthusiasm to that same song. My version of "Dock of the Bay" had been eliciting the same strong feedback from some of the greatest musicians in New York City when I'd go jam with them after hours at JP's and China Club after my songwriting and recording sessions.

I'd take the stage with their tremendous house players—all of them monster musicians who led the bands for Leno and Letterman or toured with Clapton—and somebody would say, "What key?" I'd reply, "D," and we'd be off and running.

Every time I performed that song, veteran musicians I respected would come up and encourage me to put it on a record someday. So when we were selecting songs for *The Hunger*, I told Jon Cain that we had to do just one cover, "Dock of the Bay," because the song and the response to my interpretation had meant so much over the years.

Like Stevie Wonder, Marvin Gaye, and Ray Charles, the pioneering Southern soul singer Otis Redding had been one of my inspirations and heroes. I especially love and relate to his lyric "I can't do what ten people tell me to do, so I guess I'll remain the same." Believe me, I knew better than to try to outsing any of the great soul singers. Their own definitive versions of their songs inspired me. Performing their songs is not about being like them or trying to be better than them; it's about being yourself, respecting them when you sing their songs, respecting the composition, and putting your own heart and soul into it.

All artists draw inspiration from the masters who came before them, whether they are painters, poets, authors, singers, or musicians. Feeling and acknowledging the presence of their contributions and what they've added to your own understanding of the art is essential for creative and artistic growth. I've actually always enjoyed this sense of obligation, the responsibility to bring something new to every song, including my covers of the R & B classics, just as the Beatles, the Rolling Stones, and other artists had done when recording those songs in their own voices.

My version of "Dock of the Bay" brought a slight rock edge to the classic, thanks to contributions from Neal Schon and Jon Cain, with Randy Jackson on bass. The team at Columbia Records loved it. Upon its release as *The Hunger*'s second single, the song took off. The amazing thing was that we were running strong in four formats. Our "Dock of the Bay" was getting airplay on rock stations, on adult contemporary stations, on Top 40 stations, and it started out strong on the R & B stations. We were seeing something that rarely happened: This song was a four-format hit. Rock and R & B stations rarely embraced the same music, though pop and adult contemporary often did.

Then, after the first three weeks or so, something odd happened. The record hit a wall of resistance from radio stations. Their program directors—those all-important gatekeepers who decide which songs get airplay—were suddenly saying they were reluctant to play a revered Otis Redding R & B song covered by a little-known white guy. Of course, I felt my version respected Otis, just as I did. To record his great song was an honor for me, and I'd hoped it would bring more attention to his body of music, so this was a disturbing development. Columbia Records agreed and looked for ways to get that message out to radio stations.

A promotions exec at Columbia said he'd heard that Otis Redding's widow, Zelma, had seen a performance of mine at the Apollo

Theater and she had loved my cover of her husband's song. We all knew that "Dock of the Bay" was special to the family because Otis died in a plane crash just three days after recording it. In fact, I've heard that Otis had whistled part of the song only because he intended on writing lyrics for that section when he returned from that trip.

Otis was only twenty-six years old when he died. He was one of the first black soul singers to have a huge following among white fans. Like many of his songs, "Dock of the Bay" was drawn from his experiences. He began writing it while staying on a friend's houseboat near Sausalito, California, where we shot the video for the song. As the song says, he'd left his home in Georgia, headed for the Frisco Bay, but unlike the song, he had plenty to live for. After his death, which occurred when his private airplane crashed into a Wisconsin lake, "Dock of the Bay" sold more than four million copies around the world and received more than eight million airplays. It also won two Grammy awards, for Best R & B Song and Best Male R & B Vocal Performance. Because of his tragic death, Otis Redding never enjoyed the praise and love his very personal song drew. But "Dock of the Bay" would become a major part of his enduring legacy.

I witnessed that firsthand many times, but one time stands out. During a White House event celebrating American music, I introduced President Bill Clinton to Otis's co-writer, Steve Cropper. The president responded with enthusiasm, giving an animated, heartfelt, and very in-depth description of seeing Otis's legendary performance at the 1967 Monterey Pop Festival. Steve was touched by the president's words, as was I.

We were thrilled that Otis Redding's widow had approved of my recording, and we were hoping she would spread the word. She said that my rendition was her "all-time favorite" of the song and that my performance at *Showtime at the Apollo* was "so emotional" that it brought tears to her eyes and reminded her of her husband. She said her husband would "feel the same."

Columbia took her words and ran with them. They used them in huge ads placed in the biggest music industry trade magazines that were read by radio station programmers across the country. Thanks to Zelma Redding's endorsement, walls came tumbling down at radio stations nationwide. The play the song received on the R & B stations helped open the doors for me to later perform at the Apollo, as well as the *Essence* Awards and BET Awards.

We saw the impact right away. In January 1988, my "Dock of the Bay" single entered the Billboard Hot 100, charting for 17 weeks and peaking at No. 11. It reached No. 19 on the Adult Contemporary chart and No. 58 on the R & B chart. I was grateful to be sharing the charts with hits by artists such as Michael Jackson, Whitney Houston, George Michael, and, ironically, Cher, whose comeback song, "I Found Someone," I had penned.

The Hunger's first single, "That's What Love Is All About," put my third attempt with Columbia Records in great position, and "Dock of the Bay" brought home the winner. The song was playing as often as eight times a day on rock, Top 40, adult contemporary, and R & B radio stations, which drove album sales. The combined strength of the two hit singles put me on the map as an artist. The album was eventually certified double platinum.

I am eternally grateful for the endorsement provided by Zelma Redding, because the song would never have received the airplay it deserved without her kind words and public expression of support. Mrs. Redding also provided one of the most rewarding moments of my life at the BMI Film & TV Awards show in 1988 at the Beverly Hilton Hotel in Los Angeles. Mrs. Redding was invited to receive an award for her husband's most enduring hit, which had been the year's most played song because of my cover. Backstage that night, a friend tugged on my arm and pointed to her. I walked over to introduce myself, but before I could say my last name she threw her arms around me, hugged me tightly, and said, "I know who you are."

She was crying. I had not expected her emotional greeting, nor had I anticipated how deeply it would connect me with her husband's song.

That moment is one of the most cherished of my career, so gratifying and so significant, too. Not only did I have the great pleasure of paying homage to Otis Redding through his song, but I was also privileged to experience even a small portion of the soulfulness, creative energy, and passion Otis put into his music.

STAR-MAKING MACHINERY

It was 1987 and I wasn't a real worldly guy at this stage in my career. So when executives from Sony invited me to come to Norway to promote *The Hunger*, I didn't initially see the value in it. I wasn't even at all sure where Norway was on the map. They seemed convinced that there was a market for my music in places like Lillehammer, Kongsvinger, and Steinkjer, but Oslo was my primary destination.

Louis Levin agreed with them. He thought most artists were missing out by not marketing themselves overseas. I needed convincing, especially since they were talking about an eight-and-a-half-hour flight to do seventeen to twenty interviews each day for two days with reporters who spoke in Norse code. I finally caved, stocked up on long underwear, and flew to Oslo.

Something very interesting happened on that trip. For the first time, I found myself enjoying the marketing side of the music business. The Sony people in Norway made me feel like an important part of the team, and the results were impressive. I realized that a little effort could produce big results in a small country. *The Hunger* became a huge hit in Norway.

The next thing I knew, the invitations came rolling in from Sony Sweden and their neighbors in Denmark, Germany, France, Ireland, England, Spain, and Portugal. I'd never owned a passport, and I'd certainly never even dreamed of performing for audiences around the world. Yet when I began studying the international sales reports sent by my record company, I saw that selling 100,000 CDs in Korea, 40,000 in Thailand, 50,000 in Jakarta, and even more in Australia and Canada gave me an audience around the world, which has been very gratifying as I return with new album releases and to perform in concerts year after year. As I write this, I'm preparing for shows in Italy, China, Japan, South Korea, Indonesia, Malaysia, and Chile.

Thanks to a change in direction creatively, I found my sweet spot in the mainstream, writing and recording songs I loved— without feeling any more obligation to look and sound like a hard rocker. That sweet spot grew even sweeter with my next album. I moved up from selling 500,000 copies and releasing two singles with *The Hunger* to the even greater success of *Soul Provider*, which released five singles and sold more than 12.5 million copies worldwide.

BITTERSWEET

I felt in control of my destiny as a songwriter and performer for the first time after the success of *The Hunger*. It was sweet, and bittersweet, too. My career was soaring, but I seemed to have fewer and fewer people to share my successes with. I'd lost one of my greatest cheerleaders and champions, my father, who had died seven years earlier.

My career success and all the opportunities that were coming my way pulled me farther and farther from my girls. I couldn't be there for them while writing, recording, touring, performing, and promoting during every waking hour. I told a *People* magazine reporter around this time that success sometimes felt like a video game in which the more levels you advance the greater the challenges and obstacles become.

Touring demands periods of separation that are often simply too much for relationships to endure. Many musician friends who don't tour still work such long hours in the studio that their relationships and marriages suffer. Those of us who work like that sometimes feel that maintaining a relationship is like putting a dollar down on a million-dollar debt.

Missing my daughters' birthdays and other important moments in their lives always left me horribly conflicted and anguished. I always aspired to be a good and present father to our girls. Sometimes I made it to the birthday parties by scrambling from a concert to catch a plane and then I'd have to catch the last flight out to make the next concert date. Often in those situations, I'd feel drained emotionally, fearing that I wasn't fully present.

Yet when I wasn't touring or focused in the studio, I loved spending time with them. Riding the train home from New York City, I couldn't wait to hug them and catch up on their days. I loved to read to them when they were little. All three of them shared a bedroom, and we'd sit on the floor with Taryn on my lap and Isa and Holly on either side in their little girl "footie" pajamas. I tried to find books they couldn't resist, with beautiful illustrations and great stories. I'd read to them in character, doing voices and sound effects. I loved it when they'd reach up with their little hands to peek at the next page while I was reading because they couldn't wait to see what was coming. Those were precious times. They'd also call all of their friends together while playing in the yard and have me tell them scary stories and chase them. Taryn reminded me recently of our "octopus" game, in which I would sit in one spot on the floor and they'd run around me while I reached out to pull them to me while they were screaming and laughing. They loved that simple game, maybe as much as I did. I was surprised that, twenty-five years later, Taryn remembered it being so much fun.

Still, there were times when I couldn't be there for them. I would try to explain and convey my sadness and let my girls know I loved them more than anything. One night I walked into Taryn's bedroom when she was sleeping. There was a cassette player on her nightstand and one of my demo tapes was in it. I was touched that listening to my music soothed her and that she enjoyed it. Maybe it was her way, too, of keeping me close.

You just can't make it up to a six-year-old, an eight-year-old, or a ten-year-old who wants nothing more than to be Daddy's girl. On one of these occasions, I received a little note from one of my daughters, and before I opened the envelope I thought how sweet it was of her to send it. Then I read it and felt like a stake had been driven through my heart. It was a sweet note, but she had written a heart-wrenching plea for my presence in her life. She asked me to come home, please, "whenever you can" because "I can't really explain it but I love having my daddy home."

I cried for an hour after reading her note because I knew how pure and simple the expression was. It wasn't the first or the last time I broke down. Shortly after the divorce, I had just dropped the girls off after my weekend with them when the reality of being a "visiting" parent sank in. I was driving and I had to pull the car over to the side of the road because my whole body was convulsing with grief. I wasn't crying so much as wailing in that deep guttural, primal moan you rarely hear except when a tragic death has occurred. No matter how hard men may work to deny or hide their vulnerabilities, there is no controlling that kind of overwhelming grief. You may try, but your body can't contain that volume of sorrow and loneliness. Not long after that emotional breakdown I wrote a song called "I'm Not Made of Steel." I'd been visiting with the girls and they weren't getting along and again the weight of losing them and seeing them act out because of their own grief and confusion just hit me. I told them that I wasn't made of steel, that I was hurting, too, and I just wanted them to stop fighting and have some peace with me. I was making a statement of vulnerability to them, and they responded as well as they could.

I never had as much time with them as I wished for because of so many contractual obligations to deliver songs, perform in concerts, produce records, and do publicity. I had done my share of tours over the years, but when my singing career took off, I discovered that there were no longer any borders. My world expanded exponentially. I'd look at my travel itineraries and all the stops and wish that human cloning were possible. I still feel that way.

Once an album was released, the concert tour was unleashed, which meant the publicity machine had to be fired up. I'd find myself hopscotching across Europe—Norway, Sweden, Denmark, England, Germany, France, Spain, Portugal—to do performances followed by morning television shows and interviews with local media, and then we'd hit the road to perform at the next stop on the tour.

After a long, long time of not being able to even buy my daughters new sneakers, there were some perks to being successful, especially when they could travel with me and I was able to share some very special moments with them. When Isa became a fan of boxing, I flew her out for a championship match to see her favorite fighter, Oscar De La Hoya. Once he'd won the match, we went backstage to meet him and he was very gracious. She cried as we were leaving. For me, mission more than accomplished. About a week later, an autographed pair of boxing gloves arrived at our house.

My middle daughter, Holly, was born on 7/7/77, so I'd promised her that when she turned twenty-one, we would have to put that lucky date to work. I flew her into Vegas and played blackjack at a private table at the Mirage. Her very first hand was a twenty-one. (For the longest time she was convinced that I had had the casino deal that hand as a favor. There are more than a few restrictions that I'm certain would have prevented that, no matter how much they might have liked me at the Mirage.) Holly quickly found herself up $2,100. Then she looked at me and said she'd like to quit. I was shocked but pleased and proud of her. We left the table high-fiving the occasion, enjoying our hang time. Holly's twenty-first birthday was quite a successful one and is still a great memory.

When Taryn was about ten, we took our own special trip to Disney World in Orlando. The VIP treatment by Disney allowed us to go through the back entrances of all the rides, not so much to avoid lines as to have a little privacy, away from the crowds. We pretty much did everything you could humanly do in a fourteen-hour day at Disney World, including riding Space Mountain twice. Taryn was always so sweetly appreciative of these kinds of opportunities. At the time, she probably didn't realize how much that father-daughter time meant to me, but now that she is a mother herself, I'm sure she understands.

SWINGING FOR THE FENCES

Aside from standing onstage and performing, the most fun I had in those many years of touring behind big-selling albums was playing in charity softball games with my semipro team, Bolton's Bombers. My softball team was originally called Bolton's Bad Boys.

We weren't that "bad," but we discovered that we were a couple of leagues over our heads.

When we first fielded a team in 1990, we thought it would be fun to have pickup softball games for local charities while playing against the radio-station teams along each stop. Our team consisted mostly of members of the band and road crew, but we quickly realized that the radio stations were flying in serious ringers who were professional or semiprofessional softball players. Our first hint should have been that there aren't many deejays or radio program directors with eighteen-inch biceps. When these hired guns stepped up to the plate, they blocked out the entire backstop. They were hitting 400-foot home runs and line drives that were like missiles. The infield was a dangerous place to be, as my manager, Louis Levin, discovered. He was hit with a line drive that damn near killed him.

I don't like losing, even if it's for charity, but injuries were the main reason I had to bench most of the band members. They kept jamming thumbs and spraining fingers on the ball field. You may have never heard a performance by a guitarist or keyboardist with damaged digits, and there is a reason for that. They can't play their instruments without healthy hands, and if they try, the result is music that sounds like a sore finger feels. There were other dangers on the diamond. We often played on rocky fields that weren't exactly up to professional standards, so there were a lot of bad hops on hot grounders that had the potential to behead our players.

I needed a band with a complete set of body parts. So I began beefing up the team with nonmusician, nonroadie recruits. We became Bolton's Bombers in our second season because we weren't bad anymore. The benefit of having our own string of ringers wasn't just more wins for our team. When we became more competitive, we began drawing serious softball fans and bigger crowds, which also benefited the children's charities, food banks, and other organizations we gave to. As word got around that Bolton's

Bombers had game, we were able to schedule bigger games against other celebrity teams, including one formed by the Green Bay Packers and another led by Michael Jordan, which was a memorable matchup.

We played Michael's team in July 1993 at Comiskey Park in Chicago. As you can imagine, he rounded up a few decent athletes for his Air Force Squad, including an NBA legend, a former Pro Bowl NFL star, a four-time World Heavyweight champion, an NHL All-Star, and some athletic actor types. On the field for MJ's team were Earvin "Magic" Johnson, Mark Harmon, Evander Holyfield, Ahmad Rashad, Tom Selleck, Chris Chelios, and a couple of Baldwin brothers (William and Daniel).

They had a great team, but my Bolton's Bombers managed to beat them, 7–1. I'd recruited softball players from Nashville, Alabama, and Milwaukee, my own pro and semipro ringers, to compete with those brought in by our competition. I'm not going to rub it in. I've found it wise to never taunt four-time World Heavyweight champions or their tree-size teammates. Playing against Jordan's team was a thrill. Michael had flown in one of the most famous softball players in the history of the game, a fierce slugger, but for that game we played at a baseball park without a 300-foot fence, so we just played him very deep.

Nicollette Sheridan, whom I was seeing then, was there for that game. She's extremely athletic and a competitor, and she always wanted to grab a glove and play the infield, but I had to keep her on the bench. Most of the players were capable of ripping the ball so hard that it could take your head off if you couldn't get a glove on it. Years later, I thought of that and reminded Nicollette that she would not have looked good as a headless Desperate Housewife.

In another incredible, unforgettable softball game, we played against Barry Bonds's All-Stars. His team consisted of people like Frank "The Big Hurt" Thomas, Ken Griffey Jr., Bobby Bonilla,

Matt Williams, and Ozzie Smith, some of the greatest ballplayers in the history of the game. It was an insane experience to be on the same field with them. I often wished my father, who loved all sports, could have been with me in the dugout. But I did have a new friend of mine in the dugout, and that was Joe DiMaggio. I was playing in the Legends Game to benefit the Joe DiMaggio Children's Hospital in Florida. Just an hour before showtime, there was a knock on my dressing room door. The gentleman in the doorway, Morris Engelberg, said, "Mr. DiMaggio would like to know if Mr. Bolton would like to have coffee with him in his trailer."

Imagine that. I was out the door so fast I don't think Joe's emissary had time to finish his invitation. The next thing I knew, I was sitting face-to-face with the famed "Yankee Clipper," Baseball Hall of Famer, and world-class guy. I loved his opening line, too.

"I understand you can hit a ball pretty well, Michael."

We had an amazing conversation in which DiMaggio talked about playing stickball as a boy. Since he was pretty good at hitting with the stick, he figured swinging a baseball bat might not be too big a chore, he told me.

When I wrote a song with Bob Dylan, I couldn't stop thinking that this guy playing the guitar in front of me was "The" Bob Dylan. The whole time I was talking to "The" Joe DiMaggio that day, I couldn't stop thinking that I wished my dad were there with me. That was a big one, Dad. Joe and I actually became friends on that day. In the years that followed, he came to several of my concerts and softball games.

When I met him at the gate as he arrived at one game, several thousand people stood up and applauded and Joe said, "Wow, they really like you here, Mike." I said, "I've been here all day, Joe. This is for you." And he knew. Sometime later, when he came to one of my concerts at an amphitheater in the Bay Area, I introduced him to the audience and he received a standing ovation that went on so long we couldn't start the show. He was a private guy, but he shared stories with me that I've never seen written elsewhere.

I attended his funeral in 1999, and a family member pulled me aside afterward and said, "Joe talked about you a lot. He didn't spend time with many people, but he appreciated his time with you."

I felt the same about him.

BACHELOR FATHER

After my divorce in 1991, my three girls came to live with me. They were ages twelve, fourteen, and sixteen and, since I was often on the road, I needed help with adult supervision. I tried a couple of nannies before finding women who were up for the challenge and compatible with our group. Our saving grace was Laura McKinley, who adored the girls and was with us until they were too old to have a nanny. Even then she stayed on as our property manager. It was important for me to know that the girls were safe, but I know they managed to have fun, too. Strangers often approach me all over the world to say that they loved hanging out with my daughters "at those massive high school parties at the big house on the lake." Not a very comforting visual for me. Over the years more than a few have confessed to raiding my wine cellar, too. "Awesome wine collection, sir!"

When the girls moved in, I built a recording studio on the property so I could do much of my work at home. The home studio proved to be a great move for all of us. For the first time in years, I experienced the joys of being close enough to my daughters to share meals and visit with them during my workday. By building the studio next to the house, I was able to have dinner with my girls at 6:30 every night. Many people take that for granted, but I never did. I knew I could never buy back the time I missed with my girls. We had wonderful times when I took them on my tours around the country and overseas, either by private jet or on the bus. Of course, I quickly learned that attending my concerts wasn't nearly as interesting for them as raiding the hotel minibars and ordering in-room movies.

Another great thing about the home studio was that record producers, including Mutt Lange, David Foster, and Walter Afanasieff, were willing to work there on my projects. They even joined my family for meals. At one or two of those gatherings, my male guests and I even managed to slip a word or two into the conversation. Mutt Lange joined us for dinner one night. I could see him absorbing the home environment, in which the three girls were chattering away with the nanny and the cook, making me outnumbered by women five to one. I poked around, asking questions, refereeing, and making dumb dad jokes that provoked eye rolls and looks of mock disgust (or maybe real disgust; I could never tell the difference).

When we returned to the studio to continue working after dinner, Mutt said, "Do you realize, Michael, that you are entirely surrounded by women night and day? Maybe that's why your songs and your voice resonate with the female audience so well. You are dialed into their frequency." It's true. There've been many times when I've come home from a long road trip, opened the door to my home, and smiled at the swarm of women working behind the scenes to support me and keep my crazy life running as smoothly as possible. For more than twenty years, Ronnie Milo has been the dedicated head of "mission control" for my business, operating as office manager, personal assistant, document and mail wrangler, personal and business scheduler, problem solver, mother hen, and keeper of secrets twenty-four hours a day, seven days a week.

For about ten years, she worked with Kim Downs, who always helped hold down the fort at home. I met Kim courtesy of Joyce Logan, a dear friend who created my first fan club and organized others across the country. Joyce was a true believer in me even before my songs and records hit it big. Joyce told me that I should hire Kim to work for me, saying, "You know how every person claims to be your number one fan? Well, Kim truly is your number one fan." Joyce added that Kim was also highly capable and would be a real asset to my office staff. She was right on all counts. Kim became known as "the Gatekeeper" for her determined efforts to not allow anyone without authorization onto my property and to keep me free of distractions so I could focus on being an artist. Kim became VP of Bolton Music.

Without Ronnie, Kim, and other members of my support team back home, I could easily end up lost somewhere between Singapore and Sheboygan and never be heard from again. I probably couldn't blame Ronnie if she did let me get lost, considering all the teasing and pranks I've subjected her to over the years.

She's incredibly dedicated and efficient, yet she's also a very vibrant, bubbly, and fun-loving person, which is a good thing for me. Ronnie has a great sense of humor and knows how to be a joker while developing and maintaining close relationships with people important to my business, as well as with my family and daughters. Ronnie often joins me on my insane travels across the universe. Because I can never sleep on airplanes—my curse—Ronnie usually doesn't, either. She'll go through things with me or just keep me company on most trips. Then once, on a long flight during an Asian concert tour with staff members from my record label, Ronnie did fall asleep. In fact, since this was a jet chartered by the record company, she chose to stretch out on the floor behind my seat, stealing a few winks after making sure my life was in order and my baggage was on board.

When the plane began its descent to land, I noticed her eyes flick open in recognition of the change in speed and I leaned back, waved my arms, and yelled, "Ronnie! I think we're going down!"

Everybody else laughed, but Ronnie, who was still in a bit of a sleep fog, instinctively grabbed her cell phone and began hitting numbers.

"Ronnie, who are you calling?" I asked.

"Tommy Mottola," she replied.

Apparently Ronnie's first waking thought when faced with a potential disaster was that the then head of Sony Music Entertainment, Tommy Mottola, could solve any problems we faced.

I was not surprised. Ronnie's first response to any crisis is "How can I fix this?" She is a very caring person, and when I told her I was writing about her in the book she asked that I encourage all women readers to keep up with their mammography appointments. She nearly skipped one a couple years ago because she'd just had one six months earlier and we were busy. I encouraged her to keep the appointment and, as her doctor recently noted, it saved her life. "You are the poster child for early detection," he told her.

I am very, very happy she is here for us all. So please heed Ronnie's advice.

This great lady is actually half of my highly valued superhero power couple. Her husband, Steve Milo, whom she met while working for me, has been my studio and concert technician, as well as my recording engineer and tour manager, for two decades. (Funny how they still think we didn't know they were hooking up until they made it official.) I can't leave home, go home, or be home without either of them. Steve has the complex job of handling all of the music that flows into, around, and out of my studio, whether Mutt Lange is sending fifty harmony parts that are being bounced down from analog to digital or David Foster's studio has an orchestra recording for me to work with in the home studio. Steve, forever known only as "Milo," also puts together the prerecorded music tracks I perform to when I do smaller venues like charity events or private concerts without a band or an orchestra.

I really can't perform anywhere without Milo doing his magic behind the curtain. Besides probably being the most beloved employee and member of my organization, Milo is also the first one at the studio and the last to leave. On tour he is one of the first in the building and one of the last out, too, and some wonder how he maintains his positive disposition through it all.

My support team also includes my daughters, who step in from time to time to help out in the office, back up Ronnie, and come out on the road. Christina Kline, my manager, is based in L.A., but somehow manages to work tirelessly across all time zones to support, inspire, and help drive my career. It is of great comfort to me to know I can focus on performing and recording while she is always on the watch to create opportunities and smooth the way for the next leg of my journey.

I made a decision after working with Louis Levin for twenty-five years—as well as a few others before and after him—that I wanted to manage my own career because after more than thirty-six years of experience in this industry recording, producing, promoting, and touring, nearly all decisions were coming back to me anyway; but then Christina Kline offered to represent me in 2010. She was in the thick of the music business, working with some of the most successful songwriters and producers, and she is a writer and quite a poet, too, which gave her an appreciation for every aspect of my work as well as an insight into the mentality of a creatively driven workaholic such as myself. She has been invaluable, keeping projects moving forward and networking with people around the world at all hours.

Too Sexy for Myself

Over the years, the members of my family and support team have often been amused and sometimes appalled at one of the aspects of my "public" life as a performer. My daughters were especially freaked out when they first realized that their scrambling single parent was viewed in an entirely different way by female fans.

This hit home for my girls when I was somehow named one of the 25 Most Eligible Bachelors of 1988 by (ahem) *Playgirl* magazine. (*People* magazine has named me one of its "sexiest" men on a couple of later occasions, but I'm sure it was only because they'd never met my brother, Orrin.) I was grateful, but uncomfortable with that designation, although an Italian journalist did ask me once if it was true that I had found a way to bring women to orgasm with my singing during concerts. Apparently there was a rumor in Italy about that. I did absolutely nothing to squash it. And Oprah once told me that she'd seen a marketing study that said female shoppers tended to buy more when my songs were played in stores. I'm always glad to do my part in boosting the American economy.

My daughters thought the whole idea of me as a sex symbol was either disgusting or hilarious. To them, I'm just a dad—and now a grandfather, too—and I'm very content with that role. My daughters are adults now. Taryn has made me a grandfather with two incredibly beautiful girls, Amelia and Olivia (called Gwenny), who are a constant source of joy, which starts with one look at their gorgeous faces. They are delicious in every way. (Amelia calls me G'Pa and I love it—sounds young, doesn't it?) Watching my granddaughters reminds me of my own daughters, and I look forward to every next step and stage of their childhoods. Since I am the poster child for dream chasers, I've always encouraged my daughters to pursue their passions, and they have certainly done that. I am very, very proud of them for all kinds of reasons, and I love them unconditionally.

Even though they've created their own lives, I worry about them, which is a parental privilege. I long fretted that I couldn't give them enough. Then I worried that I was giving them too much.

So far, they seem to have survived my angst and my parenting, and best of all they seem to love me despite my faults. For that, I'm more grateful than they will ever know.

Chapter Eleven

The Soul of It All

Columbia Records was eager for me to build upon the momentum from *The Hunger* by producing another big album. Leading the charge was the dynamic new president of my record company. At thirty-six, Donnie Ienner, a disciple of Clive Davis, was the youngest president in Columbia's 150-year history. Donnie, who had worked his way up from a high school job in the Capitol Records mailroom, had helped develop the careers of Whitney Houston, Kenny G, and Aretha Franklin in his previous job at Arista Records.

I certainly liked the way he described his vision for developing my career shortly after he settled in at Columbia. His focus was to help me become known as "a singer's singer," someone who could make music that crossed all genres, thus reaching a wide audience and building a long career. That sounded great to me. With his support, I tapped my songwriting connections to bring in the biggest talents in the business for this important follow-up album. Diane Warren, Doug James, Andrew Goldmark, Desmond Child,

Eric Kaz, Barry Mann, and Cynthia Weil signed on. Our team of handpicked musicians, backup singers, and producers (Barry Mann; Peter Bunetta and Rick Chudacoff—known as "Pete and Cheese"; and Guy Roche and Michael Omartian) was also chosen from the A-list.

Record producers don't receive much recognition outside the industry, but I quickly learned to respect their multitude of talents as well as their power to take great songs to the next level. I've worked with some of the best producers in the business, who have amazing track records for turning out singles and albums that sell millions and millions of copies. Theirs is not an easy calling. They and their engineers are always the first ones in and the last ones out of the studio. But the rewards can be tremendous.

A recording studio is a creative hothouse, and the environment can be volatile.

In a studio, you have several explosive elements mixed into a limited, often cramped space: talented, driven, and often insecure performers; musicians; songwriters; and studio techs who have the power to summon sounds not found in nature. These high achievers have high standards and strong opinions. When you pack so many of them into a small space for long hours, the atmosphere can go from warm and fuzzy to torridly hot and prickly. Because most studios we choose (when we can't record in our homes) are heavily booked at a high price per hour, time is of the essence, but the quality of the product is the priority. We work through the night and into the morning, and often we are reworking a song or portions of it over and over and over again until everyone feels his or her work is the best it can possibly be.

Sometimes feelings get stomped on and egos are bruised, but everyone knows it comes with gold and platinum rewards. Most of the time, all participants are collaborative and respectful because everyone wants to work with the best. When I step into the studio,

I am psyched to a level I rarely feel anywhere else except onstage. This is one of the places where I can expose myself emotionally, psychologically, and personally. I approach a vocal performance by stripping away all of the walls that guard my heart and emotions— and I feel more vulnerable in the vocal booth than anywhere else because I'm singing to deliver the soul of the song, whether it's my creation or that of another songwriter. I put all macho pride aside and let go to the flow of the lyrics and the music.

The feeling of being totally engaged with all of the elements of a song can produce a high like nothing else I've ever known. Still, there are always those moments when I'm in the flow and suddenly I'll hear a producer cutting into my bliss with a chain saw.

"Michael, buddy, that's not working. I think you should go back to the other melody."

I can take constructive criticism. Most of the time. Even when I'm not working with great people like this. I'm reminded of the importance of collaboration and one of Deepak Chopra's favorite words, *adaptability*, which spills over into other areas of our lives.

The best record producers, the ones with whom I've spent the most time and had my biggest records—including Walter Afanasieff, David Foster, and Mutt Lange—are like great film directors. They work not just on the recording of the song but on creating an environment that will inspire the best performance by all participants. Singers and bands seek out record producers who make them want to step up to the microphone and capture the full power of the song as it was meant to be sung, whether it is a quiet ballad or a defiant rock song. Walter, David, and Mutt have produced Grammy-winning songs and albums by the truckload, yet each has his own unique approach and philosophy. All three are sought out by singers because they understand what Frank Sinatra meant when he said, "People don't buy records for the clarinet player, kid."

I only wish it hadn't taken me so long to work with them. The monetary rewards of success were a great relief, but there is no greater benefit to success than the ability to collaborate with and get to know such creative and gifted people. They are all songwriters as well as record producers, which helps them understand that a song with a strong composition captured in a compelling recording can outlive its creator.

Mutt and David are command and control guys. They are intense and demanding, but respectful. David, with whom I've also done some touring and television specials, reads his singers, picking up on their moods, their health, and their readiness. He has a gift for working one on one with singers, and he always can tell whether I'm in the zone or not, and whether he'll get the performance he wants.

"Michael, man, you've got to stay away from that G note because it's not happening." Or another of his classic lines: "Michael, I've been where you are trying to go."

Like the director Clint Eastwood, who is known for allowing his actors great freedom, David—who has at least sixteen Grammys and has produced huge records for stars such as Mariah Carey, Whitney Houston, Celine Dion, Andrea Bocelli, Barbra Streisand, Michael Bublé, Madonna, and Josh Groban—also respects my decision when I tell him the magic just isn't there some days due to dry air or a cold, even though he may want to kick my ass for shutting down the vocal cords and going home. David knows how to create an environment of mutual respect and collaboration, but he is strong in his convictions about what a song needs and doesn't need. I've seen the same attributes in one of his protégés, David Reitzas, who is one of my favorite engineers, mixers, and friends.

David Foster enjoys a good joke and friendly teasing, which is a good thing. He and Mutt Lange have this friendly rivalry driven by enormous mutual respect, calling each other "Foz-Man" and "Mutt-Man." They each can claim impressive bragging rights.

Mutt co-wrote and produced the huge Grammy-winning Bryan Adams song "(Everything I Do) I Do It for You" from *Robin Hood* and David produced Whitney Houston's blockbuster Grammy-winning hit "I Will Always Love You" from *The Bodyguard*. These were two of the biggest records in the history of the music business and they generated a fortune in sales, impacting the careers of everyone involved in many wonderful ways.

Mutt, who grew up in South Africa, is a mystic among producers—a serene, sage-like Obi-Wan Kenobi. You must take your shoes off upon entering his home south of London, and he's always kept me on my toes. I'd be lucky to get in five hours of sleep before Mutt would come knockin' on the bedroom door. "Michael! Time marches on!"

He'd let me get showered and dressed, and he'd even have hot coffee and scones waiting at the breakfast table. But while I was having my wake-up meal, Mutt would strap on his guitar and play a bridge he'd been working on—in his sleep, I presume. Many performers say Mutt works them hard, but they are glad for the opportunity because he produces one great record after another. His artists have included Foreigner, the Cars, Bryan Adams, Maroon 5, AC/DC, Def Leppard, Nickelback, and most recently Lady Gaga and Carrie Underwood. He is strong, too, but in his own way. Instead of saying, "No, Michael, I don't want you to go in that direction with the song," he will say, "I see where you are trying to go and I'm thinking we should try this." And then Mutt will sing it and suggest we try a few takes both ways.

I will sing the song twenty or even fifty times for him, even if what he wants doesn't make sense to me at the time, because of what Mutt can do with a recording. I don't say that about many producers because I'm very demanding myself. I know my range and the power and intensity a song needs. But I trust that Mutt has a plan, and he has an incredible ability to transform a song.

He will say, "Okay, go away for a while and let me do my thing, Michael." And when I come back and listen to what he has done, I've often said, "I don't remember singing it that well." Mutt will reply, "I knew you had it in you."

Mutt and I co-wrote one of my favorite songs, "Said I Loved You... But I Lied," which has both romantic and spiritual elements that give it an exotic quality and spirit. The song does have special meaning for me. When I perform it, I have to quiet myself and sing it from a certain place to do it justice.

I've also written many songs, including "Soul of My Soul"—which is a father singing to his children—with the brilliant composer and producer Walter Afanasieff. He is the genius who helped me bring in a fifty-piece orchestra for my recording of "Go the Distance" for the Disney movie *Hercules*, which is one of my favorite records. The renowned record "mix maestro" Mick Guzauski, one of the greatest mixers in the world, agrees. He said, "It might be the best song I've ever mixed." The recording was nominated for both an Academy Award and a Golden Globe award and it hit No. 1 on Billboard's Adult Contemporary chart.

While David Foster likes to use a live band or orchestra in the studio so he can have all the basic tracks done in two or three days, Walter will build the tracks in the studio for a month. Mutt combines their methods. He loves the organic sound of guitars in the studio, but he can spend a tremendous amount of time on just one song or one part of a song until he thinks it's just right. Of course Mutt's idea of "just right" can elude even the most finely trained ears. He is a visionary. When Mutt is finally happy it's very likely you will be as well. It's rare to find someone who cares as much about getting it right as Mutt does.

I know I've probably frustrated Mutt, Walter, and David from time to time because I always want to have everything perfect (and so do they), but I never take for granted the fact that I get to work with producers of their caliber. I'm always excited to go into the studio and see what they can help me do. Collaboration is all about working with someone whose talents elevate your own work. With them, I know that is guaranteed. They mine for gold. They know my range and what keys to cut tracks in and what the power will be at the top notes and in the meat of the song. David likes to start me low and take me higher. Mutt is all about the nuances more than the power. He enjoys finding things others aren't aware of in a song. Walter? He just wants it all! Walter suggested that I keep my vocals restrained on the recording of "When a Man Loves a Woman," but I still sang it in a key that could cause groin damage—a key that David insisted I revisit years later during a duet with Seal. For this 2011 PBS special, David created a brilliant arrangement in which I performed "When a Man Loves a Woman" and Seal sang "It's a Man's World" and we merged our songs in the end. David said if I sang in that key the performance would sound more "urgent." He was right. We brought the house down. Later in the show I sang David's absolute masterpiece, "The Prayer," in a far more comfortable key, though I was singing in Italian.

In 2012, I had the pleasure of working on my newest album with another uniquely talented producer, Paul Mirkovich. I first worked with him during the 2011 Emmy Awards show. Paul produced my live segment of the Jack Sparrow medley with the Lonely Island trio. I was impressed with Paul's skill during rehearsals and then, during a break, he sat down at the piano and played a beautiful gospel song. I sang with him a little, and his singing and piano playing were just incredible. After that session, I sent my manager, Christina Kline, a text saying, "I want to work with Paul on a record someday down the road."

Paul and I share many experiences in the music business, including having worked with Cher. He was her bandleader and keyboardist for more than fifteen years. He also sang duets with her and married one of her dancers. More recently, Paul has served as musical director for *The Voice* on NBC. The demands of that show are insane. His job is to cut forty-five tracks in four days for each show, so the pressure is intense. We worked on the new album in L.A., and I was struck by Paul's complete grasp of every single note on each track, and his ability to stay true to the Motown sound originally created in the Hitsville USA studio.

THE GOLD MARK AND BEYOND

Soul Provider was a unique album on many levels. I'd been working with the best in the business and felt confident enough to take a greater role, as a co-producer. Of course, I had some help from Walter and other veteran producers, including Susan Hamilton, whose talents as a brilliant record producer match her long-term mastery in the jingle business.

I co-wrote the title song, "Soul Provider," with Andy Goldmark, whom I'd met through Deirdre O'Hara of CBS Songs. Andy had written songs for many singers, including Carly Simon, the Pointer Sisters, Whitney Houston, and Bette Midler. He suggested the name for the title song, which became the title of the album, too. I admit to hesitating at first, because I didn't want my female fans thinking I was singing about being a "sole provider" by taking them out of the workforce if they wanted careers.

Andy had a different concept in mind. He thought the lyrics would be more about providing a woman with love and emotional support any hour of the day over a lifetime. I was all for that interpretation. I respect Andy as a smart, soulful, and accomplished writer. We also co-wrote "By the Time This Night Is Over" for Kenny G and Peabo Bryson, which appeared on Kenny's album *Breathless*, which sold over ten million copies.

Donnie Ienner loved the song "Soul Provider" and made it the first single released. He felt the title helped establish my image and brand as a soulful singer whose music would have a wide appeal. He correctly predicted that it would receive extended airplay across many radio formats.

We had strong momentum, thanks to the success of *The Hunger*, so we knew *Soul Provider* had great potential. Still, no one was prepared for the incredible success of this album.

One of the biggest surprises was the second single. Nine years after Laura Branigan's beautiful version of "How Am I Supposed to Live Without You" hit No. 1 on the Billboard charts, my own version soared to the top. The song I'd written with Doug James became my first No. 1 on both the Billboard Adult Contemporary chart, in December 1989, and the Billboard Hot 100 chart, in January 1990.

We followed that with the release of "How Can We Be Lovers?" which I'd written with the dynamic duo of Diane Warren and Desmond Child in my New York City apartment. Desmond is brilliant and one of the best and most successful songwriters in the business. He has written huge songs for artists such as Bon Jovi, Aerosmith, Ricky Martin, KISS, Kelly Clarkson, Alice Cooper, and Cher. Desmond's songs feature the power of truth and simplicity, not to mention melodies that stick. Like Diane and me, Desmond will stand up for his lyrics and chords, so the three of us have been known to argue and debate for hours until we all agree that we have the strongest possible song. "How Can We Be Lovers [If We Can't Be Friends]?"—a simple question that goes to the soul of it all in a relationship—quickly climbed to No. 3 on Billboard's Hot 100 in April 1990.

The fourth single released from *Soul Provider* was another song by Diane Warren. I was in the studio working on some new ideas when she first called me with it. I could tell immediately from the tone of her voice that something emotional was going on.

"I was thinking about my dad and this song came pouring out. It wrote itself," she said. "I want you to listen to it."

I was aware that her dad had died a short time earlier, and I knew where she must have gone to find this song. Her father, like mine, had been her champion, always encouraging her to develop her gifts. I've spent thousands of hours with Diane. She is a quirky, eccentric genius, and she has an emotional depth that serves as the well of her creativity. I knew this song was going to be something special.

I found a quiet spot in the studio, leaned against a wall, and said, "Okay, play it for me."

On her keyboard she played "When I'm Back on My Feet Again," and it spoke to me, as it would to millions of others.

"That's beautiful, Diane," I said. "Don't give it to anyone else. I'll be in L.A. in a week. I'll do a demo of it and, if you love my version, let me have the song. If you don't love it, go ahead and give it to whoever you want."

She met me in an L.A. studio. She played keyboards when I recorded the demo of the song written for her father. I did a first take and barely made it through. I couldn't look at her and sing it. I refocused for the second take and nailed the demo. Everyone in the studio was in tears, especially the songwriter and the singer.

Diane expected that we would replace her keyboards, but we left her performance on the track because we wanted her spirit on the record. We knew it was a powerful song. "When I'm Back on My Feet Again" was released as a single from *Soul Provider* and became the second song from that album to hit No. 1 on the Adult Contemporary chart.

The success and impact of the song proved that Diane could deliver deep, emotional material beyond the love songs that she was most known for. Fortunately for me, the song resonated on first listen, reminding me of my father, and further confirming that as

My amazing and inspiring friends Del and Carolyn Bryant and fellow artist and true lover of golf Nick Jonas.

At my annual MBC event with the legendary, brilliant writer and artist Dave Mason and guitar sensation Orianthi, who is on the road to her own illustrious career.

Celebrating the release of my children's book *The Secret of the Lost Kingdom* with a signing at Barnes & Noble in NYC... and clearly my new haircut, which was very short!

At the "Shooting Star in the Desert Night" benefit with the legendary Alice Cooper, one of the most decent human beings I've ever met.

At the Atlanta Heroes Awards event with Coretta Scott King the night she was being honored by the NARAS (The National Academy of Recording Arts & Sciences) Atlanta chapter. She invited me to sing, so I wrote "The Courage in Your Eyes" and sang it to her that evening.

With Chuck Norris and Rob Schneider, two friends who were there for the unveiling of my Hollywood Walk of Fame star. Ron makes me laugh my ass off and Chuck can still kick it!

My incredible and charismatic assistant Ronnie showing her emotional support on the day I first went public with my short haircut.

Me and my buddy Bree in Sydney outside the Opera House (2012). Notice Bree's fist mid-picture. After forty-three years of sparring he just cannot help himself.

My inspired and inspiring musical cohorts David Foster, Walter Afanasieff, and Kenny G.

Me with David Foster and Dave Reitzas, the most masterful recording engineer on the planet.

Working with Stefani Germanotta (soon to be known around the globe as Lady Gaga) and Michael Mani (from the production team The Jam) on my album *One World One Love.*

A reflective moment between friends, more than twenty years in the making. Bill Clinton and me sharing the green during the Clinton Foundation–sponsored Humana Challenge event in Palm Desert, CA. I show up to support whenever and wherever I can, just as he has for me.

Clint Eastwood, not only an amazing writer, director, producer, and actor, but also an incredible philanthropist, showing up to support my annual MBC fundraiser in Ojai, CA.

The usual suspects at AT&T Pebble Beach National Pro-Am (me with Kevin Costner, Darius Rucker, and Bill Murray).

Pirate so brave on the seven seas? Or a singer dressed up like Captain Jack Sparrow in a crow's nest on Brighton Beach?

I'm reloaded! (Yes, it's all baking powder!)

much as I love writing, the singer within me recognizes the greater level of importance in embracing the right song. Many people have told me that Diane's song to her champion has inspired them and helped them get through difficult times. Henry Winkler once told me that he played that song over and over again in his car when he went through a challenging time years ago. I've also heard the song is used for inspiration by many healing organizations, such as Alcoholics Anonymous and veterans' groups. Diane's song has proved to be a wonderful legacy to her father, the man who fostered her dreams.

THE ONE & ONLY

Since fans across a wide demographic had responded so well to "Dock of the Bay," I thought it would be great to put another classic R & B song on *Soul Provider* as a tribute to another of my heroes.

The fifth single from *Soul Provider* was co-written in 1930 by lyricist Stuart Gorrell and the great composer and performer Hoagy Carmichael. Named for and written about Carmichael's sister, Georgia, it became the signature song of my biggest idol, Ray Charles, and the official song of his home state, too.

Predictably, I took some heat for covering "Georgia on My Mind." Some critics held that it was wrong to cover "a Ray Charles song," even though Ray recorded it thirty years after Hoagy Carmichael's original version. Over the years, "Georgia" has been recorded by scores of artists, including Bing Crosby, Dean Martin, and Willie Nelson, to name just a few. Still, Ray did set the bar incredibly high with his perfect and definitive rendition. He owned the song, without a doubt. I wasn't attempting to outsing him, only to pay homage with my own interpretation. What singer doesn't want to perform great songs? And "Georgia" was another of the classics that I'd learned while just starting out. I'd performed it thousands of times. People had been comparing my voice to Ray's since I was twelve years old.

Jamie Foxx did Ray Charles proud in his movie portrayal. His Oscar-winning performance in *Ray* was staggering. When I told Jamie that at an event, he kissed my hand. Jamie may just have been setting the trap for our next Ping-Pong duel. We've had some heated matches, and he once told an interviewer that I was the best celebrity Ping-Pong player he'd ever taken on. I feel the same way about him.

When the critics groused about my singing "Georgia," I tuned them out. The opinions that mattered to me were the fans' and Ray Charles's. You can imagine how thrilled I was when I was asked to perform "Georgia" with Ray for the 1991 television special *50 Years of Music Making: A Tribute to Ray Charles.* I nearly lost it while standing onstage with him at the piano for that performance. Maybe the biggest thrill of all, though, was when I was first introduced to Ray for our rehearsal. I walked up to him and said: "The student finally meets the master!"

At those words Ray flashed an ear-to-ear grin, and, honestly, the memory of his delighted expression is one of my most cherished moments as a performer. Making Ray Charles smile so joyfully felt almost as good as singing a duet with him. He was such a powerful influence and teacher for me and for countless other performers, especially with his masterful back-phrasing.

My Soul Nourished

My cover of "Georgia on My Mind" reached No. 6 on the Adult Contemporary chart in October 1992, and brought my second Grammy nomination for Best Male Pop Vocal Performance.

With five hit singles one after the other, *Soul Provider* began selling at the rate of 300,000 albums a week, reaching No. 3 on the Hot 200 chart for albums.

I learned with *Soul Provider* that scoring high on the Billboard charts is not nearly as important for an album's sales as how long it remains on the charts. The incredible staying power of *Soul Provider* transformed me into a superstar, and my first No. 1 album—*Time, Love & Tenderness*—was just around the corner. The key to the success of *Soul Provider* is that so many singles released from the album became hits—one after the other, with each receiving extended airplay—which translated into continued sales over a long period of time.

This album, a landmark for my career, remained on the charts for an incredible 202 weeks, nearly four years, thanks to its many great songs, my many great fans, and the massive support team from my record company. They conducted the sort of marketing and promotional campaign that is increasingly rare these days in the music industry because budgets are so tight and artists seldom have champions to help their careers. I benefited greatly from a record label that stood behind me, helped me grow as an artist, and then supported my work with all of its resources. That sort of artist development, which allows young people to develop their gifts, forge their identities, and build their characters as well as their brands, is also rarely seen anymore.

So if you've ever doubted the simple magic of never giving up on your dream, consider my eighteen years of singing for my supper on street corners while one record deal after another failed to generate interest or sales. I paid a price, to be sure, and so did many of the people I loved. There is always a price.

All those years, I kept in mind the words of encouragement from my father. Bullet Bolotin never gave up on me, so I couldn't give up, either. I drew strength from the encouragements I received along the way from people I respected, and I kept fighting. If that sounds like self-help-speak, all I can say is: *Soul Provider* sold more than 12.5 million albums worldwide and was certified six times platinum in the U.S. alone!

This album certainly did provide many soulful thrills and surprises. In 1989, I was nominated in the Grammy Awards Best Male Pop Vocal category for "How Am I Supposed to Live Without You." My fellow nominees included Billy Joel, Prince, Richard Marx, and another of my heroes, the late Roy Orbison, who had died the year before. Incredibly, the selection committee chose me for the award, and at the 32nd annual Grammy Awards, I took home my first gilded gramophone statue, which was a very gratifying experience. Accepting the award was a surreal moment that my mind played out in slow motion, especially because the presenter who read my name was the grown-up little girl from my past, Paula Abdul. She cracked a huge smile when she opened the envelope and saw my name, which made me think, *That's a good sign.* Given our friendship and long history, Paula's presence gave me the sense that something cosmic was going on that day.

I high-fived Louis Levin (my "date" that night), and then walked to the podium. If it's possible to be in a daze but have your mind racing and your emotions swirling, that was my situation. Overwhelmed, I forgot most of what I'd sworn to remember if I won. I tried to thank everyone involved in the album, but, maddeningly, I left out my producer, Michael Omartian, who was in the audience with his son. Afterward, I spoke about my slipup with my friend and fellow Grammy winner James Ingram. James is one of the greatest singers in the business and he's inspired me since the first time I heard his voice on the Quincy Jones recording of "Baby Come to Me," a duet with Patti Austin. I told James I messed up because I was afraid of jinxing myself if I came to the Grammys with a list of people to thank in my pocket. James and I agreed that I definitely could have used a list.

That was an emotional night, as you might imagine, given the long and rough road I'd traveled to that stage. After the Grammy Awards ceremony, Louis and I went to Wolfgang Puck's Spago restaurant in L.A. for a party. I'd never been to such an event with so many stars, celebrities, and music industry movers and shakers. It seemed like everyone who'd attended the Grammys was there. I was overwhelmed by their congratulations and kind words. Quite a few of them expressed an interest in working with me in the future, which eventually would happen in many cases. I began to feel more comfortable in the company of people I had admired for so long. I should not have been surprised to see my touchstone friend there. I don't know what it is that draws us together, because we've never spoken more than a few words to each other, but Kris Kristofferson—who had offered me encouragement while I sat on a street corner singing so many years before—has a habit of appearing at key moments in my life. Maybe one day I should ask him what that's all about.

A year later, I returned to the Grammys courtesy of another song on that same album. My cover of "Georgia on My Mind" was also nominated for a Grammy in the same category. I was in great company again, as my fellow nominees included Phil Collins, James Ingram, Rod Stewart, and, again, Billy Joel and Roy Orbison. This time, Roy's recording of "Pretty Woman," used in the sound track of the Julia Roberts movie, won. I was happy to see Roy honored posthumously. His wife, Barbara, a producer and philanthropist who died in 2011, was also a friend of mine. Roy was a sweet soul of a man with such a unique gift and a wonderful career. I heard him perform not long before he passed away and I thought that his magnificent voice was as strong and beautiful as it had ever been.

Soul Provider certainly had provided for me. With this album, I truly could say my father's prediction had come true. I'd made it big, *big, BIG!*, and I owed a debt of thanks to my parents, my daughters, and all of the family, friends, fans, and fellow travelers in the music industry who encouraged and supported me along the way. As sappy as it may sound, you just can't ever give up on your passion, because sometimes a simple adjustment in your approach or a change in circumstances can produce a dramatic transformation. During this period in which the universe suddenly shifted in my favor, I did all I could to enjoy the moment and seize the day, but honestly, I was often just in a stunned trance as a result of all the good fortune that came my way.

Never had I experienced such a series of incredible moments and mind-bending events. Kenny Rogers left me speechless when he walked up to me and said, "Pound for pound, you're the best singer in the business." Gladys Knight stepped into my elevator and lavished me with praise all the way to the lobby. Another night, I found myself locked in a warm and hilarious conversation about music and cars with Bruce Springsteen and Patti Scialfa.

But my greatest success was yet to come.

TIME, LOVE & TENACITY: THE SONG STAYS ON THE ALBUM

With the multiplatinum success of the *Hunger* and *Soul Provider* albums, I felt we'd developed a finely tuned hit-making machine, thanks to our team of songwriters, musicians, backup singers, and producers. We were on a roll, selling millions and millions of records, and so we took much the same approach to the next album. This time, however, we unleashed Diane Warren in full force. I did make her promise not to bring Butt Wings into the studio, but other than that, I asked her to give us all the songs she could. Diane responded by writing or co-writing six songs chosen for the album, including the title track, "Time, Love & Tenderness"; "Missing You Now," co-written with Walter Afanasieff and me; "Forever Isn't Long Enough" and "New Love," co-written with

Desmond Child and me; and "Now That I Found You" and "We're Not Making Love Anymore," co-written with me.

We put the new song I'd written with Bob Dylan, "Steel Bars," on the album as a final track, but we also included an R & B classic, as we'd done in the two previous albums with great success. This time, I chose to cover Percy Sledge's soulful hit "When a Man Loves a Woman." When I delivered the master copy of the *Time, Love & Tenderness* album to Columbia I thought we had a giant hit. I thought they would be ecstatic at what we'd produced.

My manager told me that the word on high was that we had a great list of hits—and one miss. The song they wanted to scratch from the album was the single that many record-business insiders had predicted would be its biggest hit. It was a solid thumbs-down to my cover of the Percy Sledge song. I felt like my dog had been kicked and then run over by an Escalade. I put everything I had into that track. Percy was another one of my longtime favorite R & B singers, and I'd been singing his songs for years.

Everyone else I'd talked to after hearing my rendition said it honored the original while adding a new flavor to it. Most thought it was a surefire hit.

I didn't understand what the objections to the song might be. Louis Levin reported that there might be resistance from radio stations about playing a song so closely identified with Percy Sledge, because there was still recurrent airplay of the Percy Sledge recording, which I personally loved and acknowledged as the definitive version.

The irony was that the head of Sony, Tommy Mottola, had just suggested a few weeks earlier that I record "When a Man Loves a Woman," without knowing that I had already recorded it.

Later, the Sony chief visited the studio and listened to my version. He was thrilled and joined the chorus of people proclaiming the song a smash.

Still, I thought it wise not to bring up Tommy's endorsement. Instead, I questioned myself.

Maybe I'm missing something?

I decided to try some other approaches to performing the song to see if another version worked. That meant calling up the record producer with whom I had just started working, Walter Afanasieff—the music industry's equivalent of James Bond's gadget guy, "Q." For our first songwriting session at the Sunset Marquis, unofficial West Coast headquarters of Michael Bolton, Inc., Walter came with a cartload of music-making gear. He was not only an amazing pianist, but a phenomenal technician.

Walter assured me that killer hits were his target. Somehow that day in our hotel room, Walter turned out a song demo that sounded better than most high-fidelity records. When my career took off, I asked Walter to produce my albums whenever possible. I was the burden he bore in long days and nights in the studio. The result was scores of killer hits.

When I called him to make another attempt at "When a Man Loves a Woman," Walter sacrificed his weekend and drove down to L.A. from his home in the Bay Area. He brought along Dana Chappelle, the studio engineer who recorded all of the vocals, to see if I could surpass the earlier version I'd done, which Walter and I had selected as my best.

I attempted seven or eight versions of the song. At one point, Walter looked as though he might pass out from exhaustion at the mixing board. He was also frustrated because he thought we'd already nailed a fantastic track. So I left the sound booth and went into the control room.

"Michael, you could sing this song one hundred more times, and there would still be nothing I'd change from the absolutely perfect way we recorded it the first time!" he pleaded. "There is nothing we should change from what we have on the album now."

He then flipped a switch to play the original recording. Sitting side by side, we listened without a word, shutting our eyes to focus on the music and the vocal. When the song was over, Walter turned to me and stared as if to say, *How could you do any better than that?*

I caught his meaning. I promptly apologized to Walter and Dana for dragging them away from their families and told them to go home. I then called Louis Levin and said: "I've made up my mind. The song stays on the record."

The song stayed on the record.

In the weeks that followed, Columbia picked up on the positive buzz for my performance of "When a Man Loves a Woman," and pulled out all the stops to promote both the single and the entire album. They brought it home in a huge way. My cover of Percy's song shot to No. 1 on the singles charts, later winning me a Grammy for Best Male Pop Vocal Performance of the Year. The success of my cover led to an opportunity to perform the song live with Percy in Chicago for a VH1 *Center Stage* show, creating another unforgettable moment in my life. The *Time, Love & Tenderness* album was also a major No. 1 hit, selling more than fourteen million copies worldwide.

The huge success of this project gave me a jolt, because I'd almost removed the song from the album. Later, Louis Levin heard a rumor that the objection to my version may have been triggered by a three-page critique written by one of the secretaries at the label.

I do think of that experience, though, on the many, many occasions when someone in an airport—including the security folks—or backstage at a concert sings it to me or tells me that it is a favorite song, or the song played at their wedding. This is the very same song that nearly didn't make it past one person's critical assessment and onto the biggest album of my career.

Everything worked out for the best. Donnie Ienner, one of the all-time great record executives, helped me sell more than fifty million albums. After all, we followed *Time, Love & Tenderness* with five more huge albums that went gold, platinum, or multiplatinum around the world, including my only classical album, *My Secret Passion: The Arias*, which went to No. 1 on the classical charts and remained there for six weeks.

I heard from another critic just prior to the release of that *Time, Love & Tenderness* album in 1991. This one was a professional, Stephen Holden of the *New York Times*, who'd once been an A and R executive for RCA and a longtime friend of mine, even though my dad once insulted him without knowing he was standing right there. Dad's hearing was shot, so he talked in a loud voice, and once when he joined me backstage after a live performance in New Haven, he said, "I hear some big shot from New York is here," referring to Stephen, then a producer, who was standing behind me. Knowing Stephen had heard my dad, I joked, "He's probably a nobody who just thinks he's a big shot." But then Dad chimed in, "Yeah, that's what your brother said."

Stephen, who'd obviously forgiven me, or forgotten that incident, remained a friend. He told me that he'd heard a pre-release version of *Time, Love & Tenderness* and thought the album was the best I'd made so far.

"It will be your biggest album to date, but I want to give you a heads-up," he said.

"What for?" I asked.

"The other critics are going to crucify you," he said.

"Why?" I asked.

Stephen, who is no softy as a critic himself, explained.

"It's a mainstream album and it will be huge, which means they'll annihilate you because they didn't make you a star, your fans did."

Holden was dead-on. My war with the critics had begun.

One of the most striking examples of this was a show at the Blossom Music Center near Cleveland. All three of my daughters were there, seated in the front row. I sang a song to them that I'd written with Diane Warren and Walter Afanasieff. The lyrics always made me think of my girls: "Soul of my soul, heart of my heart. / Some kind of miracle of my life / that's what you are. / Blood of my blood, light of my life. / You mean much more than you know, soul of my soul."

I thought the entire concert was a huge success. We performed more encores than usual, which is a good measure of audience appreciation. But on the flight home the next day, I opened the local newspaper and came upon a review of our show. The critic was harsh, particularly in his appraisal of the song I'd sung for my girls.

He mentioned that they were there and that I'd sung it to them. He then noted that it was his least favorite song of the evening, adding that he thought my kids forgave me for singing it. That throwaway comment might have stung, but the critic had not seen what I saw from the stage as I performed that song. All three of my girls were crying, with heartfelt tears running down their faces. As long as I had that memory, the critic's words didn't mean a thing.

When the critics bared their fangs, I didn't know how to respond at first. Diane Warren wasn't so hesitant. "When a man is that vulnerable and sings something that tender, women love that. They melt," Diane told an interviewer in assessing my audience.

I'd never expected to become such a divisive force. Some critics watching a television feed backstage at the ceremony even booed me as I accepted my Grammy award that year. I was on cloud nine when I walked backstage, but I came down to earth when someone told me about the boos from the critics. My indelicate response was to tell them to "kiss my ass."

They seemed shocked at that response. Were they really expecting me to say, "Please, sir, may I have another?"

I had no intention of slowing down after all those years of nothing. I had ventured too far into the desert to turn back. But even when success started to come, my extreme focus didn't allow me to celebrate. It was like being at an enormous feast where you can't taste a thing. While all the people around me were celebrating, I was already focused on the next song, the next album, the next round of promotion.

The day after I won my first Grammy, I was in a suite at the Sunset Marquis, and my entire room was full of flowers and cards. I was getting congratulatory telegrams all day long. But I had a writing session booked and I was more concerned with working than experiencing the celebration. What I did experience was a second wind, because while all this excitement was going on, my energy level was increasing. Success is a type of fuel, which frees you to continue creating on your own terms. I was on to making sure my next song would be a success.

With the release of *Time, Love & Tenderness* came my Forrest Gump moment.

DATING GAME

The joy of my success with *Time, Love & Tenderness* was dampened by the failure of my marriage, which would end amicably but sadly in 1991. Those were lonely days, mostly. I went on a few dates, but it was hard to spend time with any one person because of my crazy schedule (a recurring theme). They say a high percentage of romances begin at work and, at that point, I didn't have many other opportunities to get to know women. Often, the women who came to my concerts were on dates, which was the case when I first met Marla Maples. Her date was Donald Trump, who owned the Taj Mahal casino, where I was performing. They came backstage after the show. Donald introduced Marla as "my girlfriend, who is a huge fan of yours." I didn't quite know what to say when she stepped forward and said, "My dream man."

Donald didn't seem to notice. He said he was very happy with the turnout for my concert. That night Marla asked to interview me for a book she was doing on successful people in diverse arenas, so we met the next afternoon. Our talk wandered into the spiritual aspects of life and I found that intriguing, along with the fact that she was beautiful, but I thought of her as Donald's girlfriend.

I did see her not long after that, when she and Donald came to another concert at Jones Beach on Long Island. When we spoke, Donald and I talked mostly about our daughters. I didn't know anything about the nature of his relationship with Marla. So I was surprised to hear later on that she had broken off the engagement, which was highly publicized in the media.

After their breakup, she came without Donald to another concert and she stayed on the road a while longer with our tour, but my next stop was Europe, and we said good-bye. Then Marla and Donald got back together.

I learned some interesting lessons about being in the media spotlight during all of this. Donald is such a huge celebrity that the print and television reporters were tracking Marla's every move, and I was caught in the spotlight. That was the first situation in which I went through airports and saw stories involving me in the tabloids outside of a musical event, which triggered my awareness that my private life was no longer my own.

It never occurred to me that one day anything I said or did as part of common daily life would become tabloid fodder. Suddenly, I had to become vigilant when walking down the street or having dinner with a friend. I found myself either shying away from public life or being very selective about which restaurants I could choose. Some of my favorites were those that weren't surrounded by paparazzi.

Donald and Marla eventually divorced and I've remained

friends with Marla and also friendly with Donald. Marla is always optimistic and full of light, and I'm inspired by the depth of her loving relationship with her beautiful daughter, Tiffany.

After that story faded in the media, another work-related dating opportunity arose during the production of the music video for "Missing You Now," the fourth song on *TL&T* released as a single, which reached No. 1 on Billboard's Adult Contemporary chart. I know some singers are attracted to girls in their music videos, but how many of those guys would fall for a woman wearing a mechanic's coveralls, long johns, and a wool sweater?

In the 1992 video, Teri Hatcher played the role of a country girl whose father owned a rural gas station. She was a hottie even in an outfit designed by Exxon. In a later scene, she wore a summer dress as we kissed next to the diesel pump. At that point, she hadn't yet worked at the *Daily Planet* in *Lois & Clark*, but she had been a mermaid in residence on *Love Boat*, served a three-year hitch on *MacGyver*, and done regular guest spots on shows including *Star Trek* and *Quantum Leap*. Based on her résumé, Teri was way overqualified to be a music video girl, but I understood that she'd signed on because she liked my music. I was grateful to Teri for appearing in the video for "Missing You Now," which helped the album *Time, Love & Tenderness* sell more than sixteen million copies worldwide.

After we met on the set, we dated for ten months, but we were both very busy with our careers, so we didn't get to see a lot of each other. I was impressed that Teri was a very down-to-earth person who was also working every bit as hard to establish her career as I was to establish mine. When her career took off, I was very happy for her. Of course I would see her again on the set of *Desperate Housewives*, though by then I was dating a woman who lived a few doors down on the show's Wisteria Lane.

TL&T was certified eight times platinum in the United States. This album became the bedrock of a rewarding and fulfilling career. Its songs were the sound track to such wonderful times. Since the release of *TL&T*, I've sold many more albums and songs on CDs, DVDs, and singles. I've even had several more multiplatinum albums, but none would be so sweet, or so bitter, as *Time, Love & Tenderness*.

You see, there was one song on *TL&T* that I came to wish had not been on this album after all. It just wasn't the song Columbia Records had targeted.

Chapter Twelve

Trials, Tribulations & Triumphs

Before the turbochargers kicked in on my career, I had a
serious financial challenge. My problems stemmed from a
complex financial condition. The proper economic term, I believe,
is *broke.*

My financial spreadsheet was all outgo, no income. I couldn't
pay my bills. I couldn't pay the pizza man. I couldn't pay attention. We were so poor, in our neighborhood whenever there was
a rainbow it showed up in black and white. (Thank you again,
Mr. Dangerfield.)

One of my outstanding bills was owed to my law firm.

We are about to step into the dark side of the music business.
Most performers crack their heads sooner or later against the hard
realities of a business in which far too many lawsuits are brought
not to secure justice but to feed the wolves. My particular corner
of this hell was a multiheaded monster that would not die, a legal
torment that began shortly after the release of my most successful
album and continues to haunt me to this day.

A WONDERFUL SONG SPOILED

The definition of "cruel irony" may be found in the fact that at the center of this torment is a gloriously uplifting song entitled "Love Is a Wonderful Thing." This is the story of a song gone wrong—terribly and disastrously wrong. This joyous song was produced in 1991 by the incomparable Walter Afanasieff, and lovingly crafted with one of my favorite collaborators, Andrew Goldmark.

After our creation spent four weeks at the top of Billboard's Adult Contemporary chart, I received notice that attorneys for the R & B group the Isley Brothers had filed a copyright infringement lawsuit.

They claimed, to our astonishment, that there were many similarities between my major hit and their song of the same name. Neither Andrew nor I had ever heard their song. A quick check found that it had not appeared on any of the Isley Brothers albums before we wrote our song. After being released as a single in 1966, their song never reached the Top 100 on any Billboard charts.

Our research found that there were 129 copyrighted songs with the title "Love Is a Wonderful Thing"—and 85 of them were registered before the Isley song was written. Despite our adamant denials, and efforts to have the lawsuit thrown out, the case went to jury trial in 1994. A legal concern in these cases is the level of "access," which takes into consideration what opportunities—if any—Andrew and I might have had to hear their song and maybe subconsciously remember it. They maintained that we had subconsciously copied it. We maintained that we did not.

During the trial, our lawyers called three top rhythm and blues experts, including Motown's Lamont Dozier, who had written and produced for the Isleys and had written songs with me as well. The experts testified that they'd never heard that particular Isley Brothers song. We even brought in the president of the Rhythm & Blues Foundation, Billy Vera, an avowed fan of the Isley Brothers. He testified that he'd never heard of the Isleys' own "Love Is a Wonderful Thing."

The lawsuit and trial struck me as a great injustice and an insult to my integrity and the integrity of my co-writer. Neither Andy nor I would ever take the wrong change from a cashier or a waiter, much less take someone else's idea. I did not handle it well. I'd sit in the courtroom feeling outraged at the injustice. Worse, I couldn't leave my feelings in the courtroom at the end of the day. I couldn't sleep or think creatively. The stress affected every aspect of my life. Nicollette Sheridan, whom I was seeing then, wanted to attend the trial with me whenever possible, but the lawyers felt her presence might be distracting, and that female jurors might resent her. It was too bad, because it would have helped me to have her there.

Our team searched everywhere on the charts and airplay monitors and could find no proof that the Isley song was ever a hit. In fact, our research showed otherwise.

Our argument was that the Isleys' song was barely, much less widely, disseminated. A hit song is always widely disseminated. The appellate court found that the song was not on any album or compact disc before we wrote our song. We were convinced that no intelligent jury would find it likely that my co-writer and I could have heard the Isley composition, subconsciously locked it into our brains for twenty years, and then released it together as our own song. But I came to question the intelligence of the jury involved in this case. I felt like I was somewhere between Jimmy Stewart in *It's a Wonderful Life* and Henry Fonda in *The Wrong Man*. It was like waking into a bad dream instead of awakening out of one.

During the trial, we even produced a "work tape" recording of Andy and me that was made during the studio sessions in which we wrote "Love Is a Wonderful Thing." On the recording, the jury could hear our back-and-forth discussions during the process of creating the song from the very first note. We submitted that recording as evidence related to the question of "independent creation," which is one of three critical components in this type of case.

In the end our defense did not sway the jury, which ruled against us and in favor of the Isley team.

I felt as though a stranger had claimed one of my daughters as his own and then snatched her from my arms with the court's approval. When you create a song, word by word, note by note, and you are part of every nuance in the recorded performance, that creation becomes a part of your life. My songs are like my children in many ways. I love them all, each in unique ways, because each of them is a unique creation.

After nine draining years spent battling the copyright infringement claim, we ran out of legal options. Our side was ordered to pay what the media has reported to be the largest monetary award in the history of the music business for such a case.

The previous highest award ever given in such a case was $587,000. The late Beatle George Harrison lost that lawsuit after a ten-year court battle. The music company that owned the rights to the Chiffons' 1962 song "He's So Fine" filed the lawsuit. The Chiffons' song was a huge hit record, widely disseminated, so to us the difference between their case and ours seemed clear.

Much of the music industry was in an uproar over the decision in the Isley lawsuit because of the view that the ruling against us dramatically lowered what had been the legal standard for access in such cases. The Recording Industry Association of America and the Motion Picture Association of America submitted "friend of the court" memoranda supporting our case, saying that if the jury verdict were allowed to stand, it would drop the standard for level of access in copyright cases to an unacceptably low level.

Across the board, people throughout the industry were speaking out.

But the verdict stood. The legal ramifications reverberate to this day, and so does the emotional impact. Our song should have been one of my most celebrated creations, but I rarely perform it live. Believe me, I never judge anyone by what I hear in the news after the jury ruled that I'd somehow copied a record I'd never heard. The philosopher Seneca said, *To reach the wonders in life, we must pass through perils.*

I could certainly relate to that, but I had no idea how enormous the perils in my own life would become even as my career took off beyond my wildest dreams.

SWEET INSPIRATION

When I learned of the Isley jury's decision, I was still reeling in shock on the trip home, yet when I walked into the front hall of my home that day I found a healing gift in the stack of mail. The package was sent by Coretta Scott King, the inspiring widow of the Reverend Martin Luther King Jr. She'd sent me a signed book of photographs depicting the remarkable life and tragic death of her husband. Her message said simply, "I thought you might like this."

Martin Luther King Jr. was one of the rare giants who've passed through our time. He delivered the power of truth and then was summoned home as a victorious warrior. I sat on the floor, studying his writings and photographs, in awe of his life. His eloquence and intellect come through, even in his reports of minor events from his travels, including his visit to my hometown. I was reminded that it really was not so long ago that black men and women were barred from most restaurants and hotels. I'm sure that after Reverend King's assassination in 1968, none of the grieving civil rights freedom fighters could envision that forty years later, an African American man would be elected president of the United States.

The book sent by Coretta Scott King pulled me away from my

tormented thoughts over the lawsuit. It contained compelling photographs of the men and women who risked or even gave their lives to a cause that changed the world, and messages of peace and forgiveness were scattered through the text. These messages calmed me, as did the sense that Mrs. King had me in her thoughts. She would often send me photographs or clippings of things she was involved in, or that she thought might hold interest for me. Sometimes she'd just send me notes to cheer me up with handwritten greetings like the one on this package.

I first met Coretta at the 1994 VH1 Honors show, where a group of artists were recognized for their charitable work. Coretta was one of the presenters. We'd never met, so when I saw her backstage I felt compelled to introduce myself. I expressed my admiration for all that she and her late husband had accomplished as well as the ultimate sacrifice they'd made.

That night, a friendship formed. Coretta invited me to visit the Martin Luther King Jr. Center for Nonviolent Social Change whenever I was in Atlanta. I took her up on that invitation a few weeks later, bringing two of my daughters. Coretta gave us a tour and shared personal stories of her husband and their experiences together. Mrs. King was taken by my interest in that history, and later she invited me to speak at the center's annual march and rally in 1995. (My touchstone acquaintance Kris Kristofferson was there, too, which left me wondering what life-altering event was about to take place.)

To prepare for my appearance, I listened to a cassette collection of Reverend King's speeches, and I was delighted to hear him make reference to my hometown in one of them. He talked about visiting New Haven and feeling welcomed there as opposed to his next stop, a Southern city where he felt threatened and unwanted. My parents had been big admirers of Reverend King. I felt proud of them and my hometown for recognizing his heroic cause.

When I listened to the recording of his powerful speeches given in his booming cadence, it struck me that he was a man of my time. I was a boy in New Haven when he came there, and I was a beneficiary of his efforts. The thought kept running through my mind that these speeches occurred in my lifetime and for my benefit and the benefit of my children and grandchildren.

The Congress of Racial Equality (C. O. R. E.) presented me with the Martin Luther King Award for "outstanding achievement" in 1996 for my work with at-risk youth through my foundation. It was a thrill to be given that recognition from a great civil rights organization, especially when the award was named after one of my heroes. That award is one of my most coveted because it involved trying to make a difference beyond my own field. Michael Ovitz once told me that we don't have royalty in America, we have celebrity; and people can use celebrity as a form of currency by participating in charity events and raising important issues. I felt grateful that C. O. R. E.'s efforts to change society were aided in more subtle ways by another powerful catalyst for desegregation and mutual understanding between the races—music. Ignorance is the enemy of understanding. Racial attitudes began to shift when white kids of my generation began listening to "race music" in the form of Delta blues. Our mutual understanding and acceptance increased even more when we began attending concerts and enjoying live performances by black musicians while standing side by side with black teens.

When white kids couldn't get enough of Ray Charles, Percy Sledge, Sam Cooke, Smokey Robinson, and the Motown artists and songs, social change wasn't far behind. More than once, I've stood on the stage of the Apollo Theater in Harlem as the only Hebrew school dropout on the program. I've always been welcomed there, and I've never witnessed prejudice or racist talk on a concert stage or in a recording studio when black and white musicians work together.

I'm proud to be a part of that, but I can't pretend to fully grasp the depth of the sacrifices made by those who brought down the walls of American apartheid. Coretta often shared with me the fears, disappointments, and eventual triumphs she experienced during the civil rights movement. She told me of her anguish when her husband was jailed repeatedly on false or trumped-up charges. In many of those instances, Mrs. King and her husband both feared that he might never get out of jail alive. She told me of her gratitude when then president John F. Kennedy and his brother Bobby intervened to release Reverend King from jail.

Coretta provided me with insights into what it was like for her as a young mother alone with her children while the world seemed to rage at her door. Death threats and hateful phone calls came at all hours of the day and night. She went to bed most nights without knowing when—or if—her husband would be coming home. Hearing these stories of her bravery and perseverance called to mind a powerful quote by Winston Churchill: "Courage is not the absence of fear, but action in the face of fear."

Each day brought heart-wrenching reports of bombings, cars run off the road, shots fired, and civil rights workers simply disappearing. Those images were in my mind when I wrote a song honoring Coretta. I also drew inspiration from a beautiful photo in the book Mrs. King gave me, a portrait of her and Reverend King as a young couple. She was at his side, his pillar, his rock, the one person who truly understood all that he endured and the toll it took. I wanted to write of the powerful woman behind the powerful man—a woman who stepped up upon her husband's death and kept his dream alive.

The song's lyrics include a mention of "the endless mile," which refers to the long and often never-ending journey undertaken by those who take a stand and fight for social change—or whatever the cause might be—based on their principles and sense of purpose. Many human rights activists dedicate themselves to their causes knowing that they will likely never live to see the change they seek take hold. In some cases, including that of Reverend King, they lose their lives because of their activism. Through my own advocacy for abused women and children, I've come to know many dedicated and talented individuals, including politicians, medical researchers, lawyers, teachers, social workers, police officers, firefighters, soldiers, and clergy—all of them determined to make the world a better place. I've never met one who didn't list Reverend King and his wife among their heroes.

"The Courage in Your Eyes" is a song I wrote and performed for Coretta at the event in Atlanta, and just a short time later I sang it at the memorial service for Mrs. King upon her death in January 2006. Our audience of fifteen thousand that day included President George W. Bush and former presidents George H. W. Bush, Jimmy Carter, and Bill Clinton, whose wife, Senator Hillary Clinton, spoke that day as well. There were also three governors and three planeloads of Congress members, as well as many leading figures from the civil rights movement.

I was grateful for the opportunity to publicly show my respect for Coretta Scott King and her husband. Knowing Coretta Scott King was an honor that I will treasure all my life.

LESSONS IN LEADERSHIP

Coretta's gift to me was perfectly timed, whether she intended it or not. It was like the hand of a trusted friend reaching out to me and reminding me that love is the only right answer. The book with photographs of her and her husband had an immediate impact on the otherwise wrenching day that marked the verdict of the jury trial for the Isley lawsuit. The Kings' fight against racism put my own experiences with injustice into perspective. The struggles, sacrifices, and dangers faced by the Kings and all of their brave freedom fighters made my situation seem mundane in comparison.

Reading the book sent by Coretta calmed me in a time of turmoil. I decided to seek out other inspirational books. I am more partial to the ancient philosophers than the current ones. One of my favorites is the Roman philosopher Lucius Annaeus Seneca. I have him to thank for a quotation that has helped me immensely:

> Other vices affect our judgment, anger affects our sanity: others come in mild attacks and grow unnoticed, but men's minds plunge abruptly into anger. There is no passion that is more frantic, more destructive to its own self; it is arrogant if successful, and frantic if it fails. Even when defeated it does not grow weary, but if chance places its foe beyond its reach, it turns its teeth against itself. Its intensity is in no way regulated by its origin: for it rises to the greatest heights from the most trivial beginnings.

The trial was an excruciating experience. For me it was a travesty of justice beyond my imagination—and yet it was nothing compared to what would come hurtling at me next.

After the Supreme Court refused to consider my appeal and left the devastating jury verdict standing, I received notice that the insurance company that I'd thought was covering me in the case was instead coming after me for the full financial judgment plus interest, as well as all costs related to the case and all of the appeals.

But it got worse, much worse.

I suddenly found myself alone on the battlefield facing off against a gigantic insurance company and feeling left behind by both my record label and my music publishing company—who, combined, were reaping millions from my work. I had believed we were a team throughout this traumatic litigation, but that was not the case. The insurance company that I thought had my back was now throwing knives, swords, and axes into it. It brought a lawsuit against me in England, trying to force me to pay them millions upon millions of dollars, including the label's share of the judgment. The label that had profited from my work, in the meantime, had an insurer covering its back.

The overwhelming part was that in a worst-case scenario, I would have had another long and protracted trial in London, and if I lost that case, the rules there would have forced me to pay all the opposition's legal fees on top of the judgment, which had grown exponentially with interest.

I talked about this intense situation one day with a dear friend, Carol Genis, whom I'd known socially for years. She is a highly regarded entertainment lawyer based in Chicago.

Carol, whom I soon hired as my general counsel, dug deeply into the case. I became aware that I had yet another fight ahead of me. After a decade of battling the Isley lawsuit, I now found myself not only at war with the insurance company but also feeling obligated to bring my own legal action against one of the lawyers who represented me in the Isley litigation. This was especially painful to me given how much trust I had placed in them.

I brought in a new team of lawyers to represent me in London, where the insurance company lawsuit was filed, and new actions were filed in New York, Connecticut, and Los Angeles. So I had four cases going on at once. My legal team included Carol, David Golub, Kathy Emmett, and Doug Capuder, who were experienced in legal malpractice.

At one point in this extended and painful battle, a member of the team pulled me aside and told me what I understood to mean, "We can't get your song back for you. We can't undo what has happened to you." That proved true. Yet I survived, and fortunately there were several settlements and I avoided a financial catastrophe, but my ability to trust has been permanently...altered.

Carol, who remains my lawyer and my friend, recently offered, "We saved the patient, but he will never be the same."

How could I be the same after spending a decade and a half discovering so many things that made me feel betrayed or abandoned by some of those closest to me? I inevitably became a more guarded person. On one level, I had to implement strict methods of denying unsolicited material. This means not being able to listen to or accept outside music, whether from friends or aspiring artists. I also have never been able to look at a piece of paper in the same way. The term *indemnification* in a contract carries a very different weight and meaning for me now. Even letters and e-mails are potentially binding chains of communication. I believe there is some greater wisdom in this awareness. But in the much bigger picture, your ability to trust is hugely impaired. My perception of absolutely everything changed. The ones you're supposed to be able to put the most trust in are the ones that you start to scrutinize the most.

It was during this time that I sought guidance from my friend Bill, who was deep into his own major undertaking, writing his life's story. We met in his warm Dutch Colonial home in Chappaqua, New York, for a lunch of small, neatly cut sandwiches. At the other end of the dining table were thick stacks of paper, his manuscript awaiting edits for a looming deadline.

Out the window, amid a small forest of evergreens and maple trees, I could see sentries from the Secret Service team that had escorted me up the drive and onto the porch. They drove a convoy of American muscle cars, which seemed oddly fitting. The former president of the United States, whose triumphs and trials far exceeded mine in intensity, asked how I was doing. I told him of the issue weighing on my mind. I told him that I was in the middle of some litigation and if it went all the way to trial the worst-case scenario could be catastrophic because the matter was being heard in London, and over there if you lose you have to pay all of the opposition's legal costs on top of whatever the damages may be— and this dispute could have gone on and on and on.

When I had finished explaining the situation, Bill peered into my eyes with a knowing and compassionate look and said, "That could mean losing everything you ever worked for."

I realized he'd been in exactly the same position. I'd long respected him for his enormous intellect and phenomenal sweeping grasp of so many American, global, and human issues, but this was another Clinton moment for me. For the first time I felt the power of his empathy for other human beings. Fortunately, soon after our conversation about this matter, the other side agreed to settle.

I first met Governor Bill Clinton when I performed at a rally for his initial presidential campaign in Chicago. Dan Adler, a friend who worked for Michael Ovitz at CAA, came to me with a request from the Clinton camp to perform at the Chicago event. After the Chicago rally I went home and there was a knock on the door. My office manager told me that a presidential campaign staffer for Governor Clinton wanted to know if I could be ready for a call from the candidate in twenty minutes. I wondered what this call could be about. Exactly on time the phone rang and it was Governor Bill Clinton. He thanked me for coming to Chicago and told me that his one last big televised push was an event at the Meadowlands in New Jersey.

"I know you're just home for a few days and you are trying to spend time with your girls, but this would mean a lot to us," he said in requesting that I perform.

"Count me in," I said.

Then I stumbled because I wasn't sure how to address him after such a call. So I asked, "What should I call you?"

"Call me Bill," he said. And "Bill" it's been ever since—even when he was Mr. President.

My daughter Taryn and her best friend, Gwen, accompanied me to the Meadowlands event along with Louis Levin. They'd been to this venue only to see concerts by Jon Bon Jovi or Bruce Springsteen, so it was a different world backstage at a political event. This was my first full-on exposure to the storied Clinton charisma. I would witness many Clinton moments that boggle the mind. The atmosphere was not unlike many of the political gatherings I attended as a child with my father in Connecticut—just magnified to the tenth power.

My first impression was that we were lucky to have such a gifted leader seeking the presidency. This was not one of the backslapping, stiff-smiling pols I'd come to hold in contempt. Clinton displayed a gift for instant rapport beyond any I had ever witnessed. As he greeted one supporter after another, the Arkansas governor conversed on topics that ranged from the children and dogs of the person before him to the state of global economics and key figures in the history of rhythm and blues.

I became fast friends with Hillary and her saxophonist husband, whose wealth of interests includes a love of jazz, soul, R & B, and Motown. After one of my first performances for the Clintons, Bill made a comment about wanting to join me onstage with his saxophone someday. I laughed about that. Later, Hillary slipped me a note that said, "He really does want to play in your band."

So far, Bill hasn't had an opportunity to do that, but recently he was being honored at a USO fund-raising event where I performed, and I was impressed with his knowledge of his chosen instrument. The former president spent a lot of time in deep "sax-speak" with my amazing sax player, Michael Lington, a native of Denmark and an international recording artist who never dreamed he'd be discussing where to find the best German-made mouthpieces with the former commander in chief and leader of the free world. Bill's breadth and depth of knowledge never ceases to amaze me.

The Clintons are the most engaging, down-to-earth, and incredibly smart couple I've ever known. After I performed at the Meadowlands event, which was on the eve of the election, Al Gore spoke and offered up a surprise: "Imagine the day of the election. You wake up to the smell of fresh coffee in the kitchen. Michael Bolton is on the radio, and Bill Clinton is president of the United States!"

Thousands cheered for Bill, maybe one or two for the fresh coffee, and even some for me on the radio. After the Meadowlands event, I flew to Norway to promote a new collection of songs. When I finally trudged into my hotel room the next evening, I turned on CNN and turned down the volume before falling asleep. When I woke up, my new friend Bill Clinton was president of the United States.

My work on behalf of his campaign resulted in many invitations to perform at the White House or to simply attend events there. I was surprised to be invited to a reception for officials from the Ukrainian government. My surprise turned to stunned gratitude when Hillary hugged me and said, "We thought you'd enjoy this one, Michael, because we remembered your grandfather was from the Ukraine."

My love and respect for Hillary's keen mind, incredible strength, and poise grew exponentially at another meeting in Washington in January 1998. She'd been scheduled to take part in an event for an organization I've been active in as honorary chairman for many years: Prevent Child Abuse America. When the day of the event arrived, I was not certain Hillary would attend given her busy schedule, but she showed up, smiling, composed, looking great, and ready to speak with compassion and wisdom on specific and complex issues relating to this topic. Time after time, I observed her inquiring about the needs and desires of those around her. Her powerful speech that day sent a surge of energy through the organization that drove its members to new heights of achievement. I admire the Clintons and their determined resilience and all they have accomplished and continue to accomplish.

I flashed back to a moment just six months or so after the Clintons moved into the White House in 1993. I was in Washington for some more advocacy work. I spoke with the first lady only briefly. I asked how things were going so far because I knew she and the president were very sincere in their desire to make a big difference in the lives of people across America. Hillary didn't come out and say it, but I could tell from her tone and expressions that they were experiencing how extremely challenging it can be to get things done in Washington, D.C.

I would discover firsthand during my many visits that there are so many well-funded and deeply entrenched special interest groups as well as powerful individuals and lobbyists, to deal with that you have to wonder how anything ever gets done. I've witnessed this in my own efforts as an advocate for protecting women and children. On one trip to D.C. I met with Pennsylvania senator Arlen Specter, who was then a Republican but later became a Democrat before retiring in 2011 after thirty years. It was my understanding that Senator Specter was leaning toward supporting legislation offering protections that I supported. But this master of the political process pointed out, in a very friendly and helpful way, that some aspects of the proposed legislation as it was then written were likely to attract opposition from certain special interests.

He also suggested some solutions to potential problems. It was very enlightening for me to hear Senator Specter's perspective on how the system works and doesn't work. Just sitting in his office and watching the constant flow of people coming through to seek his advice, ask for his assistance, and present their own issues was like getting a master class in government and politics.

I learned that as proposed legislation moves through the House and the Senate, those who oppose it can find ways to water it down or even to add language that will render it ineffective, make it controversial, or result in it being rejected even by its original supporters. What was going on with our bill was just a small part of what goes on all day every day with so many other bills. It takes constant vigilance, perseverance, and political finesse to clear all the obstacles and objections and finally get meaningful bills made into meaningful laws. The more I learn about the process, the more I appreciate what an incredible system it is, and how difficult it can be to master. I have great respect for public servants like the Clintons who dedicate their lives to making our country and its sometimes messy but still inspiring democracy work for everyone.

Chapter Thirteen

Friends & Lovers

Despite the excruciating distraction of the Isley lawsuit, the 1990s proved to be an incredibly rewarding decade for me, and one of the brightest points in this period of my life was my relationship with the actress Nicollette Sheridan. It's a little complicated because after being friends for a year or so, we first became a couple around 1992 and saw each other until 1995. Then we were on and off for nearly ten years before reuniting and becoming engaged in 2006. Even during those ten years you could find us having lunch at Taverna Tony's in Malibu. Tony, who was a dear friend of Telly Savalas for over forty years, would always make sure we had our own place outside to continue our ongoing fierce but friendly Scrabble match. Nicollette and I saw each other for the next two years, until 2008, before breaking off the engagement and returning to our friendship, which continues to this day. She was at my side during many pivotal moments, from the highs of getting my own star on the Hollywood Walk of Fame to the lows of the Isley trial.

Nicollette and I first met at the 1991 wedding of my friend and frequent collaborator Kenny G and his wife, Lyndie. My date for their wedding was Teri Hatcher. Nicollette's date was her husband, Harry Hamlin. They'd just been married themselves, and we became good friends in the months that followed.

Nicollette starred in *Knots Landing* and she'd just been named one of *People* magazine's "Fifty Most Beautiful People" (a compliment I agreed with). We ran in the same social circles for several years. I often saw Harry and Nicollette at Kenny and Lyndie's house, where we'd have vicious Ping-Pong tournaments. We had cookouts and played board games. Occasionally we went nuts and watched a movie—starring someone in the room.

My friendship with Nicollette developed into the deepest and most enduring relationship of my life. Nicollette is energetic, fearless, sharp, and spirited—and she's the only person I've met who can kick my ass in Scrabble. Nic is every bit as competitive and driven as I am. She dives in and gives all she's got to everything she does, whether it's her work, a party, a charity event, or a relationship. She is extremely passionate, and I was wrapped up in our relationship very quickly.

Early in our courtship, Nicollette and I spoke a few times on the phone during a photo shoot for my *Timeless* album cover with the extraordinary photographer Matthew Rolston, known as "El Drapo" for the skillful way he arranges clothing to make his subjects look good. I was supposed to be focused on the camera and Matthew's instructions, but he picked up on the way I talked to Nicollette and the expression on my face as we spoke.

"I hope everything works out with Nicollette," Matthew said.

I was taken aback that he'd read the situation and my feelings so easily. But that's why Matthew is such a great photographer. He sees what others miss.

I was ready to fall in love without a doubt. I'd been singing about it for a long, long time, and I was eager to experience that depth of emotion. Our relationship changed my life in many wonderful ways. Having someone I could share my experiences with made them all the more enjoyable, especially when my career was soaring.

We went on great vacations to beautiful places around the world. Of course, we often were not alone, even when we thought we were. Some of our island vacation spots were invaded by little trolls with giant camera lenses hiding among the lizards and tropical shrubs. Other times, they would appear in speedboats a hundred yards offshore, carrying long camera lenses with the intent of surreptitiously photographing us at play on the beach.

Nicollette and I also had many great parties, concerts, and events to attend. Early in our relationship, she accompanied me to Washington for a presidential party. The Gala for the President at Ford's Theatre is an annual black-tie event. I was invited to perform, as were Whoopi Goldberg, Jay Leno, Boyz II Men, Natalie Cole, Kenny Loggins, and a bunch of others. Now, political events in D.C. can be stodgy, but this was during the White House years of Bill Clinton and his wife, Hillary, so it was a real party.

The event was broadcast on network television, and I'm told some people complained about jokes and comments that were a little more racy than those customarily made at White House events. It's a good thing those same people weren't backstage. Nicollette and I were socializing with a large group of other performers and their guests in the dressing room after my twenty-minute set when Whoopi walked in.

Whoopi, who was the hostess and emcee for the event, came up and hugged me.

"How was it?" I said, referring to my singing performance.

"Not a dry seat in the house," Whoopi replied.

Everyone cracked up. I laughed along, but the image conjured up by Whoopi left me feeling a little uneasy. Nicollette loved it. She laughed and laughed. She didn't love the fact that I had to leave the Ford's Theatre event before the after-party. There was another audience waiting for me in Florida, so I had to scramble to the airport and catch a plane to Boca Raton.

Proud Moments

Nicollette and I shared many big moments and great experiences, including my daughter Isa's graduation from basic training at the Lackland Air Force Base in San Antonio. Watching my daughter, the squadron leader and environmental biological engineer, march her troops made for one of the proudest days of my life. Surrounded by air force officers and other family members, I watched my firstborn march in perfect step with the other graduates. It was difficult to process that this was my baby girl, who had sat in her stroller smiling while I sang and played my guitar for her.

Earlier we had visited her barracks and she demonstrated what she had to do to prepare for inspections. I didn't know a sock could be folded into sixteenths. I kept wondering where Isa's drive and focus came from. She'd made the decision to join the air force on her own, and she did a remarkable job. We celebrated her accomplishments that day, and it was great to have both Nic and my daughter Taryn there, too.

Taryn was so excited she couldn't help but rush up and give her big sister a hug. Taryn didn't quite get the reaction she'd hoped for, though, because Isa leaped back out of her arms. "If there's one wrinkle on my uniform, they won't let me attend the ceremony," Isa said.

I was proud of my daughters and my date that day. I could see Nicollette intentionally keeping a low profile so that Isa would feel like the star of the day. I loved that about her. She did the same thing on another memorable occasion when she joined me on a visit to Walter Reed National Military Medical Center. We went to offer our respect and best wishes to wounded troops and their families, just as *Desperate Housewives* was being raved about as a hit TV show. I worried that seeing some of the severely wounded military men and women might be too intense for Nic, but she was fantastic with them. Actually, the women patients and female family members were glad to see me, but the males couldn't take their eyes off Nicollette. I was just as much in awe of her that day. She was simply dressed but stunning, and so sweet and giving as she spoke with many of them. I kept thinking, *They really don't need me in this room.*

I was grateful for the opportunity to see Nicollette in that setting. She reached out and gave it her all that day, just as she always does. Of course, I am always grateful to perform in any way for our brave troops and their families, who sacrifice so much, especially since my daughter served in the military, too. I joined a huge group of performers and celebrities, including Nicollette, in *Voices That Care*, a music video made in 1991 by David Foster for our troops during Operation Desert Storm. Aside from doing the video itself, the greatest rewards from that were the cards and letters of thanks I received afterward from men and women serving in the military around the world. We may never reach a national consensus on when and where to deploy our troops, but I think we all learned from Vietnam that we must support those who pay the price for our every freedom. They are the bravest of the brave. They don't decide where to wage their battles, their leaders do, but they fight for their country far away from home and around the world. They risk their lives and give their all to protect our freedoms and our way of life.

Magnetic Attraction

Nicollette and I spoke often of our shared experiences with the troops. I also revealed more of myself with her than I had with anyone since my divorce. Ours was never a casual relationship. It was always intense. We seemed to know each other better than anyone knew either of us.

There has always been this magnetic force at work with us. We are two very strong personalities and from time to time our passionate relationship might have been responsible for tsunamis, global warming, and the shifting of tectonic plates. There were so many pivotal moments in each of our lives that we shared with each other. Over a span of eighteen years, we came together, broke up, loved, fought, played, inspired, and provoked each other. My attraction to Nicollette was intense. We bonded intellectually and spiritually as well as physically.

A small army of paparazzi and tabloid reporters have supported their families by covering us. We're both fiercely loyal, fierce advocates for our positions, and just plain fierce. She's wise beyond her years, of course. As the daughter of actress Sally Adams and the stepdaughter of Telly Savalas, she grew up in a very sophisticated, globe-trotting family with a beloved father figure.

Snuggling with Nicollette at night made my career successes all the sweeter. Neither one of us wanted to be anywhere but intertwined. Yet the success that helped make life so deliriously enjoyable also forced us apart far too often. In 1997, when I wrote an illustrated children's book, *The Secret of the Lost Kingdom,* I named the princess Nicole after her, and another character, Gug, who saves the day, was named for her grandfather in England.

Our career obligations were always the biggest challenge to our being able to stay together. I respected Nicollette's deep commitment to her work, just as she respected mine. I marveled at her ability to bring her characters to life. Whether on *Knots Landing* or *Desperate Housewives* or in her movie roles, her characters always seemed to stand out in every scene because she's committed to developing them fully.

As busy as she was, Nicollette was great about trying to catch time with me while I was touring, but life on the road isn't as comfortable as being home together. Living out of luggage is tough enough, but a concert tour often resembles a traveling circus. I was also torn away from her to do publicity and promotion while on the road. Still, I took great comfort in having her hand in mine when we traveled. Of course, her time was precious, too, and she could never stay with me too long because of her busy career. It was much easier for me to visit her on the set, but while touring I was seldom in Los Angeles.

During our first few years as a couple, we wanted to be together whenever possible, but I resisted living together because of my demanding lifestyle and all of the travel and long hours that came with it, as well as the logistics and endless details of running your own career, a not-so-small industry that would follow me in the form of midnight faxes and paperwork requiring my signature, or numbers and scheduling that needed my approval. Give me concierge or give me death. Nicollette had an inviting British country–style home in Los Angeles that she'd made incredibly cozy. She wanted me to stay there, and I wanted to stay with her, too, but I couldn't figure out how to do that successfully, given my demanding work. I had not lived full-time with any woman since my divorce in 1991. Because of constant touring, I had dwelled mostly in places with numbers on the doors and room service at the ready.

The fact is that living in hotels best suits my vagabond vampire existence. I'm constantly on the move, either touring or bouncing between recording studios, and I usually don't get to bed until 4 a.m., which means I sleep until 11 a.m. or so. If I'm in a full-service hotel, I can sleep knowing that I can take care of my business while the staff handles distractions and relays messages and packages. My long and late nights writing songs and recording in the studio, along with touring around the world, does not lend itself to the "Honey, I'm home" model of domestic bliss. Basically, I am the CEO of a multimillion-dollar business operated on the run.

My lifestyle is not remotely compatible with a nine-to-five routine or a home office. The closest thing to a pet that I can have is a stuffed animal, because a live one would either die of loneliness or starvation. I'm just not in one place long enough to care for a pet. Maybe I can work at having plants, or at least a cactus. Honestly, I've known only a handful of couples in my business who seemed to have an idyllic, stable, loving, best-friends sort of marriage. When I've seen the real thing, or what seemed to be the real thing, I've admired it but had some skepticism, too.

Once while observing a musician friend and his wife having a conversation at the breakfast table, I was so moved and inspired by their unspoken bonds I wrote a song about it. I was simply touched by their warm banter about their kids and the things on the day's agenda. My ears are sensitive to tones. The way they spoke to each other made me want what they had, what was so lacking in my life at that point. It was the sort of Kodak moment so rare in my mad dash of a life.

While I was staying with that couple, I began to write the song, called "Once in a Lifetime," about what a gift a true, loving, and lasting relationship must be. Diane Warren and Walter Afanasieff later helped me complete and polish the composition, which we recorded soon after. It was selected for the sound track of the 1994 movie *Only You* with Marisa Tomei and Robert Downey Jr.

My "Once in a Lifetime" recording rose to No. 15 on the Adult Contemporary charts. I was happy to have written it because I am still a romantic and always will be.

THE SECOND TIME AROUND

I didn't realize how many years and incarnations my relationship with Nicollette would encompass. Even after Nic and I had stopped seeing each other romantically, we met from time to time for lunch in Los Angeles and maybe to play some Scrabble, catch up on friends and family, and just enjoy each other's company. Our romance heated up again in 2005 and soon after I asked Nicollette to marry me and gave her an engagement ring. We were reveling in love, and it looked like our time had finally come for a lasting relationship. I was recording my *Bolton Swings Sinatra* CD, and I invited her to perform a duet of "The Second Time Around" with me. I'd always thought Nic had a beautiful voice, though she wouldn't sing if she thought I was listening most of the time. She did a great job on the song, and it reflected our reuniting, which felt very good. Nicollette expressed our passionate reunion for millions of viewers on *Jimmy Kimmel Live!* in 2008.

When Nicollette appeared on Jimmy's show, he kept prodding her to reveal what brought us back together again after a ten-year split. Finally, Nic gave it up:

"We missed the greatest sex!"

Then she hastily added that there were other mitigating factors: "We're wiser and we have incredible Scrabble games that have only gotten better over the years."

I don't know what it is about Jimmy urging beautiful women to talk about me on his show. First Nicollette and then, more recently, Paula Abdul. I love Jimmy and his show, but the talk show host dearest to my heart is Oprah.

The most astounding thing that I ever heard from Oprah came from an interview she did right when she was winding down her twenty-five-year run on network television. She said her biggest fear was that she wouldn't live up to her full potential in this lifetime. Her comment stopped me in my tracks. If Oprah hasn't fulfilled her potential, how much hope is there for the rest of us? But I understand the sense of responsibility that she touched upon. She further expressed that you can't ever give less than 100 percent because people have come from all over and they're there to see you, that's their moment, so there is an enormous sense of respect, reverence, and honor toward those people. Oprah had me on her show several times, visited my home, and went on tour with me. Once she even showed up onstage singing backup at a concert. Now, there's a shocker. I'm singing my heart out to the audience and I look over and—wait, there's a new lady in my backup group and she looks an awful lot like...*Oprah?* She has given us all so much.

Five months after Nicollette revealed our shared Scrabble addiction on Jimmy's show, we called off the engagement and split up again. We made the decision just as I was heading out on another tour, this one to South America, and I was grateful for the distraction and at least the distance.

During our second time around, I had moved in with Nicollette. She did everything possible to make her lovely home comfortable for me, short of allowing me to build a recording studio in the master bedroom and a par 3 golf course in the backyard. I felt guilty every time another truckload of FedEx boxes or faxes arrived to clutter up her spotless home, wishing that she had a concierge in the lobby to handle the constant flow of correspondence and packages that had to be dealt with.

Cohabitation seems to work just fine for most human beings, and I often dream of settling down one day in a loving relationship. There is nothing that compares to sharing that accumulated life experience and the sense of being a unified team against the world outside. I miss sharing experiences with Nicollette. Ordering one box of popcorn for two people at the movies. Complete intimacy. The freedom to be exposed emotionally and to express anything and everything because you are best friends as well as lovers. I want to feel like my late friend Bart Wolstein, who said that after a round of golf, when the other guys went into the clubhouse, his preference was "to go home and see my girl," referring to his wife, Iris.

Those loving relationships aren't always the case. I've often witnessed combative tug-of-war power struggles between couples. On the road, when I eat alone, writing or reviewing projects I'm considering or in the midst of, I notice couples around me, sometimes with admiration and other times with horror. I've observed those who barely speak to each other during the meal. They seem disconnected and uninterested in each other. I would prefer to be alone than to be in that type of relationship.

TORN IN DIFFERENT DIRECTIONS

My relationship with Nicollette, and probably every woman I've been involved with, ran up against the fact that I can't just go into the studio, sing my parts, and go home. I'm involved in every aspect of the production, including recording the guitars and adding layer upon layer of keyboards and other instruments and backing vocals. While I was living with Nic, I was so immersed in recording and producing and delivering an album on time (as I'd done for the past twenty years) that my best efforts to be there for her really weren't enough. I'd go into the studio until 3:30 a.m., drive the forty minutes back to her house, and try to quietly fall into bed without disturbing her. Then she had to leave at 7 a.m. to go to the studio for *Housewives*. She would still be working when I'd awaken, have breakfast, and head back to the studio.

The time required to make records and perform on tour was not all that kept us apart. Spending time with my daughters is also important, so when I had a break in my work schedule I would often try to spend some time with them in Connecticut. Nicollette and I were living together, but we didn't get to see nearly enough of each other. Building a relationship is challenging enough for people who actually have time to talk about their issues. We didn't.

The best part of living together with Nic was having dinners with her, staying in bed on those rare days when we both had some time off, and waking up with her. In the first year or so our connection did grow deeper, and I finally had the fulfilling awareness that I was sharing my life with someone I cared about. I am not immune to the joys of that, but just as I'd begin to settle in and embrace it, the car service would show up at the front door and it was time to hit the road again for months of touring and promoting.

Working on our relationship and dealing with the issues that came up, as they do with any couple, proved to be impossible.

Little things grew into big things because we never had a chance to talk through them. Sadly, we agreed to end our engagement.

It may be true that the final break with Nicollette was made a bit easier by the fact that it coincided with my leaving for a South American tour. The distance between us, and performing for excited new fans in beautiful venues and countries, created the temporary illusion that I was turning a new page. But there would also be many reminders of our relationship as I toured cities we had visited together. I relived walking hand in hand with Nicollette along a certain beach or street. The memories were as clear as a digital snapshot in my mind. Even when I returned home, a memory would be triggered when I passed a restaurant where we'd eaten or a movie theater where we'd once laughed and recited lines from a film. I would revisit these places, which held such vivid memories, and in a second my heart would be in pieces. The memories would bring me back to the best part of what a relationship offers, which can't be found in creating a new song or performing in front of ten thousand people. At times, all you need is for that one person to hear one word from you, and just get it. That experience was gone for me. Even after getting clear and moving on from our breakup, I would occasionally hear that line in a film that would pull at my heartstrings so immediately my eyes would well up. But then I'd smile, recognizing what my heart ultimately wants—the connected power between two people. For now, intellectually and practically, I forge on and derive my gratification creatively, and with my friends and loved ones. For now.

Anyone who knows both me and Nicollette will tell you that there was a deep well of mutual love left untapped by our breakup. She knew all of my secrets and she was my best friend, the one person who knew the entire story; the one who could deftly read every nuance, tone, and expression. Nicollette was my home base.

I most recently saw Nicollette at a mutual friend's home. She said she'd been riding her horses more, which is something she has loved to do since childhood, when she competed in equestrian events. We also talked about Oliver, her beautiful golden retriever.

When Nic first walked into the kitchen, I was talking to a friend. I wasn't sure how I would feel meeting up with her that day, but she looked great and my heart skipped a beat. It may have been just the feeling you get when seeing an old friend for the first time in a while. I've come to realize there are many layers beneath that "happy to see you" feeling.

I wished her luck in her endeavors. I wanted her to know how I was pulling for her in every way, and I think she knew I was sincere. We had a brief, friendly conversation. There will always be respect and love between us, and something incredibly special, too.

When you have been so close with someone for so long and then break apart, you can't deny all of those important powerful moments and experiences that you shared. They are still part of you. The heartbreak is that when you split up, you've lost your best friend, too. The memories remain, and when you pass restaurants or other places where you had great times, those memories stir deep emotions.

Some people don't consider their spouses their best friends, but my experience is that the person you are so intimate with becomes your best friend and you build up shared moments. I often thought that I couldn't ever imagine us not being together or spending our lives with someone else. A friend once asked me after my split with Nicollette if this time we were really done forever. Other couples actually placed bets on whether we would or wouldn't eventually ride off into the sunset together. I know that I will never replace our deep and rich experiences. We really did try to make it work again and again. The sad irony of the lyrics I continue to sing night after night is that I've been so close to what I have described a thousand times onstage.

Chapter Fourteen

Reaching Higher

I was in a car in London in early 1995 when I received a life-altering phone call that expanded my musical universe beyond anything I'd ever imagined as a boy back in Connecticut. My reps at Sony in Italy had hinted that something was up a few weeks earlier. They'd asked me to block out some time in September to come to their country for a benefit concert. To entice me, they dangled the possibility that I might get to perform with one of my heroes. Then they'd told me, rather mysteriously, that a call to confirm everything would be coming.

The caller asked: "Mr. Bolton, are you available to speak with Mr. Luciano Pavarotti?"

I asked my driver to pull over so I wouldn't lose the cell connection. This was one call that I did not want interrupted. The question of the caller was still sinking in when this excited, booming Italian-accented voice blasted from my phone.

"MICHAEL!!! We are very happy you are coming to perform

with us." (The event was to take place in Pavarotti's hometown, to benefit the children of Bosnia.)

Pavarotti was off and running. He quickly suggested two arias we might perform. I'd known about his annual concert benefit in his hometown of Modena, Italy, so I'd done a little homework, buying and listening to his greatest hits collection. Neither of the arias he named was among them. I was surprised. I had never heard of either of them, so I just asked him. "Well, how would you feel about performing 'Nessun dorma' and...'Vesti la giubba'?" I suggested timidly.

Aside from being two of the most well-known tenor arias in opera, the first was Pavarotti's signature song; its title fit my lifestyle. The English translation is "None Shall Sleep."

I thought I'd come up with some winners. But there was a disturbing lack of sound on the phone. *Had I pissed off Pavarotti?*

My heart sank. My blood pressure shot up.

Did he hang up on me?

Then came an explosive outburst from the other end of the line. "BRILLIANT! GENIUS! We will do these....What key?" asked the maestro.

"Whatever key you performed them in is fine," I said.

"EXCELLENT! I will see you in a few weeks!"

I had never simultaneously felt so excited and so out of my league. I had some work to do. Aside from listening to my mother's endless playing of Mario Lanza on our home stereo system as a boy, my operatic singing had been limited to faking it in the shower. I've always had cold sweat nightmares about standing onstage and realizing I am not prepared to perform. Flubbing an appearance with Pavarotti was unthinkable. Actually, it was thinkable, but terrifying. I tracked down every recording and video of him I could find and went to work.

I practiced for hours and hours to strengthen my voice and to expand its reach. My mother's records must have had a subliminal impact because opera had always intrigued me. Other singers and singing coaches had told me over the years that my natural range was suited to opera, but I'd never tried to perform it in public.

I was not about to join the great Pavarotti onstage and insult him by doing karaoke opera. I wanted Luciano and other serious opera fans to be surprised and pleased. Once again, maybe more than ever, I had to hit the ball out of the park. The one major challenge was removing the rocker's rasp. All of my singing career I had cultivated the natural rough edges on my singing voice, which is perfectly suited to rock, R & B, gospel, and pop, but not opera. There is no rasp in opera.

Being invited to sing with Pavarotti ranked up there with the day Joe DiMaggio asked to sit in my team's dugout for a charity softball event. Actually, the Pavarotti event was up there with singing with Ray Charles, but was even more pivotal in my future love of singing. They were all moments that I was grateful for, but after each I felt I had to up my game to a whole new level. In the weeks that followed, I continued to train my voice and work on my performance as never before.

Still, performing extremely challenging operatic arias like "Nessun dorma" demanded far more of my voice than any other style of singing. As I sold more records, the stakes grew higher. I could not live with myself if I failed to deliver my best for the fans. They'd paid for their tickets and taken time from their lives to see me. I owed it to them. So I set some boundaries and rules for myself and I became more protective of my voice and my overall health over the years.

Retraining my voice for opera was an incredible challenge, but all the work brought lasting benefits. I discovered methods for protecting and preserving my vocal cords that would help me to improve the quality of my singing in general, and to both broaden and extend my career as a performer. My opera training and vocal health were aided by David Sorin-Collyer, Seth Riggs, and Bill Schuman, all great vocal coaches. I had sung higher than even opera demanded, but I'd never had to hold a high C and vibrate it, as operatic singing demands. The difference was akin to driving a car with a 400-horsepower engine and then dropping in a 600-horsepower engine.

Operatic singing also demands a much higher level of vocal care. Young tenors burn out at a fast and furious rate because many take on entire operas that are too demanding before they've fully developed their vocal cords. The more I learned about preserving the voice, the more I realized what a miracle it was that I hadn't burned mine out with all the rock 'n' roll I had sung in smoke-filled bars.

Whenever I think about all that it takes to protect and build upon my singing career, I'm reminded of some advice that came from a great athlete, a celebrated "Iron Man" who knows a little something about long-term achievement. Former Baltimore Orioles shortstop Cal Ripken Jr. performed at the highest level in major league baseball for twenty-one seasons, was an All-Star for nineteen years, and broke Lou Gehrig's "unbreakable" fifty-six-year record for consecutive games played. Cal was still playing for the Orioles when, during the off-season, he shared with me his thoughts on sustaining a career after one of my softball game fundraisers. I was playing third base and Cal was playing shortstop; I was deeply honored to be on the field with him.

The future Baseball Hall of Fame award winner told me that instead of taking it easier in the off-season in the final years of his career, he'd work harder each year. He didn't ever put his career on cruise control because he understood that good is the enemy of great. Good is not good enough. Cal Ripken Jr. wanted to always step on the field knowing that he'd prepared himself to perform at the highest level possible. His example has inspired me to always strive to do the same.

I've always been my single toughest critic, which is both a blessing and a curse. I knew early on that I could never be the guy who steps up and gets a base hit. I'm the clean-up batter and my job is to hit it out of the park. Setting my sights and goals so high propelled me to better understand and work with my instrument, to make it greater. I studied with vocal coaches and learned techniques that integrated many different genres of music, stretching me both physically and mentally. I was trained in the classical approach to arias, studying some of the most vocally challenging, centuries-old compositions in Italian or French. Then I would delve back into the bluesy rasp and phrasing of classic R & B songs, breaking all the rules I'd just been taught.

One of the things I've done over the years is to become more vigilant about protecting my vocal cords. It helps when you have the best people in their fields looking after you, and I do: Dr. Joe Sugerman on the West Coast in Los Angeles and Dr. Gwen Korovin on the East Coast in New York. I have photographs taken of my vocal cords with a scope every eight or nine months to make sure they are in good shape. Sometimes it feels like I've simply become a life support system for my two vocal cords, but when you do eighty to ninety shows a year, technique, respect, and protection are critical.

I met the amazing young singer Adele when we both performed on a television show in 2011. She was already having trouble with her vocal cords then, so she had to cut back to just one song for that appearance. She later had surgery to repair damage from a vocal cord hemorrhage, which she described as "like having someone putting a curtain over my throat."

Fortunately, Adele's surgery appears to have been successful and her amazing voice has returned. For a singer, this kind of operation is nothing less than terrifying. I experienced this almost twenty years ago, when my doctor discovered a node low on one of my vocal cords. The unusual location of that node made its removal a particularly challenging procedure, because of the risk of creating a web at the bottom of the cords that would prevent them from ever properly functioning again. My doctor at the time, Dr. Scott Kessler, removed only three-quarters of the node as a precaution.

For a week prior to the surgery and then two weeks after, I wasn't allowed to speak or even whisper. I was writing notes to people to communicate. I didn't find out whether my voice would return for four weeks. Those four weeks felt like an eternity. This could've meant the end of my singing career. It was one of the most traumatic times in my life. It also put a lot of things into perspective.

About seven months earlier I had had surgery on my knee when I tore my ACL during a ski tournament in Lake Tahoe to benefit cystic fibrosis research. I underwent arthroscopic knee surgery in Vail with Dr. Steadman of the famed Steadman-Hawkins Clinic. What followed was about a nine-month rehab with a physiotherapist. During the process, I was left wondering whether I would ski again, play softball, or participate in any other sport, for that matter. Still, all of that was nothing in comparison to the operation on my vocal cords. This one node made everything else seem insignificant.

Team Tenor

When the September day for the Pavarotti & Friends concert arrived, I scheduled an early rehearsal run with the orchestra. Luciano surprised me by walking onstage as I sang in the outdoor venue. After I'd finished my rehearsal with the orchestra, I realized Pavarotti had been listening in the wings.

"I see you have been studying the tenor," he said, his eyes fixed on mine.

I didn't hesitate: "Actually, I have been studying *you*. I don't know what I've been doing with my voice all of these years."

Then he gave me a huge smile—similar to that of Ray Charles when I hailed him as "the master"—and Pavarotti said in a soft, kind voice, "Ah, Michael, you do not sell as many records as you have if you have been doing the wrong things with your voice." That was the beginning of our relationship.

To me, Pavarotti was the greatest tenor ever. His power, his magnificence, his tone, and, behind it all, his personality were combined in a way I'd never heard elsewhere, even as I studied, as Luciano put it, "the tenor."

I will forever hold that experience in the bank and guard it as a cherished memory. I did perform with Luciano again, on *Late Night with David Letterman* and once more when he was performing in New York City, but nothing quite compared to that first night in Modena.

Other Pavarotti "friends" who performed for the concert, which was recorded and released as an album, included Brian Eno; Michael Kamen; the Chieftains; one of my favorite performers (despite my vegetarian lifestyle), the funny and humble guy known as Meat Loaf; and Bono and the U2 guitarist David Howell Evans, known as "the Edge." Bono told me his father was a huge fan of mine. I replied, "Tell your father I'm a huge fan of his son."

We were all in awe of Pavarotti. In videos of that concert, the guest performers—me included—look like a bunch of kids bouncing up and down, beside ourselves to be onstage with the greatest tenor of our time. As excited as I was, the enormity of the opportunity was not lost upon me. I'd prepared so diligently for this once-in-a-lifetime experience, but actually being onstage, in such close proximity to the maestro, hearing his powerful voice before it even hit the mic, was surreal. I was inspired by a heightened awareness of the artist I was performing next to. The moment of exhilaration was soon replaced by urgency. I had to focus on the Italian lyrics on my music stand (making sure not to mispronounce any words and give them unintended meanings), and on the cues for my parts, not to mention the thousands of people in front of me and the millions watching throughout the world. Fortunately, the arias we performed were a vocal feast for a tenor and I was swept up by a sense of musical gratification.

At showtime, as if the event itself and singing in Italian weren't challenging enough, Diana, Princess of Wales, was sitting in the front row. In hindsight it made an incredible night even more significant. We were introduced at Pavarotti's restaurant after the show, where we all celebrated the event. The princess was radiant and gracious. Although the UK was my second biggest market, Princess Diana admitted that prior to the performance she had no clue who I was.

It was clear to me how powerful a force Diana was at that time and would continue to be. She had an undeniable charm and grace. Her seemingly endless mission to raise funds for children all over the world is what remains with me.

One of my favorite moments during the performance was the grand finale, when my turn came to step up to the microphone, following Pavarotti, and sing a verse of "Nessun dorma." He was gesturing to me to take over, very visibly supportive, smiling, and joyful, which helped ease my nerves. At the same time, everything was accelerated and elevated. The tone, power, and perfect control of his phenomenal voice was felt by all my senses, setting the bar as high as it could go for my entrance. The sensation was both inspiring and demanding. The audience was pleasantly surprised when I hit the high note. Just after that Luciano walked behind me and gave a thumbs-up. I couldn't see him, but I heard the audience reaction, and of course I've only replayed that part of the video six or seven—thousand—times.

That Opera Thing

I don't want to overstate what a thrill it was, but performing with Pavarotti was one of the most important moments of my career. After the Pavarotti experience, I dived deeper into opera. One of the great things to come from that event was that the astounding soprano Renée Fleming had watched it with her sister, Rachelle. We later became friends, and I recorded "O soave fanciulla" from *La Bohème* with her, which was quite an experience. Renée sang an octave above my high C. She is not only an incredible talent, but also a wonderful mother and one of the few high achievers I've known who has managed a well-balanced life while performing with grace and gratitude around the world.

I came to enjoy operatic singing so much that I inserted an aria or two into my concert sets just to give the audience a little something different. I don't know for certain, but I may be the only performer to have sung real opera at the Grand Ole Opry in Nashville. I've taken some heat from those who thought I should stick to R & B and pop. Among friends who thought I'd lost my marbles was Jimmy Koplik, who was the biggest concert promoter in Connecticut for many years before taking charge of Live Nation's East Coast operations. Jimmy is a mensch who always takes care of his friends, especially when they want tickets that are "impossible" to find. Jimmy also is never afraid to speak his mind. We were flying to a concert he'd booked for me in upstate New York when the subject came up.

"Michael, I know it's your choice, but I don't get the whole opera thing," Jimmy said.

I laughed. Jimmy wasn't the first to say that to me. I explained how performing with Pavarotti had inspired me to do more with my vocal training. Singing opera had strengthened my voice and improved my techniques, I said.

"Besides, my audiences really respond well when I change it up with an aria or two," I said.

Jimmy looked at me as if my horizontal needed adjusting, but it was his attitude that was adjusted after the concert. He brought a big group of friends backstage to meet me after the show. One of the guys in his group rushed up to me and, with Jimmy standing there in amazement, said, "Oh my God, Michael, that Italian thing you did, that opera or whatever it was, oh my God, I don't know how you hit those notes. That was amazing!"

I thanked the guy for his praise while chuckling at his enthusiastic response. Then I looked at Jimmy, who waved a hand at me, saying, "Okay, I got it. I got it. I got it."

So did many others, apparently. When I released a classical album entitled My *Secret Passion: The Arias*, it was No. 1 on the classical charts for six weeks.

There was an even bigger benefit to my "Italian thing," which Jimmy, as a concert promoter, would understand. When Pavarotti embraced me in front of his fans, the sales of my records in Italy continued to climb for many years afterward. Italy is one of my favorite places in the world and to this day I have a substantial fan base there, which is extremely gratifying.

VIENNA WALTZ

Sometimes when you take a risk as a singer you may not hit all the notes, but if you don't push yourself, there's the greater risk of going stale, becoming boring, or even boring yourself. My adventure in opera has brought benefits and opportunities I never would have imagined, including one of the most beautiful nights of my life—spent in the company of one of the most beautiful and intelligent women I've ever dated.

About a year after I performed with Pavarotti, I recorded "Ave Maria" with another of the world's top tenors, Placido Domingo, for my Christmas album. Placido, who had great success crossing over into the international pop music world, then invited me to Austria for a holiday concert with the Vienna Symphony Orchestra.

Now, visiting the gorgeous city of Vienna at Christmas and singing with Placido to the accompaniment of a renowned symphony would have been alluring enough, but this was also during the time I was seeing Ashley Judd, who joined me on this adventure.

Christmas in Vienna, wonderful music, a stunning concert hall, and a gorgeous woman at my side: life was good in that moment! Ashley was a very sophisticated Kentucky girl, but she had never been to Vienna, and was excited to be my guest at the Austria Center concert. Because this was a black-tie affair, I ordered up a new tux with tails from Armani, and while I was at it, I bought a dress and coat for Ashley.

Fortunately, she knew how to tie a bow tie because I didn't have a clue. She was full of surprises with her great sense of humor and zest for learning all there is to know about everything. Ashley obtained a master's degree in public administration from Harvard University's John F. Kennedy School of Government just a few years ago, and she has been a leading activist on issues ranging from animal and wildlife rights to global health issues, environmental protection, and women's rights. She has infinite curiosity and fascination with the world around us, and she is committed to making it a better, safer place.

Given her intellect and breadth of knowledge, Ashley is always direct and to the point. When I first told her I'd been studying operatic singing, she looked at me and said, "Really?"

Then she teased me. "Give me a high C."

"When the time is right!" I said.

I realized that Ashley might have picked up a few notes left around the house by Naomi and Wynonna, whom I love, by the way. She knew that to sing arias, I'd need to hit the high C notes, or at least a B. Not every operatic tenor has a high C in his range. Some can't go there, so they can sing only arias limited to a B, which is still higher than most guys can sing. I can't explain where my vocal range came from. I'm guessing it came from my mother's gene pool, given her sweet soprano. If my voice comes from farther back in my family history, there may have been a rocking cantor among my Ukrainian ancestors in Kiev.

Placido Domingo had set up some major rehearsal time to make sure we hit all the right notes for his Vienna concert, which was to be televised and recorded for an album. We flew into Vienna a couple of days early, but most of my time was spent running through the program schedule and my performances again and again.

Ashley was a trouper. She sat in the audience during those rehearsals with the full orchestra. Her presence actually became a bit of a problem. She wore this beautiful low-cut dress with spaghetti straps on her shoulders. Ashley didn't notice when the left strap drooped below her shoulder. This wasn't a serious wardrobe malfunction—nothing hidden was revealed—but she is a naturally sexy woman with lovely shoulders, and I'm afraid the entire Vienna orchestra took notice. I've never heard professional musicians miss so many notes in rehearsal.

Ashley had the same effect on me and a lot of other men. We were together in Spain that same year when I appeared on a television show to promote a record. It happened that the actor Mickey Rooney, whose incredible career has spanned nine decades, was appearing on the same show. Mickey and I were talking backstage and he mentioned that he'd just seen the new HBO movie *Norma Jean & Marilyn*, about the life of Marilyn Monroe.

"The girl in the Norma Jean role, for her younger years, was phenomenal!" Mickey said.

Ashley had walked up to join us just as Mickey offered that praise out of the blue, and I said, "Well, Mickey, here she is!"

He hadn't recognized that the actress he was so impressed with was Ashley. She blushed at his words and I was thrilled for her to have this legendary performer praise her. She deserved it, of course. She was nominated for both a Golden Globe and a Daytime Emmy Award for her performance in that movie, which received five Emmy nominations altogether. I was very grateful that Ashley also appeared in my 1997 "Best of Love" music video, bringing her beauty and grace to that production, too.

Ashley and I had some wonderful times, and I remain friends with all of the Judds. It's been great to see her thrive in her career and become an international activist for many great causes. One of the things Ashley told me that has stayed with me is that "success isn't anything without a life behind it."

She was encouraging me to find more of that elusive "balance" in my own life, something that continues to elude me.

HAIR TODAY, GONE TOMORROW

I did undergo one major change while seeing Ashley. I finally cut my hair. I took a lot of flak over the years because of my long hair. The harassment began in grade school, when everyone else had crew cuts. Then as a teen I took a lot of grief from construction workers and drunks in bars. The eighties was the Big Hair Decade, so things weren't so bad, but by the mid-1990s, the time had come for a change. In October 1997, my stylist, Gemina Aboitiz, and my assistant, Ronnie Milo, who is still with my team, suggested that I go to Hollywood's "Mane Man," Chris McMillan, whose résumé includes Brad Pitt, Tom Cruise, and legions of other stars, male and female. I figured I couldn't go wrong. You can imagine my shock when I woke up the next day, looked in the mirror, and realized I still didn't look anything like Brad Pitt or Tom Cruise! The good news was that we auctioned off my big bag of hair to raise money for charity.

Chapter Fifteen

Singing On

I was ten years old when my older brother, Orrin, slapped a single with the name Little Stevie Wonder on the label onto the turntable.

"You gotta hear this!" he said.

The song, "Fingertips," was released in 1963 after being recorded live at the Regal Theater in Chicago a year earlier. Hearing it for the first time took my understanding of a singing performance into entirely new realms. The song was written as a jazz instrumental to showcase Stevie's skill with the bongos and harmonica, but "the twelve-year-old boy genius," as he was called in the introduction on the record, shocked the world with his passionate and soaring call-and-response improvisations. Stevie also may have been inspired by the fact that his drummer on this song was fellow Motown singer Marvin Gaye.

"Fingertips" was Stevie Wonder's first hit single, and of course there would be many, many more to follow. I heard him perform recently, and it's amazing how the quality and range of his voice are still as strong as ever. His voice is superior on every level—in its range, flexibility, and power. Stevie's singing also has an ethereal, inspired soulfulness that may be beyond the reach of most mere mortals.

After Orrin introduced me to "Fingertips," I couldn't wait to hear more of Stevie's music. I spent a lot of hours over the years singing along with those records, trying to match his notes. The biggest challenge was following him as he bent and turned words while still keeping the primary melodies of his compositions accessible to any listener. That ability is one of the keys to his success, and a major component of his greatness as an artist.

Stevie is also a fantastic songwriter. He has created melodies and lyrics that have become indelibly imprinted on our minds and hearts. He played a big role in the rise of Motown as a powerful presence in the music industry. It's usually late into his songs, after the first two choruses have won us over and established "the hook," when he soars into his own musical universe. His variations on melodies are always inspired and nearly impossible to reproduce. Technically, Stevie is acknowledged to have the greatest range of any singer in the history of popular music. His top notes in full voice are well above high C.

Stevie's musical compositions are as complex as they are fascinating and entertaining to hear, an opinion shared by more than one hundred million fans around the world. I learned much about the nuances of the voice from listening to his records. More than once it has occurred to me during these sessions that if God wanted to choose a voice with which to communicate with humankind, it would be Stevie's.

From what I've heard in his recent performances, Stevie has taken very good care of his voice. He still hits those high notes. I was with this amazing and enduring talent at a Fourth of July concert in Washington, D.C., in 2006. I stood backstage listening to his set and I was transformed into a ten-year-old fan again. I remember thinking, *My God, he's singing that song in the original key forty years after the original recording.* His ability to still perform at that level was inspiring and promising for me. We spoke shortly after the concert, and I asked him what techniques he was using to preserve his amazing vocal range. I was pleased to hear he's still using the techniques of Seth Riggs, the sought-after vocal coach for more than 120 Grammy winners. I work with Seth, too.

I first met Stevie in 1995 at the Thirty-Fifth Motown Anniversary concert. I was performing a medley of Marvin Gaye and Tammi Terrell duets with Patti LaBelle, another singer with an incredible voice. I saw Stevie from afar backstage and begged for an introduction. A few seconds later, I was standing in front of him. Stevie knocked me out by launching into "How Am I Supposed to Live Without You."

After all those years of singing along with his records, to hear his unique voice wrapped around one of my own songs was thrilling. He made it his own, just as he does with everything he sings. Still, Stevie's greatest gift is the joy he expresses so eloquently when he sings. Watching and listening to this unique and beloved performer always lifts my spirit. Every time he sings, Stevie bares his soul and shares his joy with his audience.

Joy in Song

A vocal coach once told me that a true singer is happiest when singing. If you are born with the gift of music, you express yourself most completely through the expression of that gift. I know for a fact that it's true. My singing releases the accumulation of my life experiences; the joy and the sorrow, the hope and the despair; all of it flows from me through song. In other areas I guard my heart, but when singing I feel no inhibition. Instead, I feel compelled to give full voice to all that is inside me.

Singing allows me to express my full range of feelings.

Most of the time you are performing from a place of great exhilaration. You're doing something you've always wanted to do. But sometimes you must perform even though your heart is in pieces. The iconic aria "Vesti la giubba," which Pavarotti made very famous, is about the fact that the show must go on no matter how much pain you're in. That's something that applies to all professionals, in all arenas—the show must go on. Put on your makeup: people have paid and you must entertain them. If I close the door on my feelings, I still may hit the right notes, but I won't bring anything compelling to the music that connects me to my audience and resonates with them. They demand that connection and they deserve it. As Khalil Gibran says, "The self same well from which your laughter rises was oftentimes filled with your tears." We all drink from the same well, and we all experience sorrow and joy. I sing to express what lies within me in hopes that others who feel the same will relate to my experiences and to me, a fellow traveler.

My passion for singing energizes me in ways that seem miraculous at times. I recently flew with our touring group to Singapore for a two-hour performance. The flight time was about seventeen hours. We were starved by the time we reached our hotel, so twelve of us went to dinner. But after we were served, the jet lag and our exhaustion kicked in. I could barely lift the food to my mouth. Even the youngest members of our troupe were falling asleep in their soup and laying their heads on the table between servings. (Ah, the glamorous lives we lead!)

Then a strange thing happened. The next day we took the stage for rehearsal. Most of us were still a little jet-lagged and weary, but as soon as the music started you never would have known that we were the same bedraggled souls who crawled off the airplane. My fellow travelers and performers weren't just being "professionals." Music lives in them. No burden of exhaustion, fear, sorrow, or despair can erase that magical, compelling force once they hear a few bars of a song.

Recently, I was walking down the street in Frankfurt, and was listening to a young man play a piano beautifully, right there on the street, for money. Oftentimes as I travel, I stop to listen to street musicians, and I think back on my own days struggling to make ends meet and knowing only one way to do it. Even amid the hardship, the love of music was present. Today, when I cross the bridges in Prague where people play guitar with their cases open on the ground, I remember my early days on the Berkeley campus playing guitar and singing in hopes of collecting enough dollars to buy dinner for the band. It's hard to believe that over forty years ago, that was me.

At fourteen, when I was hitchhiking across the country to California, burrowing between bushes at night to stop the cold wind from killing me, I wasn't exactly thinking, I better get home safe soon because in about twenty-five years I'll be receiving calls from the president, Pavarotti, Bob Dylan, and Rodney Dangerfield! Or that Mayor Bloomberg's office will invite me to the inauguration of New York's first Family Justice Center, or that Ethel Kennedy will ask me to play golf on her compound. Back on Route 66, all I knew was that it was freakin' cold and I was hungry and searching for something I wouldn't find for many years.

Talent Development

You need to have that deep-seated, DNA-encoded love of music to build and sustain a life in the music industry. It's almost a supernatural force that drives you to keep performing despite rejections, lean times, and criticism. Because of my experiences in the enter-tainment business, my friends and fans often ask my views on the current crop of television talent shows, such as *American Idol, The Voice,* and *The X Factor.* These days, my television viewing time is very limited, but I started watching *Idol* for a while because two of my buddies from way back, Paula Abdul and my former bass gui-tarist Randy Jackson, shared judging duties.

These shows are good entertainment, as their high ratings attest. I have had concerns about whether they are the best way to begin a career in music, but it's undeniable that some amazing performers might not be discovered except through this process. As my journey illustrates, though, most aspiring performers need more than one quick television season to fully develop and build an identity as an artist. If I ever served as mentor on any of these shows, I would have an off-camera conversation with the contes-tants about career development.

It is true that there are few better places to showcase your tal-ents than those prime-time competitions. Wondrous things can happen for an artist when he or she is allowed to perform for sev-eral weeks in front of thirty million viewers. Some of them step up in amazing ways. Every season there are radiant moments when the gift of music visibly flows through the bodies and souls of truly talented contestants, allowing them to rise to the occasion despite stage fright, stress, and even serious medical issues. I love to see performers totally possessed by musical forces that animate, ener-gize, and elevate them. I know the feeling, and I live for it.

Carrie Underwood, Jennifer Hudson, and Kelly Clarkson are among those with great gifts. They have clear artistic identities and strong teams. I have no doubt they will continue to work hard, find innovative ways to promote their music, and enjoy long careers.

I do worry, though, about those other contestants who lack support and guidance and seem to fall off the face of the earth into the waiting-for-a-break purgatory I occupied for eighteen years. I'm sure some who come up short in the competition will eventually find their audiences if given more time to develop their gifts under less pressure. Overnight success is overrated, as well as all but impossible to achieve, and even harder to build upon and sustain in the long term.

There are no shortcuts for fully developing your natural gifts and preparing for a long career. My first vocal coach let me know that after my first few lessons. The brilliant David Sorin-Collyer, a former Broadway performer turned voice coach to the stars, declared that while I showed promise, he could not continue to teach me if I came to him only once a week. I wanted to be there more often, but at that point I could not afford to pay him more than once weekly. I believed I couldn't get where I wanted to go as a performer without proper tools. I felt as though I needed greater range and power to stand out when I took the microphone.

I left David's Manhattan studio that day with my head down, feeling like my chances of becoming a truly great singer were out of reach. I was convinced that David held the key to developing my voice skills fully. I felt very small walking among the skyscrapers outside his office that day. Years later, my friend Valerie Simpson told me her husband, Nick Ashford, who'd once been homeless, was feeling much the same way as he walked through Manhattan's concrete canyons of stacked skyscrapers one day in 1966. He countered his despair by throwing a challenge at New York City in the form of a song he and Valerie wrote. It was called "Ain't No Mountain High Enough."

Valerie told me her husband was initially inspired to write it as a man determined to capture his dream of success as a singer and songwriter despite the intimidating world around him. That wonderful song captures the essence of what it takes to keep believing in your dreams—and Ashford & Simpson became one of the most celebrated songwriting teams in R & B history and in the history of pop music.

In my case, I vowed that one day I'd return to David's classes because I didn't want to settle for being simply a good singer. I wanted to be a great singer. (Again, as David Foster always reminds me, "good is the enemy of great.")

Ten years after David Sorin-Collyer challenged my dedication to that dream, his studio wall was covered with photographs of us together. He had become my proud teacher. As we worked then toward my goal of singing opera, David helped me build my vocal strength and range to the point that one day he said, to my lasting joy, "That is some voice you've got, Michael!" By that time I'd been singing "Vesti la giubba" in Italian.

BUILDING A CAREER

I have had far more second chances than the music business usually allows. As a result, I tend to root for the underdog. My advice to those who don't make the final cut on *Idol*, *The Voice*, *The X Factor*, or *America's Got Talent* is to follow your passion as long as it truly remains your passion and not just your fixation or an obligation. The road may be even harder than the one I encountered. Besides having a lot of talent, artists need to be disciplined and focused and they'll need to be surrounded by the right team of champions to guide them through obstacles and to recognize and create opportunities.

The refining of raw talent into professional artistry was once an integral part of every record company's business plan. Most spent a great deal of time and money coaching artists, preparing them psychologically and emotionally, and sending them out on tours to hone their talents and build their audiences. In the process, the performers learned how to handle all areas of the music industry, from the constant travel and long hours to dealing with promoters, publicists, radio station programmers, deejays, reporters, critics, fans, managers, lawyers, and accountants.

I'm grateful that my longtime manager, Louis Levin, schooled me in all of this. We eventually agreed to part ways but we had an incredible run together. He will always be like a brother to me. We shared every aspect of my work, which is my life—and Louis almost gave his life to the cause after getting hit by a line drive in one of our charity softball games.

Louis was my guide into the business side of the music business. Building an artist's brand and promoting records is like strategizing for a military operation. In my own campaigns, the record company executives had chalkboards set up in their offices plotting which stations or territories we were going after next. I came to understand that we were all part of the same team. I was the artist, but if I wanted to continue to thrive and sustain a career over many years, I had to help the promotion and marketing people build my brand nationally and internationally.

STAYING POWER

All the groundwork I laid early in my career has allowed me to travel the world, keeping and expanding my fan base. One of the great rewards of my concert tours is looking into the audience and seeing so many diverse people singing my music back to me. Part of an artist's staying power lies in reminding people of the hits.

I've been happy to discover that in countries ranging from Indonesia and the UK to right here at home, new artists who have grown up with my music are performing my songs on TV shows such as *The X Factor*, *The Voice*, or *American Idol*. I love singing duets with artists around the world and am always grateful and humbled to experience the way my songs have been shared through cultures and generations. If in real estate it's about location, location, location, a career in music is about songs, songs, songs.

Consider the all-important signature hit song, such as Aretha Franklin's "Respect," Celine Dion's "The Power of Love," or the Rolling Stones' "Satisfaction." Building a long career as an artist, however, requires a continued commitment to finding or writing great songs that will keep engaging fans while attracting new ones. What Clive Davis and Whitney Houston achieved together is a great example of this, from "I Wanna Dance with Somebody" to one of the biggest records of all time, the Dolly Parton composition "I Will Always Love You."

Motown founder Berry Gordy certainly knew hit songs and created a hit-making machine in Detroit. I recently attended the commemorative unveiling of Motown's original Steinway piano, which Paul McCartney generously offered to refurbish. Gordy recalled the year 1963, when the hot new group known as the Beatles asked to record three Motown songs for their second studio album, which would be their first release in North America. For Gordy, this would be Motown's first real introduction to the rest of the world. Gordy and McCartney, two of the greatest, most influential sources of music on our planet, both had one shared realization: songs, songs, songs. It's a testament that Lennon and McCartney, one of the most prolific and celebrated songwriting teams in the history of music, wanted to tap the great well of R & B music coming out of Hitsville USA. If there are any two people who can speak about what makes a successful, enduring career, McCartney and Gordy can. They'll still remind you that it always comes back to the right songs.

After my long climb and many years as an artist, today I serve as the president of my own multifaceted corporation, which runs on a 24/7 basis—both a blessing and a curse, but mostly a blessing.

This requires constant vigilance for incoming opportunities from around the world—there's always someone awake somewhere! From Singapore and Sydney to Moscow and Dubai, London and Germany, South Africa and Brazil, Canada and New York, and Beijing and Shanghai, my corporation is multinational, multilingual, and multifarious. My calendar is a jigsaw puzzle with not a minute to spare and fitting in all of my scheduled activities is no small feat. Then there are the unscheduled but all-important tasks of reaching out for new opportunities, alliances, and allies across many platforms. My hunger has not waned since my first successful album, and there are still many "firsts" on my wish list, including starring in my own television show, creating feature films and musicals, and writing this, my first memoir.

As much as I struggled in my climb, there were lessons learned that have helped me sustain my career over the years. I worked and I fought for nearly two decades to make what I believe is truly a great body of music. And I've never stopped working to achieve that goal. These days, I seek out strategic allies around the world, creative thinkers who understand who I am as an artist and how to stay true to my core audience while expanding my fan base.

I'm always so moved when people tell me that my music has become a sound track to their lives. Yet after all these years, I feel I'm just beginning. I'm motivated and excited to reach new audiences. People in every corner of the world still want to see live performance and still value the experience of live music.

My drive for success really emanates not from a desire for wealth or fame but from an inherent need to create and make music on my own terms. Maybe I'm not so different now than I was hitchhiking back on Route 66—fiercely independent and completely focused on fulfilling my full potential.

Recently, there's been a complete shift in the way the music industry operates. Album sales are diminishing as we move into a

digital world. Fortunately, there are some very exciting new platforms as well, like YouTube. I was surprised and thrilled when the
Captain Jack Sparrow video became the third most watched of
2011. We just may be at 100 million views by the time you read
this!

The amazing extended life of that video serves to remind
me that as long as you stay in the game, anything can happen.
Andy, Kiv, and Jorm shot for the moon and spared no expense
on the video. Of the one hundred video shorts they've done, ours
will likely be near the top in views. Now fans at my own concerts
chant for "Jack Sparrow! Jack Sparrow! Jack Sparrow!" It's the gift
that keeps on giving. I continue to hear from professional athletes, elementary school kids, business executives, and people in
show business who tell me that it's their favorite video and they
just can't get the song out of their heads. A noted author told me
it's her "happy place" to go when she needs a lift. The video has
been viewed heavily in regions from Russia and Dubai to Australia and the UK. I've just returned from Shanghai, China, to find
that even there (where YouTube is very difficult to access) people
in their teens and twenties are huge fans of the video. It's so great
that this project with the Lonely Island geniuses has been enjoyed
by so many millions of people.

That experience tapped into something I've always enjoyed—
bringing a cast of funny characters to life (which those who know
me will confirm is something I do on a daily basis). I've previously
had cameos in several films and scripted TV shows, and I felt right
at home while recently appearing as a guest on the season premiere
of the hit network television comedy *Two and a Half Men*. It helped
that director Jamie Widdoes understood how to make a newcomer
comfortable. The entire cast and crew made it a great experience
and got me thinking about how much fun it is to show up to work
surrounded by people like Ashton Kutcher, Jon Cryer, Sophie

Winkleman, Holland Taylor, and Conchata Ferrell, who are all talented and funny and an absolute pleasure to be around. All that, while the genius of Chuck Lorre and his fellow creators raised the bar for the show's team of brilliant writers, who gave us the most hysterical material, which seemed to get funnier by the minute.

GIVING BACK

It's when you're at your peak that you look back at where you came from and gratitude compels you to give back. After my first hit records came out in 1987, invitations began to pour in from organizations and individuals I'd never heard from in the frozen-broccoli days. Other performers and nonprofit groups suddenly had me on their lists as someone who might attend fund-raising events. At first I couldn't understand why I was being invited to perform—or sometimes simply to attend.

After attending a few, I got it. Without even being aware of it, I'd been thrown into the Celebrity Pool. I'd never before been aware of this part of the entertainment universe. I sang at local bar benefits in New Haven, but it was not quite the same. Champagne, not shots and beer, was served at these events—major black-tie, high-society benefits conducted by or on behalf of leading philanthropic, mentoring, and service organizations, including the American Cancer Society, the American Heart Association, the Cystic Fibrosis Foundation, the Nancy Davis Foundation for Multiple Sclerosis, the Juvenile Diabetes Research Foundation, the Center for Child Protection, and many, many others.

There was something special about performing at these events and knowing that they would benefit more than your own bottom line or those of concert promoters, booking agents, and T-shirt vendors. In my first few charity events, I was amazed at the array of talent assembled to entertain. I'd find myself backstage with Ray

Charles, Whitney Houston, and other stars who were there generously donating their time and talent.

One year, attending the Carousel of Hope fund-raiser to benefit the Barbara Davis Center for Childhood Diabetes, I found myself in a very surreal setting. Nicollette and I were seated at a table, staring at Nancy and Ronald Reagan to the left of President and Betty Ford, and to their left was Roger Moore with his wife, and Sean Connery with his wife. Two 007s, two presidents, and two first ladies. I spoke of that night recently with Barbara Davis, a beloved friend who hosted the event with her remarkable late husband, Marvin. I attended several of the Davises' charitable events, and was introduced to many incredible people there.

After singing at several such events, I was inspired to create my own nonprofit foundation for causes that resonate with me. I was brought full circle to a sense of responsibility, a sense that somehow I needed to make a difference. My original plan was to find families who were struggling in the state of Connecticut. In the process I discovered that many women and children who had suffered from domestic abuse and violence were in shelters throughout the state. I wanted to leverage my success to help them in meaningful ways.

There was a substantial learning curve to running a charitable foundation. It's difficult to track even my own business affairs when my work keeps me on the road and in the studio. Fortunately, I found a great guide into that world, Jackie Smaga, a professional in the nonprofit field, who helped launch Michael Bolton Charities (MBC) in 1992.

I met Jackie when she was helping to run a cancer-cure fund-raiser for my family friend Joel Brander, a great guy with a wonderful spirit and a wonderful family. He had been diagnosed with leukemia and, sadly, later passed away, fighting the good fight. Joel was a mensch and beloved by everyone who knew him. I performed at several events for Joel and the New York Medical College. In the process of doing these benefits, I saw firsthand that the funds raised would go straight to work in the hands of dedicated doctors and scientists who reported amazing breakthroughs in treating various types of cancer. This reinforced my feeling that we have to arm the right people with the resources needed. The list of worthy causes and issues is almost endless.

Shortly thereafter, I talked with Jackie about my interest in starting my own charitable foundation. Michael Bolton Charities would soon benefit organizations that offer assistance to abused women and children. She agreed to help me with the launch, and has been the director of the organization ever since. Assisted by Andrena Gagliardi, the dedicated woman we all know and love, they have committed such a big part of their lives to improve the quality of life for a lot of people they'll never meet. It would be impossible to do any of the work MBC does without Jackie, Andrena, the generous volunteers, and our resourceful and committed board members. MBC would be nothing without them.

Early on, we approached the Yale Child Study Center for guidance and information. Our research into families living in shelters revealed that poverty and violence were the leading factors that led to their losing or fleeing their homes. We partnered with the Yale center to provide trained family advocates to women and children at risk. They work with the mothers, helping them transition into homes or apartments with their children, escaping high-risk situations. The goal is to give them the tools and support they need so they never return to any shelter, or to an abusive relationship.

Our critical mission is to diminish and help end the cycle of abuse and violence against women and children, and to educate and positively affect young males because, as my father told me, true men are not violent toward women. Some men—and we are speaking about many husbands who are living in the Stone Age—believe for whatever reason that the way they treat the women in their own homes is a "private" or "family" matter. The Violence Against Women Act and human rights laws in this country disagree. I was a newcomer to this field, so Jackie and I consulted with experienced professionals and their organizations. We tapped their expertise, asking what we could do to help and what needs we could serve. One of our focuses has been to work with the National Coalition Against Domestic Violence to advocate for protective legislation in the U.S. Congress. I was proud to join forces with Rita Smith, the former executive director of NCADV and one of the most inspiring and enduringly committed people I have ever met, and with my friend Meredith Wagner, the former executive vice president of communications, public affairs, and advocacy at Lifetime Television, as we met with members of both houses in Washington, D.C.

We found willing champions for our efforts in Bill and Hillary Clinton. Under President Clinton's administration, the Violence Against Women Act was written into law. This law educates and guides law enforcement officials, prosecutors, and judges on the legal rights of women and children when confronted with abuse. It also provides funds for emergency hotlines that can help save lives and reduce the stress and trauma for women and children in need of assistance. The VAWA was co-authored in a bipartisan effort by Senator Orrin Hatch and then Senator Joe Biden, who shared the conviction that our laws need to be clear on protective measures for women in abusive situations. This is a perfect example of our democracy at work and at its best. Members of Congress from both sides of the aisle found common ground and created legislation that truly benefits those who have no power or clout. Many say that this vital legislation was one of the highest achievements of these two political leaders, since this law will help break the cycle of violence that has damaged and even ended the lives of innocent women and children. That's when I witnessed how powerful our system of government can be, when Democrats and Republicans pull one another toward a common goal and away from gridlock, as the Founding Fathers intended.

We continue to meet with members of Congress each year to ensure funding for the provisions in this multibillion-dollar bill. Women are well aware of the need for these protections and services, so I have focused on taking the message to men of all ages that we cannot accept violence toward our wives, our girlfriends, our mothers, our sisters, or our daughters. I am most excited about the creation of Family Justice Centers nationwide, based on an innovative approach to family violence developed by Mayor Michael Bloomberg of New York City with the help of dedicated people like Yolanda Jimenez (another one of my heroes), commissioner of the city's Office to Combat Domestic Violence. Mayor Bloomberg gave a moving speech after we all had just heard the heart-wrenching story of a single mother who had nowhere to go with her young son while living in constant danger at the hands of a violent offender. There was not a shelter in place for them. Mayor Bloomberg faced the woman and said, "Shame on us." Shame on us for not providing an alternative to a mother's day-to-day hell of trying to protect herself and her child. Mayor Bloomberg is so clearly a champion and continues his commitment to more Family Justice Centers. He and Commissioner Jimenez have set us on our present course. These are free, one-stop shelters and centers for women and children where they are provided vital services, including security, medical treatment, child care, and legal assistance in the form of an in-house prosecutor's office.

My organization is working on opening the first Family Justice Center in my home state of Connecticut, and our plan is to be advocates for replication of these much-needed centers around the country. I'm grateful that public officials are recognizing that these centers can save lives, spare victims, and help women and children stay out of the welfare and foster-care systems. The Reverend Martin Luther King Jr. said that laws don't move the heart, but they restrain the heartless. Abusers are often victims of abuse themselves, so these Family Justice Centers can help break that cycle. This is another major goal of MBC.

Since 1993, we've disbursed more than $10 million to organizations across the country, including the National Domestic Violence Hotline, Prevent Child Abuse America, MENTOR: The National Mentoring Partnership, the New York City Family Justice Center, Yale Child Study Center, the Domestic Violence Crisis Center, Mount Sinai Sexual Assault Victims Intervention Program, and the Children's Advocacy Center.

In order to heighten awareness even more, I decided to executive-produce a documentary for Lifetime, *Terror at Home*, addressing domestic violence in America. The song "Tears of the Angels," which I wrote for the film, was nominated for an Emmy.

A New Game

At first, we raised money for MBC with celebrity softball tournaments, but fourteen years ago, I took up a new game and eventually it became my favorite way to raise money for our mission to help women and children at risk. After four decades of playing baseball, softball, tennis, and almost any sport but golf, I finally gave in about fifteen years ago and joined my friends lawyer Mickey Sherman and director Barry Levinson for a round of that game while on vacation in Maui.

I'd never understood the appeal of golf before but on that occasion, I "got it," just as concert promoter Jimmy Koplik finally got "that Italian thing," otherwise known as opera, after one of my performances. I discovered that golf was very good therapy for me. I got into the Zen aspects of the game, which call for letting go of the inevitable bad shots or bad moments, so that they don't compound and affect the rest of your game or spoil the serenity of a few hours spent on a beautiful course with friends. Golf is about focusing on the moment, clearing negative thoughts from your mind, blocking out distractions, and enjoying the game, playing it one shot at a time.

I've tried to apply that same approach to other areas of my life so that bad phone calls or other unpleasant moments don't turn my whole day into a string of bogeys. Like most who play this sport, I'm not always as "Zen" as I'd like to be on the golf course or in life. I've been known to utter an occasional series of four-letter words on the course. Anyone who plays golf knows the joke that asks, "Why do they call it golf?" The answer is, "Because all the other four-letter words were taken." Once, a caddie from Scotland, where the game was created, explained to me that whoever created that joke didn't understand that golf was a far nastier four-letter word than all the others. But still, golf tournaments proved easier on our bodies than softball tournaments, and a better venue for both entertainment and fund-raising because so many more men *and* women enjoy playing that sport.

One of the perks of playing in celebrity tournaments was that I got to play a round with Arnold Palmer and the South African Man in Black, Gary Player, who gave me one of my first actual golf lessons. When word got out that I'd joined the club of celebrity golfers, I soon found myself invited to charity fund-raising golf tournaments, which quickly replaced celebrity softball games on my yearly schedule. These events have provided me with many hours of fun and much-needed time away from the recording studio and off the concert trail. I've enjoyed meeting the professional players, whose skill and focus often seem superhuman to me, and the other celebrities and guests in the Pro-Am tournaments. I've met quite a few people who are not exactly what I thought they'd be. It's also true that I've rarely laughed as hard as I have at these events.

Even if I'm not playing up to par, it's hard to have a bad day on the golf course with playing partners like one of my favorite actors, Joe Pesci. Although Joe is an Oscar-winning dramatic actor, he is also relentlessly funny out on the course.

Another of my favorite golf partners in celebrity events is the great director and actor Clint Eastwood. He and his beautiful wife, Dina, have been generous in supporting my golf tournament fund-raiser, which benefits my charitable foundation. In 2012, Clint offered up for bidders several tickets and VIP passes to his movie *J. Edgar*, which brought in some serious money for our charities.

I've played rounds of golf with Kevin Costner, Kevin James, Samuel L. Jackson, Huey Lewis, Clay Walker, and Barry Levinson, but the first celebrity I was ever paired with in a charity tournament was the infamous shock-rocker and Rock and Roll Hall of Famer Alice Cooper, whose legendary live shows combine snakes, killing machines, illusions, and horror into genre-bending performances. They say you really get to know a person if you play eighteen holes of golf together. I'd never met Alice, but that day on the golf course in my first Bob Hope Classic, I got to know a side of him that was more like Fred MacMurray, the gentle and lovable actor from one of my favorite childhood shows, *My Three Sons*. *Rolling Stone* has called Alice "the most beloved heavy metal entertainer." I can honestly say that he was one of the most courteous, soft-spoken, positive-thinking, and supportive individuals I've ever played golf with—and everyone I know who has played with him says the same thing. You will never hear a four-letter word come out of his mouth. He always has something nice to say about your swing or follow-through, some type of positive reinforcement.

Alice Cooper is also a great golfer, by the way. I believe his handicap is four or five, and he's a great putter. On the golf course, he is one of the mellowest guys I've ever played with. He never gets irritated or bent out of shape if he hits a bad shot. At one point, I hit a really bad shot, but since he had been so calm I didn't say what I was thinking. I did admit to him that I was thinking of a four-letter word, and his response was, "I thought you finished your swing very well on that."

"Don't you ever have anything negative to say?" I asked.

Alice gave some serious thought to that and replied, "Not really, no."

Golf courses and their beautiful clubhouses also provide a better setting for fund-raisers than the typical softball diamond. So I began hosting my own golf and concert charity events. In the last few years we have worked in conjunction with the Travelers Championship golf event to stage Michael Bolton & Friends benefit concerts in Hartford. We've also been putting on a Celebrity Golf Classic with several other corporate sponsors at the Ojai Valley Inn and Spa in Ojai, California. Our concerts have featured Shania Twain, Michael McDonald, Kenny G, Richard Marx, Dave Mason, Orianthi, Delta Goodrem, Wynonna Judd, Davy Jones, Bill Champlin, Paul Williams, and other great artists. I owe them all my gratitude, and we are also grateful for the generous support we've received over the years from my close friends Jâlé and Warren Trepp, Tani and Bill Austin, Terice and David Clark, Cindy and R. A. Raymond, Lisa and the late Patrick Swayze, and Michael Intoccia. My friends John O'Hurley, Tom Gross, and Jack Williams have also helped emcee, driving our auction prices upward.

THE BIGGER PICTURE

For me, the theme of the climb or struggle was not just about the disappointment of a record company going out of business or a record failing to launch. At one point, I was working against a constant backdrop of angst and fear that my family might have to confront the unbearable face of homelessness. The terrifying specter of an eviction notice was looming. Our landlord was a nice guy, but all my bouncing rent checks were causing him stress and fees he couldn't handle. I'll never forget the apologetic look on his face one day when he said he just couldn't support us anymore and we would have to leave,

But breaking down wasn't going to save my family or give us a home. Giving up was never an option for me. As it's been said, as long as there's a why you will always find the how. My family was my "why."

Although my career path looked uncertain, I knew no other way. So I put my head down and worked harder, focusing on what I could do that would make my songs and singing better than what I had done before. I believe this determination and discipline helped lead me to success. In the writing and reading of my own story, I've found that it's as hard to describe this tenacity and commitment as it is to describe how difficult and sometimes paralyzing the poverty was to me.

I recently heard that each year more than three million Americans experience homelessness, and more than fifty million Americans couldn't afford to buy food last year. That is where America is right now, and the enormity of that fills my heart with grief. How is that possible in this country?

After attending many lavish fund-raising events, built around celebrities in the worlds of music, film, television, or sports, I decided to apply my own celebrity toward a charitable cause. The original intention of my foundation was to help struggling families in the state of Connecticut, because that was something I could so closely relate to.

We discovered many women and families living in shelters

whose homelessness was rooted in domestic violence. We dedicated the foundation's mission to raising awareness and support around that plague. But today, twenty years down the road, we are coming back to the priority of writing checks to food banks and looking at ways to help families facing eviction notices.

Bruce Springsteen's recent anthem "We Take Care of Our Own" reminds me that leaders taking the oath of office to "support and defend the Constitution of the United States against all enemies, foreign and domestic" need to recognize what Gandhi was talking about when he said, "Poverty is the worst form of violence." We never thought 9/11 could happen. We had thought of and prepared for everything imaginable. Then the unimaginable happened. But the unimaginable is also happening to families all over this country who are struck by the misery and suffering of homelessness and hunger. Poverty is a form of domestic terror. In my opinion, this would be the right time to amend the oath of office that our presidents and other elected leaders take to include protecting all Americans from the banking system and special interests, which many of us believe contributed to putting our economy in the condition it's in today.

I see this often as I travel the country, and it's so painful to observe. I've heard of family businesses that have endured for generations shutting their doors and of hardworking couples who've lost their homes.

In hard economic times, it's always those with the least who are hurt the most.

It's tragically poignant that the inscription on the Statue of Liberty no longer applies only to the immigrants it was intended for but to tens of millions of Americans right here at home. The statue and the words inscribed were meant as a beacon to the whole world. It doesn't say, "Bring us your strong, your ambitious, your rich, your powerful"; it says:

Give me your tired, your poor,
Your huddled masses yearning to breathe free,
The wretched refuse of your teeming shore.
Send these, the homeless, tempest-tost to me,
I lift my lamp beside the golden door!

The American Dream once taught us to believe in our right to a decent life, to provide for our families, to have health care, and to send our kids to school. I am hopeful that dream can be revived and made a reality again. The collaborative and committed efforts of a community—the kind of efforts we're witnessing in Detroit—can become a model for the rest of the nation.

Detroit has been one of the areas hardest hit by the recession, but committed business leaders with deep roots there, particularly Dan Gilbert and his revitalization team, led by Bruce Schwartz and Dan Mullen, are fighting to bring the city back, and, in some small ways, I intend to make a contribution to their cause. While completing my latest record in 2012, I visited the Motown Museum and was struck by the great contributions that Detroit has made to both our culture and our economy over the generations. This city deserves our support now. Detroit celebrated racial diversity and multiculturalism before most people had ever considered those concepts or their implications for society. Groundbreaking black artists and pioneering African American entrepreneurs who would stir and inspire the world began their careers in Detroit, where the auto industry helped create and equip the American middle class, the backbone of our country.

My father was a proud member of the middle class. He believed in the American Dream and he taught me to believe in it as well. He believed that he could work hard, take care of his family, and achieve his dreams of building a prosperous, safe, and secure life for us all. Before the rumblings of divorce disrupted our family and our upwardly mobile lifestyle, we very much lived that dream. I was about six years old when I took a mental snapshot that has always stayed with me. I was watching my dad wash his Ford after he arrived home from work. I remember feeling very secure in that moment and protected in my environment.

We never lived in a mansion by any means, but in my early childhood we did move up to bigger homes as my father moved up the ladder in his career. My belief system, handed down from my father, was that if I worked hard and kept striving, I would be able to thrive one day, thanks to a nation that encouraged and supported its people and their freedoms. By their example—in the friends they had, the way they treated everyone around them— my parents taught me that all men and women, regardless of their race, religion, or sexual orientation, shared those rights and freedoms.

The enduring commitment to the protection of human rights and the promises of freedom makes the United States the greatest nation in the world. That does not mean ours is a perfect country, but I believe historically we are always striving to reach the highest standards and ideals in the world. In difficult economic times, those who can least afford hardship are often saddled with the heaviest burdens. In these times, we have to step up and stand together to support one another in whatever way possible, just as we have done during other national tragedies.

STANDING TOGETHER

I was staying at the Four Seasons Hotel in Dallas in the fall of 2001 when I received a morning cell phone call from Nicollette. I was surprised she was calling because we weren't seeing each other at the time.

"Michael, where are you?"

I told her I was in Dallas.

"Are you watching the news?" she said.

The concern in her voice alarmed me, so I turned on the television in my hotel room. The terrifying, horrific image on the screen was one that has become indelible in the minds of all Americans and people around the world. Smoke was pouring from the twin towers of the World Trade Center as a result of the terrorist attacks.

I told Nic I had to call home and make sure my girls were safe. I was particularly concerned about Holly, who was driving into New York City from Connecticut to attend classes at Fordham University. I had to know that she was safe. Holly answered her home phone and told me she hadn't planned on going in that day. Her sisters, Isa and Taryn, were safe at home, too. I made a few more calls checking on friends, all of whom were safe but in shock, like all of us that day.

I had assumed that my symphony concert set for that night at the Bass Performance Hall in Fort Worth would be canceled, but my tour manager said, to my astonishment, that the show was still on. I was at first put off by that, and stunned that people were still interested in attending, but he changed my frame of reference.

He said people had been calling the venue all day with the declaration that they would not concede any further victories to terrorists. I saw the wisdom and admired the proud defiance in that stance. Still, there was a heaviness in the air as I stood backstage that night. I couldn't just walk out and begin singing, as I did in other performances. The world had changed that day and I had to acknowledge that somehow. I also had to honor those who had died and those who had acted so courageously.

The lights came down and I walked out, still uncertain of what to say. I knew it had to be direct. I thanked the audience and the orchestra for being there despite the tragedies of the day. I noted that Americans put aside their differences on such occasions and pull together. Really, I was thinking out loud when I added, "Looking out into this audience, I don't see Democrats or Republicans, I just see Americans."

That statement prompted a roar of cheers that at least temporarily lifted the battered spirits of everyone in that concert hall. Tragedy always tests our spirit. Often, it requires a herculean effort to recover and rebuild from such traumatic events. Yet I am forever amazed by the power of the human spirit to rise up in the face of adversity. The heroism of first responders—especially the fire, rescue, and law enforcement personnel—will inspire us always. But the families of those who lost their lives will bear the heaviest burden.

Evil descended on us that day, but evil did not win. I couldn't wait to return to New York City after the cowardly attack. I wanted to make my own statement about my feelings for the place where my talents were nourished and my dreams were formed. With New York City as the center of my world, the bar was set at the highest level and I am grateful for that. I made it a point to thank police officers I saw that day, and I know they appreciated it.

Long before 9/11, I had developed an appreciation for law enforcement and the extreme circumstances they encounter. During the late 1980s, when I needed security just to get through an airport or from a hotel to a concert venue, a lot of the security people who worked and traveled with me were once police officers or detectives who had spent their careers working in some of the toughest cities in America. I would ask them what a day in the life was like and the stories were beyond what most of us think comes with the job of keeping us and our families safe. The weight of what their work consists of, and the weight of that work on their families, is something I never take for granted.

Ironically, tragedies often have the effect of reminding us that we are all in this together; it's just too bad we don't feel more of a sense of unity at all times. It was almost a year before I saw the bounce return to the stride of New Yorkers. I performed in several fund-raisers for the families of firefighters, police officers, and other responders. I am always open to opportunities to do more to heal our country and to bring us together not because of tragedy but for the greater good.

It starts with dreamers. At the heart of the American Dream is the human spirit. The human spirit is the driving force behind all the greatest achievements that humankind is capable of, whether the achievers are Olympic champions, scientific visionaries, or creative artists.

I am a dreamer, and a believer in the principles upon which this country was founded, as recorded in the Declaration of Independence:

> We hold these truths to be self-evident, that all men are created equal, that they are endowed by their Creator with certain unalienable Rights, that among these are Life, Liberty, and the pursuit of Happiness.

Since 1776 people have been risking and sacrificing their lives to uphold these principles. We have inherited a responsibility to these ideals. The greatest argument for prosperity is human dignity. But if we are to be the legitimate beacon of freedom for the rest of the world, it's time for our leaders to bring the focus home and, as Springsteen recently put it, "take care of our own."

GAINING STRENGTH THROUGH ADVERSITY

As I've revisited so many chapters of my life in this writing process, I've realized that eventually a person can come to grasp the full

meaning of even those experiences that once seemed beyond reason or comprehension. One such experience occurred during the
turmoil and confusion of my fourteen years in litigation. I reached
a point where I was facing a potential worst-case scenario—one in
which I might lose everything I'd worked for, including the ability
to support my family.

During this time, I was pained because I misplaced my trust
in those whom I thought would protect me and my career and all
that I had accomplished to that point. I remember one afternoon,
in the midst of it all, walking across my backyard, looking at the
home I'd built, the office where my staff worked, and my recording
studio. I was thinking about my daughters as I took all of this in,
and I was bracing myself for the worst. The eighteen years of the
climb and the successes I had achieved were endangered by a complicated lawsuit in which the stakes were unbearably high.

Those fourteen years became my Odyssey. I felt exiled from my
home and from my heart. But the fighter in me, the son of Bullet
Bolotin, would not give up. While the legal battle raged and volu-
minous documents rained on me at every stop, I continued to tour
and perform on stages around the world. My survival strategy was
to compartmentalize my experiences, walling off the trauma and
angst over the lawsuit so I could embrace and enjoy what was good
and hopeful.

This was vital, because while the depressing battle raged on,
my career was soaring. I recorded a new album nearly every year
and each project bolstered my spirits and fortified me. With *Timeless: The Classics* in 1993, I drew positive energy from soulful
anthems like Holland-Dozier-Holland's "Reach Out I'll Be There"
(which I recorded with the Four Tops as well) and the classic "To
Love Somebody" by Barry and Robin Gibb, which I continue to
perform with gratitude in all my shows.

The following year, during the recording of the album *The One*

Thing with Mutt Lange, it was impossible to not focus on the music and connect with the spiritual elation of songs like "Said I Loved You...But I Lied." I dedicated the song "Soul of My Soul," written by my genius cohorts Diane Warren and Walter Afanasieff, to my daughters.

This creative process was uplifting and soothing. In 1996, I had the opportunity to work with Placido Domingo and Wynonna Judd, both of whom I love personally and professionally, during the making of my first Christmas album, *This Is the Time.* A year later, while making the album *All That Matters,* I enjoyed writing and working with Kenneth "Babyface" Edmonds, another wonderful artist. All these projects were rewarding and stimulating, yet throughout each of them, the litigation loomed over me.

In 1998, I managed to channel my deep concerns over the litigation into my work, using that negative energy for positive effect as I focused on a very challenging project, a performance in which I sang one of the most demanding arias from *My Secret Passion* with an eighty-six-piece orchestra. To prepare physically and mentally, I worked with a vocal coach, Bill Schuman, and also a linguist, Daniella Orlando, since I was singing in Italian and French (I'm still working on my English). This project was inspired by my experience singing with the great Luciano Pavarotti, who was so gracious and generous with me. Once again, I was grateful to have a creative outlet in music.

One day, in the midst of one of the oh-so-much-fun stages of the litigation, I met my friend Barry Levinson (the brilliant Oscar-winning director and very gracious person) in Milford, Connecticut, for a round of golf with his father-in-law and another friend. It was a great day on the course, and definitely took my mind off troubling matters for a while. When it came time to head back home for more work in the studio, I said good-bye to the three of them and drove away, but missed my entrance to the highway. As I started to make my way back around along the side streets, I noticed a car following me, seeming to mimic my every turn. Abruptly, I took a hard left into the driveway of a bank parking lot and slowly looped behind the building. I pulled out onto the main street again, glancing into the rearview mirror, and, sure enough, the car had followed my turn and was right back on my tail. I spotted the highway ramp and got on, and the car stayed close. Quickly, I grabbed my car phone and dialed, shielding my face as I slowed down and forced the car to pass me. Kim in my office picked up and I explained to her that I was being followed. Alarmed, she immediately called my friend Vito Colucci, a private detective who had done security for me in the past. Vito met me at my studio within the hour. It was pouring rain by this time. I was now so paranoid that I insisted Vito and I speak outside in case the house was bugged. (Just because you're paranoid doesn't mean there aren't people out to get you.) Vito and I walked the property, sharing an umbrella, which I was apparently unconsciously tugging toward me, leaving him partially exposed to the rain. I explained who I thought might be up to this act of intimidation and Vito agreed I should take precautions and be careful about what I said on phone calls until he could find out more.

I went back to my recording, but just thirty minutes later, Vito was on the phone. "I have the information for you." My heart raced. Vito went on. "The car that was following you belongs to a guy named Barry Levinson." I was mortified and of course relieved and explained to Vito it was "The" Barry Levinson, and we had just finished a round of golf.

It turned out that Barry, who had apparently driven by himself to the course, was as lost as I was, and thought if he followed me I'd lead him home. A few days later I got a call from my good friend Mickey Sherman, who was close with Vito. "Let me know if Martin Scorsese or Francis Coppola starts stalking you, Michael." Everyone thought it was quite funny, including me, at least in hindsight.

There was another source of light in the midst of the chaos of travel, recording, publicity, and lawyering—the occasional call from Rodney Dangerfield. Many say Dangerfield was the single greatest stand-up comedian we've ever known. The first call came just after I had done a few minutes of my best Dangerfield impression while on the *Tonight Show* with Jay Leno. (Jay and I would continue to do a minute or so of Rodney on every show for years to follow.) I was at home when Kim from my office rang in and said, "There's a guy on the phone who wants to speak to you. And he says his name is Rodney Dangerfield." I smiled. The next thing I knew, there was Rodney's voice on the receiver as clearly as I'd ever heard it. "I tell ya, Michael, I just wanted to thank you for the Leno show! You're on top of the world and there you are, doing *me!* It means a lot to me, I tell ya." I told Rodney I was a huge fan of his work. That was the start of a good friendship. He showed up for me at This Close, a cancer-research fund-raiser, and joined me in a music video for one of my albums. He later invited me to cameo in two of his films.

Radio interviewers were soon asking me to "do some Rodney" when I was on my promotional tours. I usually led with Rodney's "My wife's a terrible cook" jokes:

"In my house, we pray *after* we eat."

"One night my wife told me to take out the garbage. I said, *You* cooked it, *you* take it out."

"My wife's cooking is so bad the *flies* chipped in to fix the hole in the screen door."

Or another favorite: "I was an ugly kid; when my dog humped my leg he closed his eyes."

When my assistant, Ronnie, told me that Rodney actually did the cooking in his house and that none of his pots and pans matched, I bought him a full set of Revere cookware for his birthday. Next thing I knew, he was on the phone to thank me. I told him I couldn't believe he was the cook at home. His reply: "You don't think I married my wife for what she does in the *kitchen*, do ya?"

I called Rodney after one of his last rounds of surgery to see how he was feeling. "I tell ya, Michael, I've been cut up so much lately I feel like I'm back in my old neighborhood." After Rodney's passing, his wife, Joan, asked me to be a pallbearer at his funeral. There was quite a cast of characters at the service, including generations of the greatest comics around, from Chris Rock and Adam Sandler to Jim Carrey, Rob Schneider, and Tim Allen. They all shared stories that had us laughing and crying. There will only be one Rodney Dangerfield.

Perhaps the album I wrestled with most during those endless years of litigation was *Vintage*. The court case was coming to a head during this project, and though I was staying in a great hotel in Miami, I was unable to sleep even after putting in ten- to twelve-hour days. I was working with Rudy Pérez, my dear and brilliant friend who is a Grammy-winning producer. We had set out to record an album of authentic, timeless American classics, which Rudy arranged masterfully. That's what Rudy does. I drove back and forth to the studio each day, feeling weary to the bone. I struggled to find my full voice for those sessions. Some days I delivered; other days I was just a mess. Still, being in the studio, immersed in music, was my saving grace, along with the support provided by Rudy and his lovely wife, Betsy.

One night I was working with Rudy when the very gracious and generous Julio Iglesias came into the studio, bringing a bottle of La Tâche (my favorite red wine) with him. He smiled and said, "I'm going to be having dinner with someone who loves you very much." Later that night the phone rang in the studio and Rudy said, "It's Julio and he's got President Clinton on the phone to speak to you." Every musician and engineer in the studio went quiet and stared as I took the phone. I listened to Bill's familiar voice on the other end: "I hear you're doing an album of standards, Michael. What songs?" I started in on the track list, beginning with "The Very Thought of You," and Bill chimed in without missing a beat, "I see your face in every flower / Your eyes in stars above." This was yet another endearing Clinton moment for me, and I was once again blown away by the wealth of information the man has at his fingertips and his ability to connect so personally.

By 2005, I was recording the live album *Til the End of Forever*, which was mostly co-produced by Steve Milo and reunited me with a close friend, the supertalented writer and producer Billy Mann. This CD included my composition "The Courage in Your Eyes," dedicated to and inspired by Coretta Scott King. I have read all I could find on the teachings of Socrates, Seneca, Buddha, Christ, Gandhi, and Montaigne, as well as the King family. These spiritual warriors practiced compassion during the most intense and perilous times of their lives. They rose up in the face of adversity. Rather than becoming absorbed or overwhelmed by their own suffering, they led by example, offering messages that impacted and inspired generations to come. Love and compassion are at the center of all their messages, which share a universal human quality reflecting the soul of it all—that which fulfills us beyond all else and gives our journey purpose.

We each have our own journey. Life brings trials, tribulations, and challenges to us all. Nothing great comes without challenge. It's not just surviving the battles that determines our character, it's persevering with dignity, with grace, and with kindness. That can be the hardest thing to do, of course. The power of the human spirit is manifested when we rise above our hardships and discover what we are truly made of.

THROUGH THE FIRE

It was around 2005 and I was on a short vacation in Mexico with Nicollette. We were relaxing and enjoying each other's company all day, but that night I couldn't sleep. My one remaining legal battle was haunting me and my mind would not let go of it. In the wee hours of the night, I got up, turned on my computer, and checked my e-mail. There appeared a message in the in-box and I saw the five words "Your case has been settled."

I had spent all of my forties and half of my fifties in litigation. I just sat there, very calm, internally quiet, motionless. Trying to process it all. Thinking back upon all that had happened. Suddenly, I realized, fourteen years of litigation had come to an end.

Even when your odyssey has ended, there is a process of healing that takes as long as it takes. Home is where the heart is, and if yours has been broken or injured in some way, you may feel alone and displaced. I felt as though an important part of me had been torn away. My song had been taken from me along with years of my life that were stolen by the emotional burden and my sense of betrayal. Songs are like your creative offspring: You get to be a part of that birthing process and watch your songs live on throughout the world, affecting and touching people. You hope your songs will outlive you.

Even once you accept that you've lost a part of yourself, you may struggle to fix it or to make yourself whole again. What helped me was to step outside myself, connect with the courage of others, and to feel empathy for those facing their own challenges. I was reminded again and again that we are all connected through our humanity, and from that I gained strength.

I was also reminded that the ultimate and most effective use of power is to practice kindness at every opportunity. I see the soul of it all in many remarkable people who have touched my life and the lives of others. They are often anonymous, unsung heroes, such as social workers or volunteers, who commit their lives to helping people and families, one by one. They are like an army of compassion and we can help give them the instruments and resources they need to succeed. Then there are people like Frances Preston and Bill Clinton, both of whom won admiration and achieved greatness by wielding power with abundant doses of kindness.

I often look at a photograph of Bill and myself on a putting green, captured in a reflective moment. I see in that photograph the result of a friendship some twenty years in the making, encompassing great jovial times, as well as our individual triumphs and tribulations. President Clinton, the most powerful person on the planet for (at least) two terms in the White House, always remained a kind and empathetic man, one who always supported and encouraged me in good times and in bad.

Many considered former BMI president Frances Preston the most powerful woman in the music business, yet she wielded her power with rare compassion and humanity. As Vince Gill put it, "Frances was kind." His description resonated with everyone gathered at her funeral service.

And how poignant was the use of that simple word: *kind*. It comes back to this recurring theme of compassion, the best of human traits. How poignant our lives can be when we wield kindness in the face of adversity. Without all the challenges, developing such powerful a trait is simply not possible. One allows for the other.

A Day in the Life

As you may have noted while reading this book, I don't give up easily on my dreams or on love, so I'll keep pursuing both, and will keep on singing and writing about them, too. My schedule is often dense, especially when I'm making records in a studio in L.A. or in New York City. I'll leave the studio at two or three in the morning after working all night and return to my hotel too wound up to sleep. I'm physically exhausted, but my mind is still going over the songs we're working on. I'll take my laptop and my headphones into bed and make notes while I listen to each of them over and over.

The next thing I know, the sun will be shining through the curtains in my hotel room. I'll look at the laptop, the notebooks, and the CDs scattered next to me on the bed.

Like many artists, I've come to terms with the fact that a creative life can often be a solitary one. But it's the career and life that I've chosen, or that's chosen me.

Since the end of my long on-again, off-again relationship with Nicollette, I've met some great women, but maybe I am more guarded now. Many people have told me that when the right person comes along, you just know it. I want to know that feeling. I am ultimately a romantic, with the emphasis on ultimately.

I am the descendant of Russian immigrants, a Jewish rebel who found Jesus and Buddha and studied ancient Eastern scriptures so I could learn to be in the world but not of the world. I like nice things, but I am not attached to them, because they are replaceable and human beings are not. I believe we are all passing through this world as transient beings, except for our souls. Singing is my joy and my method for expressing all that lies within. My purest happiness comes in the flow of connecting internally and then performing and feeling connected to the musicians and the

audience, hitting notes that travel out into the universe and resonate there as part of the whole.

More simply, I've learned to enjoy life moment to moment—
laughing with friends; having a cup of coffee at Oscar's Deli with
Tommy Febbraio, the unofficial mayor of Fairfield County; sparring with Bree Belford until either our ribs crack or we collapse
in laughter; playing golf with Mickey Sherman; playing tennis
with Scott Marona; or playing both golf and tennis with my buddy
Brad Salter (preferably twenty-seven holes of golf and then two or
three sets of tennis, until we're painfully aware of what we've done
to our no-longer-twenty-one-year-old selves). Then there's holding my granddaughters and making them smile, meeting them
with love whenever they look at me, watching my daughters grow
and thrive, even just hearing their voices in quiet conversation,
and knowing that in a given moment—right now, for example—
everyone I love is okay.

My daughters have basically owned me, each from the day she
was born, and I think they've always known it. Although I can't
control the trajectories of their lives and their individual journeys,
as long as they know how much I love, respect, and treasure them,
at the end of the day that is one of the only things in this world
that truly matters to me.

Albert Einstein had quite a few good theories, but one that I
find very compelling is about choice. He says, "There are only two
ways to live your life. One is as though nothing is a miracle. The
other is as though everything is a miracle." He chose the latter.
And so do I.

I encourage you to choose the inspired life. Whether you create art or you marvel at the works of others, we all share a greater
purpose, the desire to come together in our shared humanity,
expressed through kindness, compassion, and awe: the soul of it
all. I still believe that love is the most powerful force and ultimately

the only choice to make. It is the only intention, the only direction meant for the soul to take. Love is the lesson, the destination, and the exercise. The hardest challenge is to allow the journey to be the destination. Live and love fully, and you will never miss the soul of it all.

Acknowledgments

So many people have enriched my life and helped, guided, and befriended me in many ways. As I've already told you, it's been a soulful journey, full of family, love, companions, and collaborators. I feel blessed to have such a long list of people to acknowledge and thank.

My beloved family... I carry you in my heart wherever I go:

Isa	Micah Bolotin
Holly	Sandra Christoferson
Taryn	Adam Christoferson
Robbie	Paul Christoferson
Amelia Rose and Olivia	Amelia and Olivia
("Gwenny")	Guimond
Helen "Lila" Bolotin	Cousin Kaye Innamorato
Orrin Bolotin	Maureen McGuire
Oliver Bolotin	Olivia Sklar

ACKNOWLEDGMENTS

Paul Sklar

Rita Sklar

Ken and Elizabeth Cleary

Rose Mary DeGrand

My A team...my greatest appreciation for all you do at all hours to support me always and in all ways:

Gail Atkinson

Helen Burnett

Ronnie Falana

Virginia Fernando

Jackie Gill

Eric Greenspan

Michael Karlin

Christina Kline

Steve Milo

Sonia Muckle

Victor Trevino

Creative cohorts...the magic that's captured in a great musical collaboration can only really be described by the work that outlives that moment of creation. Thanks to all those who've created the timeless magic with me:

Walter Afanasieff

Gary Burr

Jonathan Cain

Bobby Campbell

Desmond Child

Dave Delhomme

Lamont Dozier

Bob Dylan

Nathan East

David Foster

Andrew Goldmark

Randy Goodrum

Berry Gordy

Mick Guzauski

Patrick Henderson

Brian and Edward Holland

Dann Huff

Randy Jackson

Doug James

Ted Jensen

Eric Kaz

Robert John "Mutt" Lange

Johnny Mandel

Barry Mann

Billy Mann

Steven Mercurio

Paul Mirkovich

Rudy and Betsy Pérez

Greg Phillinganes

Phil Ramone

Dave Reitzas

Paul Riser

ACKNOWLEDGMENTS

Al Schmitt and Steve
Neal Schon
Valerie Simpson
Michael Thompson

Jorge Velasco
Chris Walden
Diane Warren
Cynthia Weil

Allies across time ... who have championed my creative endeavors and whose expertise has supported me in what I love to do:

Jenna Adler
Martin Bandier
Mark Burnett
Clive Calder
Barbara Cane
Ryan Cavanaugh
David Cole
Cousin Brucie
Clive Davis
Fran DeFeo
Jody Gerson
Dan Gilbert
Mike Green
Stephen Holden
Bob Holmes
Bill Hopkins
Donnie Ienner
Quincy Jones
Yue-Sai Kan
Jimmy Kimmel
Jimmy Koplik
Dr. Gwen Korovin
Kelly Kulchak
Honey Labrador
Michael Landau

Jay Landers
Jerry Lembo
Jay Leno
Louis Levin
Rob Light
Chuck Lorre
Pat Lucas
Kevin McCollum
Allison Miller
Doug Morris
Peter Morse
Dr. Moy
Dan Mullen
Mason Muñoz
Keith Naisbitt
Deirdre O'Hara
Danielle Orlando
Nicoletta Pavarotti
Dr. Perrault
Regis Philbin
Neil Portnow
Rosi Pritz
Allen Rawls
Marty Richards
Seth Riggs

ACKNOWLEDGMENTS

Rory Rosegarten
Dr. Ronald Rudin
Tami Sagher
Bill Schuman
Bruce Schwartz
Harvey Shapiro
Andy Sheldon
Marty Singer
Leslie Sloan

Dr. Joseph Sugerman
Al Teller
Robin Terry
Charlie Walk
Joel Weinstein
Ron West
Oprah Winfrey
Donna Young

Artist collaborators…the inspiration of working or singing with artists of such genius and talent has been an honor, and fuels my desire to reach higher goals:

Paula Abdul
Chris Botti
José Carreras
Cher
Alice Cooper
Celine Dion
Placido Domingo
Paula Fernandes
Melanie Fiona
Helene Fischer
Renée Fleming
Aretha Franklin
Kenny G
Delta Goodrem
Rita Guerra
Sammy Hagar
Ying Huang
Naomi Judd
Wynonna Judd

B. B. King
KISS
Gladys Knight
Dave Koz
Patti LaBelle
Lady Gaga
Coco Lee
Richard Marx
Dave Mason
Agnes Monica
Ne-Yo
Orianthi Panagaris
A. R. Rahman
Rascal Flatts
Martha Reeves
Smokey Robinson
Kenny Rogers
Kelly Rowland
Leon Russell

ACKNOWLEDGMENTS

Andy Samberg
Akiva Schaffer
Judith Sephuma
Percy Sledge
Barbra Streisand

Barrett Strong
Jorma Taccone
Joe Walsh
Stevie Wonder

Friends and acquaintances dear and new…thank you for the laughs, support, and friendship when it really counts:

Dan Adler
Andre Agassi
Bruce "Bree" Belford
Mark Berg
David Black
Barry Bonds
Doug Capuder
Dave Carroll
Joe Carter
Jeffrey Donovan
Kim Downs
Chris Everett
James Falana
Frederica Famea
Marc and Richard "Ribs"
    Friedland
Carol Genis
Mark Gimple
Toni Hudson
Michael Intoccia
Samuel L. Jackson
Shae Jacobson
Michael Jordan

Ashley Judd
Barry Levinson
Wayne and Joyce
    Logan
Anita Lomartra
Marla Maples
Laura McKinley
Cory Morrison
Chuck Norris
John and Lisa O'Hurley
Sean Penn
Lydia Powell
Dr. Ed Rabiner
Coach Pat Riley
Brad Salter
Rob Schneider
Nicollette Sheridan
Mickey Sherman
Ken and Gale Sitomer
Donnie Slye
Lisa Swayze
Joe Torre
Kim Turner

ACKNOWLEDGMENTS

Great gratitude... for all your generosity in time and spirit, and for the example you set for the rest of us:

Bill and Tani Austin

Del and Carolyn Bryant

Dave and Clarice Clark

President Bill Clinton

Secretary of State Hillary
Clinton

Dick Cook

Barbara Davis

Nancy Davis

Clint and Dina Eastwood

David Gest

Dinesh and Ila Paliwal

Cindy and R. A. Raymond

John and Patty Rowland

Warren and Jale Trepp

Hachette and the literary team... for all your diligence and faith throughout this tremendous birthing process:

Kate Hartson

Rolf Zettersten

Michele McGonigle

Andrea Glickson

Shanon Stowe

Harry Helm

Bob Castillo

Carolyn Kurek

Melissa Mathlin

Hannah Boursnell

Lauren Rohrig

Louise Sommers

Shannon Marven

Jan Miller

MBC and allies... thank you for all the work you do, which often goes uncredited but which makes a real difference to the lives and well-being of others:

Joyce Abousie

Patricia R. Beauregard

Lois Beekman

Joe Biden

Laura A. Cahill

Dr. David G. Carter

Robert P. Doran

Robert J. Epstein

Tommy Febbraio

Andrena Gagliardi

Richard Gephardt

Tom Gross Jr.

Orrin Hatch

Joan Lunden

ACKNOWLEDGMENTS

William J. McNamee

James P. Sandler

Jackie Smaga

Rita Smith

Meredith Wagner

Very special thanks...to the hardest-working touring team on earth, and to everyone who keeps me on track for sound and lights, camera and action:

Andy Abad

Gemina Aboitiz

Catte Adams

Sandra Allen

Alisha Ard

Christopher Austopchuk

Sammy Balfour

Brian Becvar

Rebecca Blake

Keary Braxton

Mary Bush

Melinda Cabral

Tommy "Mugs" Cain

Chris Camozzi

Kevin Cassidy

Kiku Collins

Errol Cooney

Sal Cracchiolo

"Booby" Daniels

Toby Davis

Schuyler Deale

Jason DeLaire

Elizabeth Dotson-
   Westphalen

Tom Friga

Earl Gabbidon

Darren Gilcrest

Cameron Handel

Mike Harris

Pat Hawk

Lee Hawkins

Jennifer Ismail

Carol Jarvis

Vann Johnson

Naomi Kaltman

Jesse Leal

April Leslie

Kelly Levesque

Janis Liebhart

Everice Lindesay

Michael Lington

Moyes Lucas

Andrew Macpherson

Herman Matthews

Scott Mayo

Amy McCabe

Drew McKeon

Chris McMillan

ACKNOWLEDGMENTS

Jerry Mele
Joey Melotti
Rebecca Mink
Katherine Mlynar
Tracy Monaco
Monty Montford
Dani Olorenshaw
Ryan Parrino
Mark Pasquale
Daniel Pearl
Geoff Perren
Tiffany Phillips
Mike Revell

Land Richards
Dennis Rodriguez
Carmine Rojas
Steve Scales
Jessica Spinella
Karen Straw
Joe Turano
Jacques Voyemant
Timothy White
Tara Wilson
Gaylin Winkler-Cates
Chad Wright

Sponsors and partners…thanks to all the leaders and amazing employees, in America and worldwide, of these great organizations:

Ali Foundation
American Airlines Special
    Services
AT&T Pebble Beach
    National Pro-Am
Barking Dog
Beverly Hills Hotel
BMI
Bullseye Studio
Creative Artists Agency
Callaway Golf
Christophe's (especially
    Alex and Hilda)
CityKids Foundation
City of Hope
Clinton Foundation

Columbia Records
Congress of Racial Equality
Dr Pepper
Emerald Studios
EMI Music Publishing and
    Sony/ATV
FIJI Water
Gentlemen's Club
Harlem School of the Arts
Harman
The Hit Factory
The Ivy
Jive Records
Lifetime Television
The Lodge at Pebble Beach
Louisville Slugger

ACKNOWLEDGMENTS

T. J. Martell Foundation

Martin Luther King
Jr. Center

Motown Museum

Music Express

National Academy of
Recording Arts and
Sciences

National Conference of
Diocesan Vocation
Directors

National Mentoring
Partnership

New Act Travel

Ocean Way Recording

Ojai Valley Inn and Spa

Passion Studios

The Peninsula (hotel)

Polo Lounge (especially
Jerome, Pepe, and Nancy)

Quicken Loans

Record Plant

Resolute

Rockrimmon Country Club

St. Regis (hotel)

Sony Music Entertainment

Steadman Clinic

Sterling Sound

Toscana Country Club

Travelers Insurance

Tree House

United Negro College Fund

Universal Studios

USO

Vail Valley Medical Center

Valbella

Verizon Wireless

VH1

Vincent Limousine

Wally's World

Walter Reed National
Military Medical Center

Westlake Recording Studios
(especially Steve Burdick
and Steve Rusch)

Yellow Elephant Music

The bravest of our brave...the men and women of our armed forces

In everlasting memory of...

George Louis Bolotin

Isadore "Izzy" and Rose
Gubin

Nick Ashford

Bobby Brooks

Ray Charles

Dick Clark

Rodney Dangerfield

ACKNOWLEDGMENTS

Laura Branigan

Joe DiMaggio

Gary "Gaz" Douglas

Tom Dowd

Marvin Gaye

Whitney Houston

Coretta Scott King

Reverend Martin Luther
  King Jr.

Marvin Davis

Paul Newman

Maestro Luciano
  Pavarotti

Frances Preston

Otis Redding

David Sorin-Collyer

Patrick Swayze

Tammi Terrell

Index

Abdul, Paula, 73–75, 216, 256, 282
Abdul, Wendy, 73–75
Aboitiz, Gemina, 275
Abramowitz, Alan, 69
Abramowitz, Jack, 69–70
AC/DC, 110, 207
Adams, Sally, 252
Adele, 162, 267
Adler, Dan, 241
Aerosmith, 94, 110
Afanasieff, Walter, 156–157, 166, 195,
    205, 208, 210, 218, 220–221, 223,
    230, 255, 306
Aguilera, Christina, 169
Allen, Woody, 121
All That Matters, 145, 306
Anspach, Susan, 79
Ashford, Nick, 112, 283
Augusto, Carl, 9
Austin, Bill, 297
Austin, Patti, 114, 138, 216
Austin, Tammy, 297
"Ave Maria," 272

Bad Company, 105–106
"Bah Bah Bah," 67–68
Baldwin, Daniel, 193
Baldwin, William, 193
Beatles, 10, 22, 24, 37, 67, 85, 89, 103, 143, 170
Begley, Ed, Jr., 84–85

Belford, Bruce ("Bree"), 45–48, 98, 314
Berniker, Mike, 94, 95, 97
Biden, Joe, 292
Blackjack, 106–109, 121, 157
Blackjack, 107
Blood, Sweat & Tears, 77, 94
Bloomberg, Michael, 281, 293
Bloomfield, Mike, 10, 77
Bocelli, Andrea, 206
Bolotin, George (father), 12–24, 41, 49, 63,
    73, 94, 124–126, 194, 212, 217, 222, 300
Bolotin, Helen (mother), 11, 13–17, 21–25,
    28, 30, 40–41, 49, 72, 73, 141, 217
Bolotin, Sandra (sister), 12, 16–17, 29
Bolton, Holly (daughter), 78, 98, 117,
    124, 129, 173–174, 188, 191, 195–196,
    199–201, 218, 223, 258, 302, 314
Bolton, Isa (daughter), 6, 78, 97–99, 117,
    124, 167, 173–174, 188, 190–191,
    195–196, 199–201, 218, 223, 250–251,
    258, 302, 314
Bolton, Maureen (wife), 72–75, 92, 96–99,
    102–104, 132, 180
Bolton, Orrin (brother), 9–11, 15–21, 27–28,
    32, 43, 50, 68, 70, 76, 92–95, 102, 109,
    124, 127–136, 131, 170, 172, 200, 277–278
Bolton, Taryn (daughter), 78, 98, 117, 124,
    129, 173–174, 188–189, 191, 195–196,
    199–201, 218, 223, 242, 250, 258,
    302, 314

INDEX

Bolton Swings Sinatra, 255
Bonds, Barry, 21, 193
Bon Jovi, Jon, 147, 211, 242
Bono, 269
"Bop Bah," 66
Bova, Fred, 54, 59, 71
Boyer, Clete, 19
Brander, Joel, 290
Branigan, Laura, 135–138, 147, 151–152, 155, 176, 181, 211
"Breathe in My Ear," 9
Brockway, Bob, 59
Bublé, Michael, 206
Bunetta, Peter, 204
Butterfield, Paul, 10, 42
"By the Time This Night Is Over," 210

Cain, Jonathan, 75, 118, 179–180, 182–183
Camiletti, Rob, 148
Capuder, Doug, 239
Carey, Mariah, 156, 206
Carmichael, Hoagy, 213
Champlin, Bill, 297
Chappelle, Dana, 220–221
Charles, Ray, 93, 107, 146, 182, 213–214, 235, 265, 268, 289–290
Chelios, Chris, 193
Cher, 147–150, 185, 209, 213
Cheung, William, 47–48
Chicago, 94
Chiffons, 232
Child, Desmond, 147, 151, 160, 203, 211–212, 219
Chopra, Deepak, 205
Chudacoff, Rick, 204
Churchill, Winston, 236
Clapton, Eric, 10, 85, 88, 89, 107, 161, 182
Clark, David, 297
Clark, Dick, 114–116
Clark, Terice, 297
Clarkson, Kelly, 213, 282
Clinton, Bill, 18, 184, 237, 240–243, 245, 249, 292, 310
Clinton, George, 127
Clinton, Hillary, 237, 242–245, 249, 292
Cocker, Joe, 85, 88, 93
Colavito, Rocky, 20
Cole, Natalie, 249
Collins, Judy, 28
Collins, Phil, 217

Colomby, Bobby, 77
Colucci, Vito, 307–308
Connery, Sean, 290
Cooke, Sam, 235
"Cookie Man," 68
Coolidge, Rita, 80
Cooper, Alice, 96, 160, 213, 296–297
Cooper, Ken, 62, 65–67
Cordell, Denny, 85–86, 88, 89, 121
Costner, Kevin, 296
"The Courage in Your Eyes," 237, 310
Cousin Brucie, 35
"Cowboy's Theme," 76
Creach, Papa John, 97
Cropper, Steve, 182, 184
Crosby, Bing, 213
Cruise, Tom, 275
Cryer, John, 288
Cy, Joe, 85, 87, 90, 92, 96

Dangerfield, Joan, 309
Dangerfield, Rodney, 11, 69, 174, 229, 281, 308–309
Davis, Barbara, 290
Davis, Clive, 94–96, 121, 203, 286
Davis, Marvin, 290
Davis, Miles, 146
Def Leppard, 110, 207
De La Hoya, Oscar, 190
Diamond, Keith, 180
Diana, Princess, 270
DiMaggio, Joe, 194–195, 265
Dion, Celine, 87, 156, 206, 286
"Dock of the Bay," 58, 182–186, 213
Domingo, Placido, 272–274
"Don't Press Your Luck," 9
Doors, 36, 68
Dowd, Tom, 107–109
Downs, Kim, 196
Dozier, Lamont, 143–145, 154, 230
"Dreaming Dreams," 131, 180
"Dream While You Can," 90, 94
Drysdale, Don, 20
Dylan, Bob, 28, 77, 160–167, 194, 219, 281

Eastwood, Clint, 206, 296
Edmonds, Kenneth ("Babyface"), 143, 306
Edmunds, Dave, 105
Einstein, Albert, 314
Ellington, Duke, 146

INDEX

Emmett, Kathy, 239
Engelberg, Morris, 194
Eno, Brian, 269
Epstein, Bob, 96
Everybody's Crazy, 174–175
Every Day of My Life, 98
Ezrin, Bob, 158

Febbraio, Tommy, 314
Ferrell, Conchata, 289
"The Fire Keeps Burnin'," 71
Five Satins, 35
Fleming, Renée, 271
Fonda, Henry, 231
"Fool's Game," 127–134, 137
"Forever," 159–160
"Forever Isn't Long Enough," 218
Foster, David, 170, 195, 198, 205–209,
    251, 284
Four Tops, 305
Foxx, Jaime, 214
Franklin, Aretha, 107, 203, 286
Friedland, Alice, 50–51
Friedland, Bob, 33
Friedland, Ida, 60–61
Friedland, Marc ("Marky Doodle Ham-
    burger"), 33–35, 41, 48, 52, 54, 58–60,
    65–66, 69–75, 78, 79, 80, 83–84, 85–91,
    131, 176, 181
Friedland, Richard ("Ribs"), 33–35, 50–52,
    54–59, 61–62, 65, 69–72, 79, 83–86, 92,
    176, 181

Gaga, Lady, 167–171, 207
Gagliardi, Andrena, 291
Gandhi, Mohandas, 310
Gaye, Marvin, 129, 182, 277, 279
Geffen, David, 149, 150
Gehrig, Lou, 266
GEMS, 77, 295
Genarro, Sandy, 106
Genis, Carol, 239–240
George's Boys, 48–49
"Georgia on My Mind," 58, 213–215, 217
Gephardt, Dick, 18
Gibb, Barry, 305
Gibb, Robin, 305
Gibran, Khalil, 103, 280
Gilbert, Dan, 300
Gill, Vince, 127, 312

"Going Back to New Haven," 68
Goldberg, Whoopi, 249
Goldmark, Andy, 203, 210–211, 231, 235
Golub, David, 239
Goodman, Bobby ("Goody"), 35, 50–52,
    54, 57
Goodrem, Delta, 297
Gordon, Michael Z., 71, 76
Gordy, Berry, 143, 154, 286
Gore, Al, 243
Gorrell, Stuart, 213
"Go the Distance," 208, 209
Griffey, Ken, Jr., 193
Groban, Josh, 156, 206
Gross, Tom, 297
Gubin, Isadore ("Izzy" grandfather),
    13–14, 140
Gubin, Rose (grandmother), 13–14, 17
Guzauski, Mick, 208

Hamilton, Susan, 113, 116, 180, 210
Hamlin, Harry, 248
"Hard Enough Getting Over You," 147
Harmon, Mark, 193
Harris, Richard, 157
Harrison, George, 66, 88, 161, 163, 232
Hartman, Lisa, 134
Haslip, Jimmy, 106
Hatch, Orrin, 292
Hatcher, Teri, 226, 248
Haughwout, Bill, 43–45
Henderson, Patrick, 131–133
Hendrix, Jimi, 33, 101–102
Holden, Stephen, 94, 98, 222–223
Holiday, Billie, 101
Holyfield, Evander, 193
Houston, Thelma, 138
Houston, Whitney, 185, 203, 206, 207, 210,
    286, 290
"How Am I Supposed to Live Without You,"
    16, 134–137, 181, 211, 216, 279
"How Can We Be Lovers If We Can't Be
    Friends," 15, 212–213
Howell, David, 269
Hudson, Jennifer, 282
Hullen, Dan, 300
The Hunger, 175, 179–187, 203, 211, 218

Ienner, Donnie, 203, 210, 221, 222, 229
"I Found Someone," 149, 185

INDEX

Iglesias, Julio, 309–310
"I Heard It Through the Grapevine," 145
"I'm Not Made of Steel," 190
"I'm Riding Home," 90
"I'm Still Thinking of You," 133
Ingram, James, 216, 217
Intoccia, Michael, 297
Isley Brothers, 230–233, 239, 243–244, 247
"It's About That Time," 61
"It's a Hard Life," 90
"It's for You," 66
"I Work for Freedom," 71

Jackson, Michael, 104, 128–129, 146, 185
Jackson, Randy, 75, 183, 282
Jackson, Samuel L., 296
"Jack Sparrow," 5–7, 209, 288
Jagger, Mick, 36, 180
James, Doug, 133, 136–137, 146–147, 160, 203, 212
James, Kevin, 296
Jefferson Airplane, 98
Jefferson Starship, 98
Jett, Joan, 110
Jimenez, Yolanda, 293
Joel, Billy, 94, 129, 216, 217
Johannsen, Brad, 54
John, Elton, 85
Johnson, Magic, 193
Jones, Allen, 108
Jones, Davey, 297
Jones, Quincy, 146–147, 216
Joplin, Janis, 56, 94, 101
Jordan, Michael, 193
Journey, 76, 118, 182, 186
Joy, 54, 56–57, 60, 65, 68, 71–72, 75, 77, 84–86, 121
Judd, Ashley, 273–275
Judd, Naomi, 273
Judd, Wynonna, 273, 297

Kaline, Al, 20
Kalodner, John, 147, 150
Kamen, Michael, 269
Kaz, Eric, 179, 204
Kennedy, Ethel, 281
Kennedy, John F., 236
Kennedy, Robert, 236
Kenny G, 156–157, 203, 207, 210, 222, 248, 297

Kessler, Scott, 268
Kimmel, Jimmy, 74, 255–256
King, B. B., 10, 42
King, Coretta Scott, 233–234, 236–238, 310
King, Martin Luther, Jr., 233–234, 236–238, 294
KISS, 107, 129, 157–160, 213
Klatzkin, Alan ("Klatty"), 7, 92–93, 95, 109
Kline, Christina, 6, 153, 199, 209
Knight, Gladys, 218
Kooper, Al, 77
Koplik, Jimmy, 271–272, 294
Koufax, Sandy, 20
Krebs, David, 110–111, 123–124
Kristofferson, Kris, 79–80, 126, 217, 240
Kulick, Bruce, 106, 127, 158–160
Kutcher, Ashton, 288

LaBelle, Patti, 279
Landers, Jay, 155–156
Lange, Robert John ("Mutt"), 195, 198, 205–206, 208–210, 306
Lanza, Mario, 22, 170, 264
Lauper, Cyndi, 129, 151
Leber, Steve, 109, 110, 111, 123
Led Zeppelin, 105–106
Lennon, John, 11, 66
Leno, Jay, 23, 249, 308
Levin, Louis, 109, 111–112, 118, 123, 137, 175, 186, 199, 216, 219, 221, 242, 285
Levinson, Barry, 294, 296, 302, 306
Lewis, Huey, 296
Lewis, Steven, 71
Lington, Michael, 242
Linzer, Sandy, 68
Logan, Joyce, 196
Lorito, Phil, 105, 106, 109
Lorre, Chuck, 289
"Love Is a Wonderful Thing," 230–232
"Love Me Tonight," 108

Madonna, 168, 206
Maharaj Ji, 102–103
Maharishi Mahesh Yogi, 103
Mangold, Mark, 147
Mani, Michael, 169
Mann, Barry, 151, 154, 160, 165, 204, 310
Mann, Suzanne, 161, 165
Maples, Marla, 224–226
Marley, Bob, 89

Marona, Scott, 314
Marx, Richard, 115, 135, 216, 297
Mason, Dave, 297
Mason, Marsha, 79
Mayer, John, 6
McCartney, Paul, 66, 286
McDonald, Michael, 132, 297
McKinley, Laura, 195
McMillan, Chris, 275
Meat Loaf, 269
Medley, Bill, 138
Melanie, 28
Merman, Ethel, 22
Michael, George, 185
Michael Bolotin, 96–97
Michael Bolton, 127, 128, 130
Michaels, Hilly, 71, 75
Midler, Bette, 210
Milo, Ronnie, 196–199, 275
Milo, Steve, 198, 310
Mirkovich, Paul, 145, 209–210
"Missing You Now," 218, 226
Moody Blues, 85, 89
Moore, Roger, 290
Morrison, Cory, 28–29, 49–50, 54, 131,
    180–181
Morrison, Jim, 36–37, 101
Mottola, Tommy, 115, 156, 198, 219–220
"Murder My Heart," 169
Murray the K, 35
My Secret Passion: The Arias, 222, 272, 306

Nelson, Tracy, 59
Nelson, Willie, 59, 85, 213, 214
"New Love," 220
Nickelback, 206
"Now That I Found You," 219
Nugent, Ted, 110

Ocean, Billy, 180
Odyssey, 134
O'Hara, Deirdre, 133–135, 146, 210
O'Hurley, John, 297
Omartian, Michael, 204, 216
Omley, Jordan, 169
"Once in a Lifetime," 255
The One Thing, 305–306
One World One Love, 167
Orbison, Barbara, 217
Orbison, Roy, 161, 216, 217

Orianthi, 297
Orlando, Daniella, 306
Osbourne, Ozzy, 108
"O soave fanciulla," 271
"Our Town," 76
Ovitz, Michael, 235, 241

Palmer, Arnold, 295
Parton, Dolly, 286
Pavarotti, Luciano, 167, 263–266, 268–270,
    272, 281, 306
Pérez, Betsy, 309
Pérez, Rudy, 309
Perkins, Wayne, 89
Pesci, Joe, 296
Petty, Tom, 85, 161
Pink Floyd, 94, 160
Pitt, Brad, 275
Player, Gary, 295
Pointer Sisters, 138, 210
Pollard, Tom, 68, 79–80
Presley, Elvis, 104, 143
Preston, Frances, 126–127, 312

Quinn, Larry, 76

Radle, Carl, 89
Raitt, Bonnie, 179, 259
Rashad, Ahmad, 193
Raymond, Cindy, 297
Raymond, R. A., 297
"Reach Out I'll Be There," 305
Reagan, Nancy, 290
Reagan, Ronald, 290
Redding, Otis, 107, 108, 182, 183–184,
    186
Redding, Zelma, 183–186
Reitzas, David, 206
Richardson, Jack, 96, 97
Richie, Lionel, 129
Riggs, Seth, 266, 279
Ripken, Cal, Jr., 266
Robinson, Smokey, 235
Roche, Guy, 204
Rogers, Kenny, 138, 218
Rolling Stones, 10, 36–37, 88, 143, 286
Rolston, Matthew, 248
Ronstadt, Linda, 179
Rooney, Mickey, 274
Roth, David Lee, 55

INDEX

Rozen, Jimmy, 33, 234
"Running Away from the Night Time,"
    71, 76
Russell, Leon, 33, 85–92, 121, 131

"Said I Loved You...But I Lied," 208, 209,
    306
Salter, Brad, 314
Samberg, Andrew ("Andy"), 4, 5,
    6, 288
Sanborn, David, 97
Santana, Carlos, 70, 94
Savalas, Telly, 72, 252
Schaffer, Akiva ("Kiv"), 4, 5, 6, 288
Schmitt, Al, 72
Schon, Neal, 179, 183
Schuman, Bill, 266, 306
Schwartz, Bruce, 300
Scialfa, Patti, 218
Seal, 209
Seger, Bob, 87, 96, 127–128, 130, 137
Selleck, Tom, 193
Selwitz, Glenn, 71, 75
Seneca, 233, 238, 310
Serling, Rod, 174
Shags, 9, 35, 61
Sheridan, Nicollette, 193, 231, 247–253,
    255–260, 290, 301–302, 311, 313
Sherman, Mickey, 294, 308, 314
Silver Bullet Band, 127–128, 137
Simmons, Gene, 158
Simon, Carly, 28, 210
Simpson, Valerie, 111, 283
Sinatra, Frank, 146, 156
Sledge, Percy, 219, 221, 235, 241
Smaga, Jackie, 290–291
Smith, Ozzie, 194
Smith, Rex, 133
Smith, Rita, 292
Snow, Phoebe, 85, 89
Sorin-Collyer, David, 266, 283–284
"Soul of My Soul," 208, 223, 306
Soul Provider, 187, 211–218
"Soul Provider," 15, 210
Specter, Arlen, 244–245
Springsteen, Bruce, 94, 107, 218, 242, 299,
    304
Stagg, Warren, 80
Stanley, Paul, 158–160
"Steel Bars," 166–167, 219

Stewart, Jimmy, 231
Stewart, Rod, 106, 217
"Still Thinking of You," 133
Stoller, Mike, 151
Streisand, Barbra, 94, 155–157, 206
Summer, Donna, 180
Swayze, Lisa, 296
Swayze, Patrick, 296

Taccone, Jorma ("Jorm"), 4, 5, 6, 288
Taylor, Holland, 289
Taylor, James, 28, 157
Teller, Al, 123, 130, 174–179
Terrell, Tammi, 279
"That's What Love Is All About," 16,
    181–182, 185
This Is the Time, 306
"This Man," 61
Thomas, Frank ("the Big Hurt"), 193
Til the End of Forever, 310
Timberlake, Justin, 3–4, 135
Time, Love & Tenderness, 156, 167, 215, 219,
    221–222, 224, 226–227, 252
Timeless: the Classics, 248, 305
"To Love Somebody," 305
Traveling Wilburys, 161–162
Trepp, Jâlé, 297
Trepp, Warren, 297
Trump, Donald, 224–226
Turner, Tina, 181
Twain, Shania, 297

Underwood, Carrie, 207, 282

Vandross, Luther, 111, 114–116
Vera, Billy, 230–231
"Vesti la giubba," 264, 280, 284
Vintage, 309

Wagner, Meredith, 292
"Wait on Love," 75
Walker, Clay, 296
Warren, Diane, 136, 147, 150–152, 154–155,
    160, 165, 179, 203, 211–213, 218, 223,
    255, 306
Warwick, Dionne, 133
Weil, Cynthia, 160, 165, 204
Weiss, Steve, 105–107
"We're Not Making Love Anymore," 151,
    155, 157, 219

INDEX

"When a Man Loves a Woman," 15, 150, 209, 219–221
"When I'm Back on My Feet Again," 212
"Where Do We Go from Here," 76
"Why Me," 145
Widdoes, Jamie, 288
Williams, Jack, 297
Williams, Matt, 194
Williams, Paul, 297
Williams, Ted, 20
Winehouse, Amy, 101
Winfrey, Oprah, 256, 260

Winkleman, Sophie, 288–289
Winkler, Henry, 213
"Without Your Love," 108
Wolstein, Bart, 257
Wolstein, Iris, 257
Wonder, Stevie, 182, 277–280
"Working Girl," 147
Worlds Apart, 107

"Your Love's Much Too Strong," 90

Zimmerman, Bob, 162

About the Author

Michael Bolton, the multiple Grammy Award–winning singer, songwriter, and social activist, has sold more than fifty-three million albums and singles worldwide. Known for his soulful voice and poignant lyrics, he continues to tour the world, all while writing and recording for a wide array of projects, spanning the realms of music, film, television, and theater. Bolton remains committed to humanitarian causes, especially through his Michael Bolton Charities, and donates his time and talent to several social and political organizations. His timeless style, charm, and good looks have earned him a spot in several *People* magazine "Sexiest Man Alive" issues, most recently in 2012. In 2011, he was featured in the Lonely Island's hugely popular "Jack Sparrow" video, which became a viral sensation after it launched on *Saturday Night Live*. The Emmy-nominated video has racked up more than ninety million views on YouTube, where it was the third most viewed video of 2011. Bolton credits his fans with being the best in the world, and loves nothing more than bringing his timeless hits to audiences globally.

In recognition of his artistic achievements, Bolton won two Grammys for Best Pop Male Vocal Performance (he was nominated in this category four times), six American Music Awards, and a star on the Hollywood Walk of Fame. As a songwriter, he has earned more than twenty-four BMI and ASCAP awards, including Songwriter of the Year and the Million-Air Award, as well as the Howie Richmond Hitmaker Award from the Songwriters Hall of Fame. To date, he has seen eight of his studio albums rank in *Billboard*'s Top 10; from these albums have come nine number one singles.

Bolton has recorded and performed with musical icons who have inspired and influenced his own career. He joined Luciano Pavarotti onstage in a highly praised rendition of "Vesti la giubba" and pays homage to the Italian tenor when performing the aria "Nessun dorma" at each of his concerts on tour. He has sung with Placido Domingo, José Carreras, and Renée Fleming, and has played guitar with B. B. King. He earned a Grammy nomination for "Georgia on My Mind," and was invited to sing the classic song to Ray Charles when Charles was honored at the International Jazz Hall of Fame Awards in 1997. Bolton performed duets with both Seal and Lara Fabian to standing ovations for a 2011 *David Foster and Friends* PBS special.

A versatile and prolific songwriter, Bolton has collaborated with some of the greatest songwriters and producers of our time, including Lady Gaga, Diane Warren, Desmond Child, David Foster, Walter Afanasieff, Kenneth "Babyface" Edmonds, Robert John "Mutt" Lange, Dann Huff, A. R. Rahman, Phil Ramone, Ne-Yo, and Billy Mann, among others. He is one of the very few artists to have co-written a song with the legendary Bob Dylan, resulting in the megahit "Steel Bars." He has penned songs that have been recorded and performed by a diverse list of more than one hundred artists, ranging from country-and-western legend Conway Twitty to hip-hop superstar Kanye West, in concert with Jay-Z and John Legend. Other greats who have performed Bolton's songs include Marc Anthony, Wynonna Judd, Joe Cocker, Peabo Bryson, Kenny Rogers, and Patti LaBelle. Bolton has written number one hit singles that have boosted the careers of artists such as Laura Branigan ("How Am I Supposed to Live Without You"), KISS ("Forever"), Barbra Streisand ("We're Not Making Love Anymore"), Cher ("I Found Someone"), and Kenny G ("By the Time This Night Is Over").

Bolton has always balanced a love for writing new songs with a passion for covering the classics. On his breakthrough album, *The Hunger*, he authored the number one single "That's What Love Is All About" and sang his chart-topping version of Otis Redding's "(Sittin' on) The Dock of the Bay," which was a hit in four radio formats. That album was certified double platinum and shipped four million copies worldwide.

He seized his true signature success with the album *Soul Provider*, which sold more than 12.5 million copies worldwide and showcased several hit singles, including the number one song "How Am I Supposed to Live Without You," which earned him his first Grammy. This pivotal album also includes "When I'm Back on My Feet Again," "How Can We Be Lovers If We Can't Be Friends," "Soul Provider," and, of course, the Grammy-nominated "Georgia on My Mind."

Soon after, Bolton released the number one album *Time, Love & Tenderness*, which has sold more than sixteen million copies worldwide and features his Grammy Award–winning vocal performance of the blockbuster hit "When a Man Loves a Woman." This album also produced the hit singles "Love Is a Wonderful Thing," "Time, Love and Tenderness," and "Missing You Now," as well as "Steel Bars," co-written with Bob Dylan.

Bolton followed this album with a collection of soulful classics on *Timeless*, delivering the hit singles "To Love Somebody" and "Reach Out I'll Be There." *Timeless* sold more than seven million copies worldwide.

From his next album, *The One Thing*, came Bolton's massively popular single "Said I Loved You...But I Lied," which spent twelve weeks at No. 1 on the adult contemporary charts and earned him another Grammy nomination.

Bolton has always been attracted to a wide array of musical genres, from Sinatra favorites (*Bolton Swings Sinatra*) to classical arias (*My Secret Passion*, which stayed at No. 1 on the classical charts for six consecutive weeks). His most recent studio album features an authentic approach to Motown and soulful classics, as well as original songs written in the same vein.

Bolton's songs and performances have been featured in numerous television and film sound tracks, including that of Walt Disney's blockbuster animated film *Hercules*, for which Bolton wrote the Oscar-nominated theme song, "Go the Distance." He also executive-produced the documentary *Terror at Home*, which addresses domestic violence in America, and wrote its Emmy-nominated theme song, "Tears of the Angels." Most recently, he was cast to act and sing in the season premiere of CBS's hit prime-time television show *Two and a Half Men*, and has landed his own new comedy series on ABC, entitled *Michael Bolton's Daughter Is Destroying My Life*.

For his dedication to social activism, Bolton has been honored with several philanthropic awards, including the Humanitarian of the Year Award, granted by the Congress of Racial Equality (C.O.R.E.) at their annual Martin Luther King Jr. dinner; the Lewis Hine Award, from the National Child Labor Committee; the Ellis Island Medal of Honor, from the National Ethnic Coalition of

Organizations; and the Frances Williams Preston Lifetime Music Industry Award, from the T. J. Martell Foundation. He is especially proud of the initiatives carried out by his own foundation, Michael Bolton Charities, now in its twentieth year of advocacy on behalf of women and children at risk.